AF469065

BARTON

part one – 1908 – 1949

by

Alan Oxley

Series Editor Alan Townsin

BARTON

part one – 1908 – 1949

CONTENTS

ISBN 903839 52 0 [limp]
ISBN 903839 64 4 [case]

Other titles in this series:

North Western (two volumes)
West Yorkshire
Potteries Motor Traction
Southampton City Transport
Nottingham City Transport
Provincial - Gosport & Fareham
Birmingham trams
Alexander Coachbuilders
Plaxtons
Northern Counties
etc. etc.
(Illustrated list of all titles available from publishers)

Designed and Published by
The Transport Publishing Company
Glossop, Derbyshire

Typesetting, Artwork and Photography by TPC Studio
Printed by Nene Litho, Northants
Bound by Woolnough Bookbinding, Northants

Introduction

From an early age I adopted the red, maroon and cream buses which passed my home at regular intervals, and over many years this attachment grew until I became almost part of the Company. Now I have had the opportunity to put in writing the rise of Barton Transport Ltd, from the small beginnings to the largest independent stage carriage operator in Western Europe. Hopefully, I would have called this a definitive history, but this is impossible as items and memories have been lost for ever. However, from the exhaustive information I have accumulated, there will, I am sure, be something to stimulate everyone's interest. Particularly as Barton's area of operation is not confined to the East Midlands, but nationwide, with Road Cruises and Express Services reaching most points North, South, East and West.

In preparing this book, research into the early fleet operation has been made rather difficult as many vehicles were purchased for resale, and on occasions ran for only a short period. My enthusiasm will, I am sure, spread once the eccentricities and enterprise of the family and Company have been read. This interest has rubbed off on my own family, so much so that Jonathan, my six year old son, was able to spot a Barton coach on the North Yorkshire Moors seconds before my own keen eye. My wife, Barbara, says little but knows far more than she will say and daughter Claire now aged eleven wrote the following three years earlier:-

Buses

Buses Buses Buses
Double-deckers, singles, any kind of buses
Blue seats, green seats
Just any sort of buses
80 wheels 10 wheels or even only one!
Any kind of buses just will do.

July 1983

Alan F. Oxley
Attenborough, Notts

The Leyland Journal staff visited Barton's headquarters in May 1935; as a major Leyland user Barton merited substantial coverage. This photograph, taken during the visit, shows, from left to right, Maurie Barton [Works Manager], T. H. Barton senior, Tom Barton [Chief Engineer] and Carl Barton [Traffic Manager]. Behind is No. 2, the Leyland Bull breakdown vehicle delivered in April 1934.

A delightful scene on Derby Road, Long Eaton, during early 1926. The cyclist gives the impression of overtaking No. 27 Morris-Barton 6-wheeler with 24 seat Strachan & Brown body, which has been posed for this photograph. The spare wheel at the side of the driver gives the impression of a most uncomfortable driving position.

BARTON

Chapter One : Sowing the seeds

Thomas Henry Barton was born in 1866, during the twenty ninth year of Queen Victoria's reign, at his quarry-owning parents' house in Duffield, Derbyshire. A member of a large family, he led an eventful early life, and at the age of fifteen months almost died a drunkard's death. He was taken downstairs early one morning, and placed by two beer coolers, whilst his father lit a fire; suddenly gurgling sounds were heard coming from one of these vats. He was fished out, saturated with beer and held face downwards, saving his life. Even so, the alcohol had some effect, but gradually he became sober in the arms of his mother.

As a youngster living in the open countryside, he was anxious to buy a gun and acquired a muzzle loader with shot bag, powder flask and ram rod for five shillings. There were rabbits in the quarry and ducks on the river, so he and his sister made ample contribution to the dinner table for many weeks. However, funds for ammunition were not plentiful, so he filled the powder flask from blasting powder barrels at the quarry — unfortunately it was of coarse grain, causing misfiring. This was perhaps the earliest record of his inventiveness, as he hit upon the idea of using a coffee mill for grinding down powder to fit the gun nipple. This resulted in comments from the breakfast table about black and salty-tasting coffee, but he could not explain the phenomenon without prejudicing his powder supply. However, the family eventually became accustomed to the unique taste, and he retained his secret! He decided to try pigeon for a change, and with his muzzle loader well charged, shot at two pigeons on a chimney pot, both of which fell down the flue pipe. When he had rescued them from the fire back, the owner appeared, demanding two guineas for the birds — however, Thomas Henry contended they were wild, and offered 8d each for them. He received a summons demand of two guineas, but as evidence could not be produced in court, it having disappeared in the pie, the case was adjourned to find out if wild pigeons settled on chimneys. As it was not proved one way or the other at the adjourned hearing, the case was dismissed on payment of £4.10s. 6d. costs; it was an expensive pigeon pie, so it was back to duck and rabbit!

His father was a yeoman, providing three horses and ten men for ten day's Spring training, and to meet judges at Derby Assizes. He was also a local preacher, taking his family to London, to hear Dr Talmadge at the City Temple and Dr Sprigeon at the Tabernacle.

At the age of 8½ years, when his mother died, he helped in his father's office; later he was apprenticed for a short time with a saddler in Duffield.

It was then that he took up a second apprenticeship as an engineer at Ruston Hornsby Ltd, Grantham, earning 7 shillings (35p) for a 54 hour week of which 3s 6d was paid for lodgings and washing. This income was augmented by overtime and Sunday work bringing the wage up to 10 shillings a week. Unfortunately he had served only two and a half years when his father died, and his stepmother appropriated the home and income, leaving himself aged 17, the younger brothers and sisters penniless and homeless. A year later the firm went on short time, so he returned to his native heath walking from Lincolnshire in two days with only 2 shillings in his pocket. After sleeping out for a few nights on the Derbyshire moors, he found work helping to build a stone house, but as he could not carry stones up a ladder on his head, he was given a timekeeper's job in the office, doubling up as night watchman. He slept in the cabin with a horse rug and cement bag for bed clothes, for which he was paid 16 shillings per week. Having saved £4 in a few months, he asked for his release, which his employer reluctantly granted.

Eventually he arrived in Manchester, where he went back to engineering, becoming an expert in torpedo boat boilers. He accepted the opportunity of six months probation on engine room work and was appointed to the 'Lord Walden', travelling to the China seas. From there he crossed to Russia, travelling from St. Petersburg over to the East coast fixing lighting on railway stations.

He had saved £30 in threepenny bits and decided to marry. The lady of his choice turned him down, and a rich aunt backed her up, saying he had a grubby trade, never had a good suit of clothes, thinking more of his work than he did of a woman. The young lady's mother, however, was on his side, and a wedding date was fixed, but the day before he received a letter from his intended saying "Don't come as I shall not marry you". Undaunted he turned up, and persuaded by her mother, the young lady was hustled into a cab, bouquet in hand. Immediately the ceremony was over, he was back at work, for a honeymoon was unknown in those days.

By this time he was living in Barker Gate, Nottingham, working at Manlove, Alliott & Co, entirely on the construction, development and repair of internal-combustion gas engines, which were at an early stage of development. During the evening he sold paraffin from his home.

After twelve months of somewhat

tempestuous married life, the husband found himself almost forgotten with the arrival of the first child, Thomas Andrew, born during February 1888. It was during this period that the new father came to give up smoking. The baby woke, father was unable to find a match to warm the drink, and was blamed in no uncertain manner for using matches to light his tobacco. From that day onwards he never smoked again. Hardship and experience had taught him self-reliance and thrift.

He then attended Professor Robinson's classes at the Nottingham University College technical workshops. Professors Robinson and Simpson were acquiring data for a book on gas and oil engines, and he helped in the evenings for no pay. The old University was situated on Shakespeare Street — now the site of Nottingham Polytechnic.

During 1890 the family had moved to Grantham where T. H. Barton was again working for Ruston Hornsby and Son, soon almost exclusively on the Ackroyd Stuart hot-bulb crude oil engine which had been patented, and built on an experimental basis in 1890. It was far from satisfactory, and under the direction of Robert Edwards, Hornsby's Chief Engineer, Tom Barton was involved in the development of the Hornsby-Ackroyd engine, as it became known. The development of a cam-operated fuel-injection pump was a key step forward in the development of the oil engine and important improvements were made in other features. The success of this venture ensured Barton the management of a department at a good salary, and he had the satisfaction of knowing he had helped in the development of one of the first successful oil engines. So successful was his work with this engine, that Hornsby's presented him with one in 1894 when he left to take over the family quarry after his stepmother's death. T. H. Barton always complained that credit for the first successful oil engine rightly belonged to England, not Germany. He considered the Ackroyd Stuart engine was the forerunner of all oil engines since developed, never acknowledging Diesel.

Upon arrival back at his family home, on Rigger Lane, between Little Eaton and Duffield, he set the engine to work operating a drum to grade limestone. As a youngster, son Tom soon found himself helping dad and one of his jobs every Friday was to fetch the wages from Derby; this left him only four days a week for school.

The quarrying business never really flourished. Moreover with the head of the family suffering from ill health, accentuated by inhaling fumes from experimental engines, it was decided to leave the quarry in a manager's hands, and to move to a small rented poultry farm at Mablethorpe on the Lincolnshire coast. Another venture involved hiring out a pony and trap for transporting passengers from the station, the first involvement of the Barton family in passenger transport, and for collecting scrap iron which the family sorted and despatched by train to Sheffield.

In 1897 Barton visited a London exhibition where he saw single-cylinder engines fixed on what amounted to little-modified horse wagonettes, driven by belt, with two speeds and no reverse. He took the bold decision to purchase one of these 9 hp Benz-engined eleven-passenger vehicles, but as he had never driven one of these new-fangled machines, the vendor drove it as far as Barnet. T. H. Barton, young Tom and sister Kate were then left to get it back to Mablethorpe. It took them three eventful days, during which tyres burst and were then stuffed as tightly as possible with grass; this was far from successful, and so when they came to a wheelwright's, narrow pony-trap tyres were purchased, cut to length and forced on the rims. These worked perfectly. There were other mishaps. On the first hill the low speed belt was lost; after measuring up with string the saddler in the next village made one up for 15 shillings. This stretched so much it had to be shortened every ten miles or so! Their arrival in Spalding attracted a very large gathering who admired the new motorised wonder, and it was over two hours before they could make a start on the final part of the journey. It was eventually completed by a very tired, dirty but happy trio of adventurers.

This vehicle was immediately put to work carrying passengers between the 'Pullover' and Victoria Road, Mablethorpe at 2d a journey, as long as they could keep the temperamental engine working long enough to complete its task. It must have been one of the earliest petrol-engined buses to have operated in the British Isles.

The family pose for the camera at the Duffield, Derbyshire, quarry during the mid-1890's. Shown from left to right, Nanny[?], Maurice, John, Tom, Kate, [Mother] Mary, Ruth and Tom Senior. John died at the age of six. T. H..Barton in his wisdom could see the cameras future and used it regularly during the early part of the 20th century, thus recording many items of interest during this period.

At the end of the holiday season, the decision was made to return once again to Derbyshire. By late September 1898 the family had resettled at the quarry, using the wagonette on public service in the Little Eaton and Derby area throughout the winter of that year. The Benz was now giving a lot of problems so the engine was removed. The wagonette was fitted with shafts, and sold separately.

Ill health again resulted in a move, this time to Weston-super-Mare, and within a year father had purchased a 6 hp 10-seater 1898 Granville wagonette for £75. It had been dismantled for repairs, its running costs having been prohibitive. However, the family soon had it operational, and it turned out to be a very reliable machine. Working in conjunction with a friend they obtained three further similar vehicles, having successfully applied for licences to meet boats from Wales and Bristol at the pier. They would then take passengers to the Gower Pier, or on excursions to Bridgwater, Cheddar Gorge, Wells, Glastonbury and Clevedon. They were ridiculed by the horse cab fraternity, who were nearly all town councillors, but fierce opposition developed as they took most of the cab trade. Restrictions were imposed on the licences so that they could operate only in July and August, when there was more business than the horse buses could handle. To overcome this, they picked up fares in the front gardens of friends. Charges were made against them, and they had as many as seventeen summonses to answer in one day. One magistrate had faith in the future of the motor vehicle, somewhat easing their burden, but still not preventing the opposition from putting them out of the driver's seat.

On one occasion Mr Barton senior had a load of passengers ready to start their journey, when the cab owners frogmarched him down the pier, with the intention of throwing him into the sea. After a few hundred yards or so it was concluded that it was not worth the trouble! Upon returning to the wagonette, he found his passengers had gone and he had to wait for the next boat.

After the season had closed, the vehicles carried apples from Devon to Bristol, and while consideration was being given to a proposition for regular work, an approach was made to T. H. Barton by a deputation from the opposition. Would he take over management of their business, which it was proposed to motorise? As he considered he had been unfairly treated, a coin was tossed; heads he left the district, tails he accepted the job. It came down heads.

By the end of 1903, T. H. Barton's health had improved markedly on the Somerset coast, so it was decided to return to Little Eaton in the wagonette. The quarry, which was still being run by a manager, was providing only a small return as the demand for limestone had dwindled. Father then heard of a Derby hosiery manufacturer who left a large amount of money when he died, and thought there must be something in it.

He obtained a new hand machine from Nottingham, and 20lb. of wool. Production proved difficult until he sent his eldest son

Working in Weston-super-Mare with T. H. Barton at the wheel of the Daimler-Granville, and a full complement of ten passengers. The chain drive to the rear axle is clearly shown.

and one of the daughters for a day's instruction on the use of the machine. T. A. Barton was quoted as saying "Soon I could make twelve pairs of socks in a day, my sister doing the toes, pressing, wrapping and winding wool on to the bobbins. Working by hand, it took from 6 am to 8 pm five days a week to achieve this output. On Saturdays we took socks, stockings and wool by pony and trap to the surrounding villages of Horsley, Coxbench, Kilburn, Denby and then on to a stall at Ripley market.

Another quarry was purchased at Tansley Moor, near Matlock. The stone being dug from these works was suitable to make grindstones for which there was a big demand in Sheffield. The daughters continued the stocking business and the Granville was used between the two quarries until the Little Eaton site was sold. Later a house was built at Tansley, where the family had, in addition to the quarry, some 27 acres of grassland on which cows were kept. The children milked and stabled the cows at night and early morning before putting in a days work at the quarry.

During this time father was involved in a steam bus service from Herne Bay to Canterbury before moving on to Wales, where he was asked to take over an established route from Llandaff Castle to Cardiff Town Hall. He found the obstinate vehicles ran very irregularly, his comments afterwards were "The whole concern would have done credit to a first class music hall entertainment, which was certainly too good an institution to attempt to spoil".

The wagonette had been working around Matlock, being disposed of before the sale of the Tansley Moor quarry. It was evident that these workings had to be sold, as the family worked without wages. The accounts showed it was just holding its own; as it turned out later, it was then at its peak.

Yet another move followed, this time to Derby, where a monumental mason's business was purchased, including a house. From the proceeds of the quarry sale, T. H. Barton was persuaded to purchase a 20-seater 20 hp Durham Churchill charabanc, this being kept in an old lean-to shed which had a low roof. To overcome this the ingenious father jacked it up 3ft. Soon, however, the Town Clerk to Derby issued instructions for its demolition, but they refused to take any action until the Corporation took the case to court, and won. On appeal to London the authority won again. Many years later when relating this, his son Tom said "It cost us £100 to fight the action for a building which was probably not worth £10 anyway." In partnership with two other persons, T. H. Barton was licensed to operate the charabanc in the Derby Borough. Young Tom had been plying the vehicle for hire in the Derby and Little Eaton districts for three years when, on Monday 3rd October 1908, he drove nineteen people to Edwinstowe, in the Dukeries for the day. While lunching in Mansfield. he was approached by a Mr Lock, who questioned him about the vehicle. Lock wanted to know if it would pull a load, and was it for sale? The answer to the second part was easy "Father will sell anything if the price is right, as to the first, why not watch it pull this load up Leeming Street Hill". Mr Lock saw it do just that,

The Clarkson steam bus purchased by Barton in 1909 [see page 94, top left] is seen at Herne Bay, in this official view. The Herne Bay & Canterbury title has been obliterated on this copy, but it is known that the company never operated the vehicle as it passed to the East Kent & Herne Bay Co, from whom it was obtained by Barton. There are no records of Barton's involvement in this service, although this was claimed some years later. The author believed the gentleman with cap sitting facing rearwards was similar in appearance to TH, but it is now known it is the editor of the local newspaper [detailed on original photograph].

and the vehicle was sold by the time the outing had returned home.

Father and son had a candid discussion that evening, as Tom junior really did not like to lose the vehicle, and it was decided they would catch an early train to London to find another bus. During the journey they chatted to the only other occupant of the carriage, who turned out to be a Director of Durham Churchill, and offered them a nearly new 28-seater for £450. It had, he said, only worked for three months in Scarborough, from where they had repossessed it because instalments could not be met. Father said it was no use to him at that price, so it was offered on a month's trial for £12 and, if proved satisfactory, they would purchase it at £12 per month thereafter. An order was written for the vehicle to be collected, filled with petrol, oil and water. The Bartons never reached London that day. Breaking their journey at Luton, they discussed where this new purchase could best be employed as they waited on the platform for the return train.

Mr Barton senior recollected a lot of people travelled between Long Eaton, Beeston and Nottingham, particularly on the coming weekend, which was the time for the annual Goose Fair, located in the Market Place. This fair was over 600 years old, having grown in size over the years, until it had reached enormous proportions.

Whilst T. H. Barton was arranging for printed timetables, and permission from the local authorities, T. A. proceeded to Grimesthorpe, Sheffield, to collect the vehicle. Registered W 963, it was chain driven, fitted with a four-cylinder 28 hp Aster engine and four-speed gearbox. Passengers sat on crossbench seats, including the driver's. After the second set of seats each row was raised several inches, giving all passengers a clear forward view. It is understood the roofed but open-sided bodywork was constructed by Tomlinson of Sheffield.

The following day he collected his sister Kate from Derby and they met father in Long Eaton, where final arrangements had been made, except for the distribution of timetables which they completed that day. That evening the trio stayed overnight at Wilsthorpe Farm, Long Eaton, not realising this was to be the dawning of a very different chapter in their lives.

Believed to be the 20 hp 20-seat Durham Churchill charabanc which the Barton family operated in Derby and the Little Eaton district between 1906 and 1908. Cloth-capped T. A. Barton is in the front passenger seat.

Chapter Two: Andrew's progress

The start of the new era was marked when, at 8am Thursday, 6th October 1908, the Durham-Churchill charabanc left Long Eaton Market Place carrying one passenger. It travelled through the small hamlet of Toton, and on to Chilwell village, where six people boarded; by the time Beeston was reached they had a full load. The service continued at two-hourly intervals throughout the rest of the day, with practically a full load on each journey; it was the same on Friday and Saturday. Encouraged by the response, they continued the service, but the passenger receipts did not meet expectations, particularly over the section between Beeston and Long Eaton which was discontinued. The charabanc did not match the railways for comfort, of course, being fitted only with tarpaulin side curtains to keep out the elements; these curtains whipped and cracked in the wind. The road surface was bumpy and dusty and turned to mud in the rain. Lighting was provided by candles, which dripped fat on to passengers' clothing. To extract the grease a hot iron and blotting paper were carried as standard equipment!

Long Eaton was a rapidly developing Derbyshire market town with the lace industry laying the foundation, but had been greatly influenced by the arrival of the railway, which had established a marshalling yard for assembly and dispersal of coal wagons from the Nottinghamshire and Derbyshire coalfields.

The Midland Counties Railway Company commenced operations between Nottingham and Derby on Thursday 30th May,

Durham Churchill W 963 surrounded by the family, stands in the Green, Long Eaton, with a full load for Beeston and Nottingham. The author's great grandfather is on the second row holding his straw boater, whilst T. A. Barton is sat on the end of the fifth row of seats. The chain drive to the rear wheels is plainly visible. Other members of the family are assembled around the front, including Maurice [against radiator], Alfred and Carl [standing at front]. Seated on front row from left T. H., Kate, Mabel and Edith.

The advertisement placed in the 'Advertiser' for the new service, a year later in 1909.

LONG EATON, TOTON, CHILWELL BEESTON and NOTTINGHAM

MOTOR CHAR-A-BANC SERVICE.

A well-appointed Motor Char-a-Banc Service will Commence on WEDNESDAY, OCTOBER 6th (Goose Fair).

TIME TABLE.—Leaves Long Eaton Market Place: 8.30 a.m., 10.30, 12.30 p.m., 2.30, 4.30. Leaves Stamford Street, near the Fountain, Nottingham: 9.30 a.m., 11.30, 1.30 p.m., 3.30, 5.30. Passengers picked up en route. Theatre and other parties by arrangement with Driver.

FARES: Long Eaton to Nottingham, 6d.; Toton to Nottingham, 6d.; Chilwell to Nottingham, 4d.; Beeston to Nottingham, 3d.

Communications to be addressed to Mr. Andrew Barton, c/o "Advertiser" Office, Long Eaton.

1839, serving Beeston and Long Eaton, the line running parallel to the highway and the River Trent, but some distance from the townships. This was overcome when a link Erewash Valley line was opened on 6th September 1847, by the Midland Railway, which had succeeded the Midland Counties Railway. This link provided a station in the centre of Long Eaton, named

The scotch or wedge attached by chain to the underside of the body, adjacent to the white-painted stakes was an early form of brake. This has been faithfully reproduced on a replica vehicle introduced in 1952 and photographed in 1981.

Toton until 1862 , when the old Long Eaton station was closed. On 1st May 1862, a second station, Trent, was opened approximately one mile away; this was on the junction of four railway routes, and gave access to Leicester and London. A little later Attenborough station was built to serve the village and Chilwell.

An old-established carrier's cart was operating twice-daily to Nottingham via Chilwell and Beeston, collecting passengers and goods, and taking in finished lace and bringing material for making up by outworkers. Beeston was also served by two more carriers, one offering a twice-daily service; some years earlier a horse bus had also operated the four miles into Nottingham.

Beeston, with a population of almost 10,000, had lace and stocking frame knitting as its main industries. Thomas Humber had established his first cycle factory here, but had moved on to Coventry by this time. As a near neighbour to Nottingham, new industries were finding Beeston an ideal area in which to establish themselves, and so the short service to Nottingham survived, helped by the railway station being some distance out of town.

From Beeston the route to Nottingham went via Beeston Lane towards Derby Road, passing by Wollaton Park, the home of Lord Middleton, and meeting the Nottingham Corporation Tramways service 9 terminal at the Lodge Gates. Shortly afterwards the vehicle turned into Lenton Boulevard (to avoid the steep Derby Road hill) and on to Castle Boulevard. It then followed the line of tram service No. 6, reaching the terminus at Stanford Street, just off Greyfriar Gate, which was, incidentally, only a few hundred yards from the Midland Station.

Nottingham evolved around two small sandstone hills. The site was a crossing over the River Trent, and the Normans built a castle on one of the hills to control this point. The industrial revolution brought the factory system, with its overcrowding, slums and, for a time, unrest. Factories and equipment were destroyed by cottage industry workers, who could see their livelihood destroyed. However, by the late nineteenth century the city had developed lace and hosiery, side by side with engineering, tobacco and pharmaceutical industries, making it a major industrial area.

Horse tramways had commenced in Nottingham during 1877. Nottingham Corporation acquired the 19 1/8 route miles in 1897, converting these to electric operation in 1901 and extending the track to 25½ miles. During 1901-2 three rival projects to build tramways were proposed, covering an extensive area of Nottinghamshire and Derbyshire. None of these was built, but it is of interest that the Derby and Nottingham Light Railways intended to run from Long Eaton, Chilwell and Beeston to join up the Corporation track at Lenton. The Nottinghamshire and Derbyshire Tramways Company, however, did build one route from Ripley to Heanor and Cinderhill, before joining the Corporation's line into the city. They also had grandiose plans, including a Stapleford, Bramcote and Beeston to Lenton route. Nottingham Corporation made an unsuccessful attempt in 1908 with Ilkeston Corporation to join their systems, via Beeston, Chilwell, Toton and Stapleford.

Barton's was not the first motor bus to operate in the city, as the Corporation had already operated three Thornycroft double-deck buses for a short period between the Market Place and Carlton Road. There was an abundance of carriers' carts serving Nottingham from most of the surrounding villages, particularly on Wednesday, market day. Regular horse bus services were still operating just beyond the city boundary to Arnold, Ruddington and West Bridgford.

It was decided to run the service from Long Eaton again during the Goose Fair of 1909. The weekly local newspaper, the Long Eaton Advertiser, carried a report on 8th October:

> "A motor charabanc has commenced between Long Eaton, Nottingham and intermediate villages. The appearance of a charabanc in Long Eaton streets this week has been the subject of much comment. The service was initiated on Wednesday, when about 30 schoolchildren were treated to a free bus ride round the town."

Nottingham Corporation, supported by Beeston Urban District Council, granted the application to Andrew Barton, subject to restrictions inside the city area, which allowed passengers to be set down only after the boundary on inward journeys and picked up only when leaving.

The family had by now moved into shop premises with living accommodation at 69 Chilwell Road, Beeston, giving access to an area of land at the rear for maintenance and garaging. Vehicles entered by way of Ellis Grove, a short distance from their home.

Successful applications were made by Andrew Barton Bros to Nottingham Corporation in January and September, for licences for additional buses, one being a replacement vehicle for repair purposes. The subsequent timetable which appeared showed Long Eaton being served every two hours, Monday to Saturday, with an additional two-hourly service to Beeston only on Saturdays, giving an hourly headway on this section. On Sundays Long Eaton was reached on two journeys only, with one run to Beeston. An application was refused by the City Authorities for a conductor's licence to Mary Barton, aged 20, in connection with a vehicle for touring purposes.

A second vehicle, a Scott-Stirling, registered in London as LE 8000, fitted with ornate 18-seat coachwork, and complete with roof rack, had been obtained late in 1909 to cope with the additional work. This chassis was manufactured at Twickenham, with a two-cylinder 14 hp engine, over which was directly mounted the driver's seat and controls. Rather than the then normal chain drive, it was fitted with 'bevel crown' transmission and thus of quite advanced design for the period. Most of these chassis had been manufactured for London Power Omnibus Company, but were withdrawn from service in 1907; by April 1908 the firm had gone into liquidation due to lack of orders.

During September of 1910, neighbouring premises at 71 Chilwell Road were also acquired, about the same time as the first double-decker came into Barton ownership. This was a Clarkson driver-over-engine steam bus produced at Chelmsford some four or five years earlier. Rather unusual bodywork was fitted, having a front entrance to the lower-deck, accessible from the near and offside, and a rear-entrance landing to both floors, with an open staircase. Limestone water furred the boiler which had to be replaced frequently, as T. H. Barton recalled some years later, saying at the same time that the Durham-Churchill vehicle had been a real step forward in development of the motor vehicle, and for the period was very reliable. The Durham-Churchill was still in regular use, and to overcome passenger heating problems, a novel idea was to divert the exhaust pipe through the centre of the bodywork to discharge above the roof, with effective results. On these vehicles the driver took the full force of the weather; T. A. Barton suffered frost-bite in both fingers and toes during one day's driving through snow.

Modifications and repairs were now being carried out in a wooden garage in Ellis Grove, employing staff from outside the family. They included Jack Bloor, who had moved to Beeston from Little Eaton with the Barton family, also two local lads who were to serve for many years, Charlie Parker and Tommy Shirley. Often it was necessary to work through the night to keep vehicles running. Drive chains were removed and boiled in oil to clean off the grit and mud which so often caused them to break. Solid rubber tyres were very expensive, so complete wooden wheels were fitted; in dry weather these were soaked overnight to make the spokes fit. These wheels soon wore down, exposing knots, which gave a very uncomfortable ride, particularly as the road surfaces were often rutted and unmade. Brakes were ineffective, requiring scotches to be carried, together with long stakes which were attached at one end to the back of the vehicle. If rolling back occurred, they were released, digging into the road surface to halt the vehicle. T. H. Barton was now developing general engineering work and commercial motor sales, which was to cause a large influx of vehicles over the next few years, many of which were never operated, being directly resold.

T. A. Barton was interviewed in 'Coaching Journal and Bus Review' of March 1954. A part of that interview is reprinted as follows:

"The opportunity arose to purchase 20 brand new double-deckers due to liquidation of a London bus company. Indeed, some of them were not quite finished, and were secured at an incredibly low price of £50 each. We tried them on the Beeston route and they ran beautifully. However, my father said they were too good for Beeston and we must sell them. A dozen were sold to a Bedford operator at £250 each, and the balance on similar terms. At last there was a little money in the kitty, although our two older vehicles were beginning to prove very unreliable on our own service route."

These vehicles were purchased during 1911 and at least one of them was retained, being registered AL 68. Described by T. H. Barton as of Farcot make, these were Lacoste-Battman with Farcot engine, being chain-driven chassis imported from France. Burridge of Bedford (Bedford Motor Omnibus Co) purchased one (AL 1895) as a single-decker, and re-registered it as BM 1815 in January 1912. An Argyll (AL 1141) also passed to Burridge but was not re-registered.

At this time Mr Barton senior had been approached by Merthyr Tydfil local authority, asking if he would operate a Merthyr Tydfil to Aberfan service; an application was made on his behalf and approved by six local authorities. It is not known if this was operated, but there is a possibility of the Clarkson decker operating in the area. This may also have been the reason for retaining one of the Farcot vehicles. There was an interesting motif on the side of the Clarkson, of a clock tower and a heron from the defunct Herne Bay & Canterbury Co, coming to Barton from the East Kent & Herne Bay Co. The Llandaff-Cardiff was licensed in 1910 at the same time as the Merthyr service.

During December the first of many conflicts with Nottingham Corporation and the Constabulary was to arise. The Company was approached following reports of illegal picking up and setting down within the city boundary; they were reminded that the first stopping place from the terminus was the west side of Wollaton Lodge on Derby Road (in effect immediately after the tram terminal), although in November 1912 they successfully applied for a stopping point at Lenton Boulevard/Derby Road, being the junction of tram routes 5/6 and 9.

Another large batch of vehicles arrived in 1911-12 and again T. A. Barton's comments are taken up in the article previously mentioned:

"Another slice of luck came our way, however, when Ryknield Motor Co Ltd, Burton-on-Trent, failed and offered my father 30 bus chassis, some ready for delivery, others ready for assembly. Some of these chassis were quickly sold, ten of them going to the Argentine."

Several of the vehicles may have been purchased with bodies as these were sold to Burridge of Bedford (BM 1698), Arnold of Nailsworth, Gloucestershire in February 1912, and one, in September, to Boyer of Rothley, Leicestershire. It is known that two such vehicles were sold to Boyer's, one two-cylindered, one four-cylindered (AY 1798/R6).

Mr Barton was persuaded by son Tom to run one of these vehicles (AL 1700) and a body was built for it in one week. To increase the seating capacity, two rows of three seats were fitted longitudinally alongside the bonnet, on top of the wings, making it somewhat difficult to drive with passengers in front of the driver. Obviously the passenger potential required either larger vehicles or duplication, and so they ingeniously decided to lengthen the Ryknield chassis by cutting it in half and inserting another section of metal to extend the wheelbase. This procedure was to be repeated on many later Barton vehicles. A similar vehicle, AL 2360, entered service later in the year. The Ryknields proved reliable, except for a problem with the engine lubrication, which eventually was cured.

It was decided at this time to separate the motor and engineering side of the business, which was to operate under the old title of Andrew Barton Brothers, whilst the omnibus section was renamed as Progress Motor Services Ltd.

It is of interest to note the title Andrew Barton Brothers was used inferring the business was run by the founder's sons, although applications to Local Authorities after 1910 were made in the name of T. H. Barton, the father.

By early 1913 Nottingham to Beeston was the only service operating, with six journeys each way Sunday to Friday, and with an extra ten each way on Saturday.

On 16th April they were granted patent rights on an invention; this was to secure a solid rubber or other band to a wheel when it is slightly larger than the rim of the wheel. The principle was to drive bolts or distance pieces into the space between the wheel and the tyre, so as to fix concentrically with the wheel, the space between the bolts being filled with hot sulphur or other cement. It is not known if this was a success, although there is a photograph of a Ryknield fitted with tyres which resemble this description.

The motor and general engineering work had developed so rapidly that new premises were erected 300 yards along from 71 Chilwell Road, where the registered offices remained. This building, at High Road, Chilwell, fronted on to the main road, having eight glazed sliding doors running the whole length, and forms the

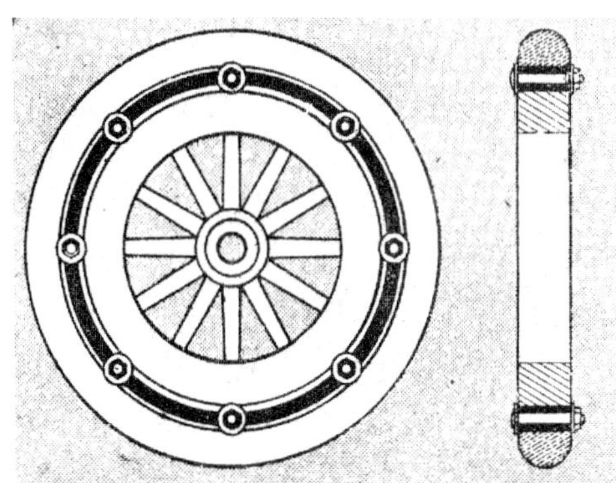

A diagram of the patented wheel described on the previous page.

nucleus of the present headquarters.

This area was earlier known as New Chilwell, being almost an extension of Beeston; Old Chilwell was a mile distant. Cottage industry of shawl knitting had been the main employment of the villagers, although there was a large shawl knitting factory in West Gate, very near to the new garage premises.

The Barton concern was really progressing now. They were gearing themselves to the new demands of the motoring age by providing welding service, oil and Mex spirit supplies. They also had an Enfield Autolette 8-10 hp car agency and commercial vehicle sales, tyre agency with press facilities and acted as commission agent for second-hand vehicles, attracting customers from a very wide area.

The bus fleet was increased with a further two Ryknields (AL 2653/2986) and a Thames 40 hp charabanc, but the Scott Stirling had been scrapped, and the Lacoste-Battman double-decker (AL 68) converted to a lorry for another venture — a haulage and taxi fleet. Additional lorries — three Ryknield, one Brillié, vans — two Thames, one Ryknield, one Argyll, two Belsize, one Napier Hawker, one Panhard, and a Thames taxi supplemented the fleet. The Thames were rather strange vehicles, manufactured by the Thames Ironworks Shipbuilding and Engineering Co Ltd of Greenwich from 1906 until 1913, and unusual for the period in being driven by six-cylinder engines, with final drive through roller chains to large rear wheels.

During this time vehicles often saw service for a short period, either being sold if the opportunity arose, or cannibalised, due to unreliability of mechanical parts. Whatever parts were salvagable were reused. Very often a radiator would disguise a completely different engine or chassis.

T. H. Barton's three daughters, Kate, Ruth and Edith, together with their mother, now operated two knitting machines, making wool stockings in the shop window of their premises on Chilwell Road. In between times Kate would drive, and her sisters act as conductors, as required.

Standing outside the new premises on High Road, Chilwell is a taxi with Kate Barton at the wheel, and a straw-hatted passenger. This photograph may have been taken on Sunday, as all the boys in the group seem well-dressed, and flowers indicate a special day. The house in the background eventually became Barton's premises, firstly as general office, now housing the advertising, printing, buying departments, and Director Peter Barton's office.

This pioneering spirit was to hit the national newspaper 'Daily Mirror' on 3rd July 1913, when the caption "Girl as chauffeur of omnibus: Sisters as conductors" appeared. This was before the use of women conductors became commonplace in the 1914-18 war and, at the time, for a female to appear as a driver or conductor was something of a sensation, but not to the hard-headed T. H. Barton. Sons Maurice (Maurie), Alfred (Peggy) and Carl were now also working, being fully employed either in the garage or on the road.

By October 1913 a good relationship had been established with another operator, Lewis of Cotgrave, who was working in the rural area of eastern Nottinghamshire; this entailed the supply of a Thames van, hiring of vehicles and carrying out repairs.

Motor vehicles were now becoming more common, and with them the inevitable competition. On Goose Fair Saturday the Long Eaton Motor Company operated a 16-seat Napier from Long Eaton (Market Place) to Nottingham (Fountain); this was so successful that a licence was granted for regular charabancs to run parties between Long Eaton and Nottingham. Undaunted, Progress Motor Services Ltd applied to operate once again from Long Eaton, this being granted on 8th December. By March 1914 Long Eaton Motor Company had successfully applied for transfer of Progress licences to them, but for some reason these were not taken up.

Ruth, acting as conductress, looks over the side of Ryknield AL 2360, parked in Ellis Grove, Beeston, with Chilwell Road in the background. In this posed photograph dated July 1913, it is believed the small girl third from front is sister Mabel with brother Carl directly behind.
Ruth is seen again in the lower picture on the step of the vehicle, with a roll of tickets in her hand.

The ex-GPO Thames van E526 had been converted to carry passengers by Barton for Alfred Lewis of Cotgrave, who commenced operating during 1912. It was used on the Wednesday and Saturday service from Cotgrave to Nottingham. A Dennis 28 hp charabanc/lorry from Barton replaced this in 1915, when it was sold to Burrows & Sturgess of Derby.

Once again Long Eaton became a regular part of the timetable, but Bartons were still in conflict with Nottingham Corporation Tramways Committee, who requested they cut services short at Derby Road, Lenton Boulevard junction in January 1914, and a little later asked them to stop at the County boundary to connect with their own tramways. In December the Committee was informed that buses were still operating to Greyfriar Gate, and T. H. Barton advised them he would continue to do so. Very often drivers became involved in the conflict by driving along the tracks in front of trams, at their own pace, collecting all the passengers. In January of the same year a second service was commenced from Long Eaton (Market Place) to Draycott, a large Derbyshire village, operating a distance of three miles on Wednesday and Saturday market days via Wilsthorpe and Breaston village.

During this period the build-up of the bus fleet enabled a further service to be added between Nottingham and Sandiacre, operating Friday to Wednesday; vehicles did not operate on Thursday, which was Nottingham shopkeepers' half-day closing. From Nottingham to Beeston Lane, the same route as the Beeston/Long Eaton service was used, but then continuing along Derby Road on the north side of Beeston, passing very little population until reaching the outskirts of Bramcote village. The route continued to the small township of Stapleford, with a population of approximately 4,000, whose main industry was lace making. It crossed the Erewash Valley line of the Midland Railway, with its station separating Stapleford from Sandiacre, a township of similar size and population to Stapleford. Sandiacre could be regarded as a town of contrasts, having lace making and railway line manufacturing as its staple industries.

Again opposition was evident; Trent Motor Traction Ltd of Derby, the local branch of the BET empire, started a Nottingham-Sandiacre service at the same time, using a vehicle which entered Nottingham from Mansfield via Bulwell. This was the first of many meetings the two companies were to experience, particularly over the next sixteen years.

Office premises were now opened in Lister Gate, Nottingham, close to the motor bus terminus; at the same time the Company became an agent for Berna and Dennis. Two more buses were added to the fleet, a Ryknield, AL 3365, and a further Durham-Churchill from Atyeo of Weston-super-Mare. The Thames charabanc was converted to a lorry, now registered AL 4304, joining two Dennis 28 hp and a British Berna, AL 4407, in the haulage fleet. T. A. Barton drove a ubiquitous Model T Ford car, AL 4406, which also stood in for taxi work.

The outbreak of the 1914-18 war in August was to radically affect the country and had its effects on Bartons. The Government then requisitioned certain types of vehicles from all sources, Barton supplying at least two Dennis lorries. Repercussions of the war affected the motor transport industry — though it was not on its own — by restriction of supply of petrol. This led again to the cutting back of the Long Eaton service to Beeston, with occasional journeys to Chilwell, and one only Saturday afternoon extension to Long Eaton. This did not produce the economies required without further reduction in services, but to avoid this, Mr Barton senior remembered his days working with gas engines, and hit upon the idea of driving vehicles with town gas. The main problem, the difficulty of carrying gas in sufficient quantity, was overcome by fitting large rubberised canvas bags — with stitched joints — on the roof, with a 6in. board fixed to brackets to hold it in place. The gas was taken direct from the mains, by hose, and fed from the gas bag to the engine. Initial starting was made with petrol, switching over to gas once the engine was warm. T. H. Barton, now referred to by his employees as 'The Guv'nor', recalled the following story, 26 years later, in the Company's magazine 'Gas Bag':

"The very term 'Gas Bag' seems to be regarded as somewhat in the nature of a huge joke, or humorous vapouring. We all know the type of individual referred to as such: much cry and little wool, as the man said who clipped the pig.

Well, the Gas Bag on motors appears to uphold this tradition, big bulk, small results: quite a humorous proposition, that often causes a tolerant smile, or vulgar laugh on the face of almost every person you encounter on a journey; the effect of the gas is very harmless to the engine and very soothing and pleasing to the driver who is not anxious to break speed records, and I feel sure the police one passes look with sympathy on those who venture to carry the tremendous superstructure overhead. On one of our early journeys in the last war, a dear old lady said, "How kind it was to put such a good protection from bombs on the top of the bus," although I really think many observers expected at any moment a violent explosion to carry away the whole caboodle and driver into oblivion.

In our first venture during the last war, we arrived at Nottingham terminus one morning at 10.30. I was driving the bus and saw, drawn up on the pavement, several gold-laced officials, several police officers, two University professors, one with gown and mortar-board, and some councillors. The whole appearing to be a civic reception, with the absence of a fanfare of trumpets, which made it appear a bit flat. The passengers and myself alighted with some little trepidation, and the waiting crowd loaded up. The Carriage Inspector, with several councillors, proceeded to put me through a catechism of enquiry, while the other members of the civic party walked round the bus at a discreet distance, looking at every gadget and examining the gas filling pipe; smelling at it to assure themselves of the presence of gas. This caused a lot of comment, as the general idea seemed to be that a big explosion, like that of a time bomb, might occur at any moment.

The questioners required information as to the manner of the operation, and particularly what precautions we had taken for the safety of passengers with regard to explosions if such an event occurred; this was more than I had anticipated in my calculations, and I had to explain that our intentions were not to let off the gas in one big bang (so we had put it in a bag to keep it safe from passengers taking it home to fill their meters) and we only meant to dole it out to the engine in very small quantities at a time; to keep the wheels turning and the business running.

This simple explanation seemed to soothe the fears of the inquisitors, and they held a group meeting on the path, after which Professor Robinson called me to the group and enquired the reason which induced me to adopt this power system, whereon I explained that as one of his pupils in applied mechanics at the University, I had learned these principles and put them into practice on the bus.

In the meantime, passengers sitting in the bus began to fear the terrible result of a charge of aiding and abetting in this diabolical plot, and some, with bowed heads, made off in shame to the station, and those who faced it out complained of getting home late for their husbands' dinners.

Well, after another meeting on the path, it was decided that under the Carriage Inspector's supervision, the Gas Bag should be allowed to operate for one week only, as the Professor was of the opinion that a disastrous explosion was not a very likely occurence, and should the gas ignite in bulk the result would be a flare that would take an upward direction, and in the main be less dangerous than petrol; so ended our Civic Reception and, up to date, no great calamity or devastating explosion has happened to the gas bags, which are still received with indulgent smiles or a vulgar laugh at times, as best suits the observer."

A driver did recall later the dangerous practice each evening of lighting acetylene lamps inside the vehicle. These were suspended from wooden slatted ceilings, upon which rested the gas bags! At least three Ryknields were converted, having 18ft. x 6ft. diameter holders, containing 504 cubic ft. of gas, which was equal to only two gallons of petrol. There were refill points at their depots in Chilwell and Nottingham, and possibly one at Sandiacre, as it is doubtful if one fill could have covered a return journey. As the holder emptied, the surplus material hung down the side of the vehicle, obscuring passenger's view, and often on windy days the vehicles were difficult to steer. It was not unknown for the bags to blow off, resulting in a rescue from the most obscure places.

On a less adventurous note, the Thames van was taken back from Lewis of Cotgrave in exchange for a Dennis 28 hp lorry, but did not re-enter service, being resold shortly afterwards.

Various makes of chassis were sold during 1915, very often one of the sons driving to the purchasers in various parts of England and Wales, and staying on to give driving lessons.

Buller of East Bridgford operated into Nottingham on Wednesdays and Saturdays, but for three weeks in May 1915 had to hire a bus and driver from Progress to keep his service running.

The war in Europe did bring unexpected prosperity to the district, when it was decided to build a shell filling factory at Old Chilwell. This involved the closing of the road to Toton, diverting the occasional bus through Attenborough village, on to a new road and bridge over the factory's internal railway system, then rejoining the Long Eaton road on the outskirts of Toton. From September, Barton provided lorries to work on this site, supplementing his fleet with Numbers 9, Thornycroft 'J'; 10, Daimler; 14, Milnes Daimler; 6, Seldon two-tonner, and 21, a Durham-Churchill converted from a charabanc. Fleet numbers were also given to earlier lorries:- 7, Thames; 8, Berna (British); 18, steam roller and 17, a cultivator. Several showmen's or farmers' steam engines were hired on a day-to-day basis, being allotted fleet numbers for reference purposes; at least one 'showman' stayed with the Company until after the war, working in the garage. Various haulage work was undertaken during construction, including carting of slag from Stanton Ironworks, near to Sandiacre, for use in concrete, due to the shortage of sand, gravel and ballast. Perhaps the strangest job was the carrying of one shell from each batch over 200 miles to Shoeburyness, for testing by firing into the sea. This entailed a regular overnight journey of up to twelve hours, which was rather hazardous, on poorly surfaced roads, with restricted acetylene lighting. They often used a fully exposed vehicle such as No. 6, the Seldon with solid wooden wheels in all weathers.

Demands of the Central Shell Filling Company necessitated additions to the fleet in 1916:- numbered 25, another Thornycroft 'J'; 24, Foden steam wagon; 22, steam roller; 5, Clayton steam wagon, and 16, an unidentified vehicle. One of these steam wagons was purchased in the South of England. Young Alfred was duly despatched with one of the employees to collect it. Despite not having experience in the finer arts of steam-manship, they quickly adapted themselves on the homeward journey, which took several days, very often sleeping on the wayside.

Meanwhile at Barton's premises in Chilwell, all available hands were involved in the manufacture of the patented 'Gas Bag' which was being sold to transport operators throughout the country, including Bath Electric Tramways, Harrogate Road Car Company and United Automobile Services Ltd at the latter's Bishop Auckland branch. Gas holders were fitted to the roof of Barton's own Model T Ford, which now regularly taxied personnel to the shell filling factory from the railway; a tractor was converted, and a trailer attachment gas holder was hooked on to a Ford Model T for a local customer.

The Ministry of Transport Act of June 1916 allowed omnibuses plying for hire two years before 14th March 1916 to continue to do so without consent of the Local Authority, though charges would be made for road maintenance.

Ryknield AL 2653 was sold to Lewis of Cotgrave in October 1916, being fitted some months later with a 'Barton Gas Bag'; during the same year a Berna, AL 4297, entered service to replace the Ryknield. Reference was also made to Dorman buses AL 1700 and a Little Dorman. Since Dorman were known for their engines, it must be

Seldon lorry No. 6, imported from America, looks totally inadequate to undertake the 200 mile journey overnight to Shoeburyness. It is not surprising the driver is so well wrapped in heavy clothes to face the elements. This was a regular journey to delivery a sample shell for testing purposes. Note the OHMS lettering on the bonnet.

assumed these were original Ryknields which had been overhauled. The life of engines, and very often vehicles, was quite short. This enabled the mechanically minded to buy at very reasonable prices, and then to rebuild, using spares from other vehicles, or making their own.

The livery of the vehicles had by now been standardised on post-box red; it is understood earlier vehicles had been green, though many had operated in the colour scheme of previous owners.

As in 1915, there were no additions to the 1917 bus fleet, however, steam wagons 3/4/11 were purchased for work at the shell filling factory, plus a Ford T van. Three steam wagons were sold to Ericsson Ltd of Beeston, the telephone manufacturer, thereby ending their hiring contract which had been in operation for the previous two years.

Experiments were made with Benzole fuel. This was a petrol substitute, a by-product of coal supplied from Bolsover collieries. Unfortunately this required further refining — dirt clogging the carburettors — which in turn raised the price far above the cost of petrol. It is worthy to note that, sixty years on, experts are considering coal-derived motor fuel again, with world fuel shortages bringing demands for another alternative.

Another Thornycroft 'J', AL 2360, with a 31-seat body and registration number from a Ryknield, was a new addition, as were 3/4, two American Signal 2-ton lorries and Ford T car, R 115, during 1918.

A 'Gas Bag' being tested for leaks by filling with smoke. Seated on the holder are Alfred [Peggy] Clarice Stapleton, and Carl. The buses behind are unidentifiable.

A Model T Ford taxi, proudly advertising its ability to be propelled by coal gas. It was probably photographed in Devonshire Avenue, Beeston, whilst taking its complement of army personnel to the Chilwell shell filling factory.

Also in 1918 Nottingham Corporation for the first time approached Bartons in friendlier vein, asking them to provide a service from the city centre to Bagthorpe hospital, which housed wounded soldiers. This they reluctantly declined, due to a labour shortage at the time.

Wedding bells rang out twice in 1918 for the family, when Kate married employee Jack Billingham, at Beeston Parish Church in the March and six months later son Tom married Miss May Woodhouse at Attenborough.

Construction was virtually complete at the shell factory, which had by now been renamed the National Shell Filling Factory, production having commenced in March 1916 with many workers being recruited from around the country. This was hazardous work — there were nineteen explosions, four being fatal, including one on the evening of 1st July 1918, which virtually destroyed the factory, with a resounding blast and pall of smoke crossing over Beeston and Nottingham. Every available vehicle was called upon to carry the injured to Nottingham General Hospital, and the Voluntary Aid Detachment Hospital at Long Eaton. Mr and Mrs T. H. Barton ferried bodies to Nottingham in the Model T Ford car, not knowing if some were dead or alive. Many inhabitants of Beeston remember the long line of wagons wending its way, reminiscent of war time evacuation.

Greyfriar Gate offices and works in Nottingham had by now replaced the Lister Gate branch, and the offices at Beeston moved next door to 73 Chilwell Road, on the corner of Ellis Grove, under the title Barton Bros.

Although war ceased in November, many of the restrictions continued into the next year. However, with the increase in population due to the shell filling factory, the family decided to try their luck in Long Eaton once again. On the 20th April a two-hourly Monday to Wednesday, Friday and Saturday service was started, with three return journeys on Sunday, all advertised as offering fares at third class railway rates.

Long Eaton Advertiser on 15th August carried the following editorial:

> "We have seen Barton Bros and henceforth each week the timetable will appear in our advertising spaces. This obviates uncertainty and complaint. The benefit of starting promptly from the Market Place on a pleasant fresh air journey and land in the heart of Nottingham at the price of a railway ticket is too obvious to comment. When buses ceased to run frequently, owing to exigencies of war, we grumbled much. Now that Barton Bros are again providing for our comfort and convenience we should patronise them."

Although still running on the same headway, the service was an extension of the Sandiacre route, via Longmoor Lane and Wilsthorpe, into Long Eaton along Derby Road. During October Long Eaton Urban District Council requested that services commenced from Hall Green on market Saturdays.

Chilwell Hall and Estate was sold in 1919, Bartons purchasing three lots of land adjacent to their Chilwell premises for future expansion.

Fleet additions were lorries 5 and 7 Berna (Swiss), AL 2360/4878; Ryknield AL 6306; a second 7, this time an AEC; followed by two ex-London General Omnibus Co AEC 'B' models, purchased from the War Department, which had converted them to ambulances, operating with these bodies as LGO2 and 1, LH 8139/41. The seventh lorry was a Four Wheel Drive, commonly known as FWD, having final drive of bevel type to all four wheels as the trading name implies. The bus fleet was not forgotten; with increase in services the following were received:- a Thornycroft 'J', AL 4408, with Todd 42-seat two-doorway bus body from a Ryknield; an AEC, AL 5872, also with Todd 42-seat body, this time with centre-entrance, both of which were evidently on lengthened chassis; a Karrier 35-seat charabanc, AL 6870, and a Daimler 'Y' open-top double-decker O18/16R, AL 7028. Gas bags were still in use in late October, with Thornycroft AL 4408 being put into service with this conversion.

Nineteen-twenty saw a new decade opening with Barton and Nottingham Corporation once again in conflict; in January Barton had support from Nottinghamshire County Council who successfully opposed the Corporation's proposal to extend its boundaries and establish a motor bus service between Nottingham and Chilwell. In October Barton applied to run entirely within the city, with a service from the centre to Dunkirk. This was refused as the Corporation intended to run this themselves, with a proposed tram service passing through Dunkirk on to Beeston. This was opposed by the trustees of Sir Jesse Boot's pharmaceutical empire, who had left this area of land to the city for development of a university.

Another rival was granted a licence by Nottingham Corporation when Clayton Transport commenced a daily service to Beeston from Trinity Square, a prime position near the centre of the city; immediately Barton applied for Upper Parliament Street termini for their services but were turned down. However, they were more successful at Long Eaton where they were granted licences from there to Castle Donington and Derby. Trent were also granted a licence to Derby, which was never operated, but possibly kept as an insurance and a reminder to Barton that they ran into Derby from Sandiacre.

During June, the Long Eaton-Sandiacre-Nottingham service became daily, and two additional services were introduced using the traditional route via Beeston; these were extended from Long Eaton Green to College Street, and Royal Oak, Tamworth Road, Sawley, each on a two-hour headway daily, giving an hourly service on the main route, with a half-hourly service on Saturday between Beeston and Nottingham.

These routes from Long Eaton were short-lived, for on 1st October the extension from Sandiacre was detached, thus making this service again a Sunday to Wednesday, Friday and Saturday operation using the same times. This amendment was covered by a new link between Old Sawley - New Sawley - Long Eaton - Sandiacre - Stapleford, giving three journeys daily, with regular short runs from Long Eaton to New Sawley to cover an amendment on the Nottingham route. One leg of the Nottingham to Long Eaton service from Royal Oak was withdrawn on 7th October, being replaced by a further extension of the College Street section, along Derby Road to Wilsthorpe, and terminated at Wilsthorpe Road, New Sawley. Business was now so good on this service that it became half-hourly from mid-day each day of the week.

New Sawley and Wilsthorpe had become a part of Long Eaton Urban District Council the previous year. Wilsthorpe was a very small hamlet of a few farm buildings, but New Sawley was an adjoining suburban area of modern housing, with several industries on Wilsthorpe Lane. The population increase during the war had been absorbed, taking up property which had previously been vacant, and transferring employment from the now run-down shell factory to local industries. Long Eaton now diversified into furniture and piano making, several firms of importance setting up around the town. Beeston also had a boost with the new Ericsson's telephone factory being rapidly developed. Old Sawley, a small rural village, remained as a part of Shardlow Rural District Council.

To cater for these demands, the bus fleet was expanded considerably, receiving eight open-top double-deckers, two ex-LGOC AEC 'B' types, LF 8351/8424; another AEC locally registered as AL 9410; two Daimler Y-types also from LGOC, LE 9696/LC 7379, (LE 9696 originally licensed as Leyland), the second having a 1906 chassis! The remaining three were again Daimlers, NN 49/289/302. It is possible some of these may have been re-registered locally after being War Department ambulances, as mentioned earlier. A large capacity single-decked AEC, AL 9410, with 38 seats, was followed by Maudslay AL 3365 which entered the haulage fleet earlier in the year, receiving a 45-seat Ryknield body, upon removal of the lorry structure. A later Ford T car, AL 7025; two vans, Willys Overland and a Lewis, AL 3288, supplemented the fleet. Ryknield AL 2635 was returned from Lewis of Cotgrave, who received AL 4297 Berna in exchange.

During this time Barton experimented with a Daimler road train, which it was proposed to use on the Nottingham to Beeston route. It looked a good proposition, but they had difficulty starting the engine, and when it was moving used a large amount of petrol. Carriages were not built; it was only run as a chassis. This was possibly obtained from Daimler who, in 1907, had acquired exclusive British rights from Colonel Renard, a French engineer. He had designed the Renard Road Train in 1902, each of the six-wheeled carriages having its drive shaft and differential coupled to the drive transmitted from the rear axle of the train. Several were supplied to other countries, although one did operate at the Franco-British Exhibition, London in 1908. They were not successful and production had ceased by 1914.

Tragedy was to strike the family just after the war ended; within a week the death of daughter Ruth from pneumonia had occurred on 17th November 1918, aged 26. And within another two years, Thomas Henry's 52-year old wife Mary passed away on 8th October 1920.

The Renard train, which T. H. Barton had hoped to fit with passenger bodies for the Nottingham to Beeston route. The venture did not get beyond this stage.

Chapter Three: Thinking big

At the meeting of Progress Motor Services Ltd, held on 5th November 1920, at 73 Chilwell Road, Beeston, it was decided to take over Barton Brothers operations, at the same time changing the name of the parent company to Barton Brothers Ltd. T. H. and T. A. Barton were both appointed directors, T. H. being Chairman, with T. A. as Vice Chairman and Manager. Further appointments were made amongst the sons:- Maurice (Maurie) becoming Assistant Manager, Alfred (Peggy) as Checker and Carl appointed Inspector. Father ensured that they should still be mindful of the business at hand, and added the following:- This does not preclude any of them from working on the buses when needed. At the end of the month, a further meeting was held to confirm these proposals, and increase the capital from £1,000 to £6,000, by creating £5,000 of £1 shares, ranking for dividend.

A new fleet name was adopted, being very similar to LGOC style and lettering, using a larger B and N, with the intermediate letters underlined. This was to be used in various forms, but the basic outline is still in use at the present time.

The haulage fleet was now being run down, particularly as most of the contract work was being lost as a result of business concerns purchasing their own vehicles.

It was also decided to number all buses and lorries in a general group; these numbers were carried in the top left-hand corner of the drivers' screen and the centre of rear panels on saloons. Double-deckers had them placed on upper front and rear panels.

During the next three years there was to be an intake of AEC and Daimler vehicles, most, if not all, being of War Department or other military origin. Many of the single-deckers had large seating capacities, and it seems almost certain that most of the chassis frames had been extended. However, there were no national regulations on seat spacing and some vehicles of that period had relatively high seating capacities due to close seat pitch dimensions.

A close relationship had existed between AEC (the London General Omnibus Co's bus-manufacturing subsidiary) and Daimler from 1913 until the war years and the two designs incorporated many interchangeable units. Hence it was relatively simple to fit engines and radiators from one make into chassis of the other, Barton being by no means alone in doing so.

So, for 1921 the following vehicles were installed in the Barton fleet: Daimler 'Y' No. 9, a 36-seat double-decker, and No. 15 with Hora 29-seat centre-entrance body. Lorry LGO2 was rebuilt as a 31-seat rear-entrance bus numbered 7, and a second-hand Straker-Squire double-decker entered the fleet for a short period. AEC 'B' No. 12 received a 20-seat body, taking its registration number, AL 6306, from a Ryknield lorry. Louth Motor Bodies Ltd of Louth, Lincs, fitted a 32-seat bus body structure on No. 14, a Daimler 'Y'. Double-deckers entering service had a seating capacity of 36, which was a meagre total when some of the saloons were carrying more passengers. It was, therefore, inevitable that Barton should extend two Daimler 'Y' chassis which received open-top open staircase bodywork seating 34 over 30, becoming numbers 21 and 22, an unprecedented capacity for a motor bus at the time. These were so successful it was decided to similarly rebuild No. 16, an AEC 'B', Daimler 'Y' Nos. 5, 15, 18, 19, 20 and AEC 'B' No. 1, the latter seating 30 over 28. Nos. 5 and 15 were renumbered 23/5 respectively. The Berna bus returned from Lewis of Cotgrave during June and was numbered 17.

There is an increasing tendency to employ double-decker buses with a seating capacity almost equal to that of the largest types of tramcar. The vehicle shown above, which is in service in the Midlands, has accommodation for 64 people, and was built by the Hickman Body Building Co., Ltd.

At least three earlier double-deckers — 16, 19, 20 — were lengthened and rebodied by Hickman Body Building Co Ltd, to accommodate 64 passengers, during 1921. Clearly visible on the side the full-length BARTON BROS LTD title became an almost standard feature until 1927, although the style was changed slightly when all but the outside letters were underlined. The shortened legend of Barton introduced just prior to 1920 and after 1927 again had the inner letters underlined.

Bartons were granted a terminal point in Wollaton Street, Nottingham, in January 1921. This was closer to the city centre and so the Sandiacre service was transferred. In March it was decided to link the Beeston and Long Eaton service through to Sandiacre and return via Stapleford, joining up the existing terminals in Nottingham by way of Market Street and Wheeler Gate. This circular service ran each way on a daily two-hourly headway, with the times of the existing Long Eaton route remaining the same. When this service was announced Barton proclaimed "Cheaper and more frequent than trains". Nottingham Corporation, however, did not take kindly to this intrusion, refusing permission for vehicles to run into the city centre. During April, the route was reduced to Wednesday, Saturday and Sunday morning and afternoon journeys only, being withdrawn completely a little later.

All train services to and from Long Eaton were suspended during May giving Barton Bros the opportunity to do considerable business, far in excess of previous holiday times.

Further competition on the Beeston to Nottingham service came from J. Atkin of Beeston, a former employee, who used a Ford T with bodywork by Lambert of Thetford.

Almost a year after being granted a licence to Derby, a daily service commenced on 28th June giving extra journeys on the Draycott section, then extending through to Borrowash, and Spondon villages, and terminating in Cheapside, Derby. T. A. Barton did the driving, with Alan Farnsworth conducting, on the first day. Loadings were good, as it was a long walk to Trent station from Long Eaton, then 30 minutes railway travel, and another long walk back into Derby. Derby is located on the River Derwent to the south of the Pennine foothills. It is renowned for the manufacture of Crown Derby porcelain; railway repairs, maintenance and locomotive construction. The famous car manufacturer, Rolls-Royce, moved from its original Manchester address to Derby before the First World War, during which aero-engines became a major product for the first time.

Open-top deckers did not operate without incident. On 22nd July 1921, Annie Osborne was awarded £12 costs against Barton Bros Ltd, at Long Eaton Assizes. Whilst travelling from Breaston to Long Eaton, she was hit violently in the face by an overhanging branch resulting in two black eyes, cut nose, and damaged dress. It was adjudged that the driver should have driven on the opposite side of the road to take avoiding action, an indication of the attitudes of the period.

In defence, it was stated that warning notices were displayed on every seat, advising passengers not to stand whilst the vehicle was in motion, due to low bridges and trees. A week later, Long Eaton Urban District Council wrote to Barton Bros Ltd, drawing their attention to the dangers of running double-deckers under Nottingham Road railway bridge. Clayton's Transport were granted a licence to serve Long Eaton by the extension of their Beeston route, and they also were warned of the low bridge. The local authority had received a lump sum for the lowering of the road under this bridge by 2ft., but it was many years later before the work was completed, even though there were three accidents in 21 days at this point. At this time a far-sighted Councillor Truman suggested that the time was not too far distant when they, as a town, should institute a service of motor buses between Nottingham and Derby.

During August, Clayton's commenced their daily, two-hourly service, which by early September had become hourly on weekdays. Clayton's Transport and Motor Bus Co Ltd of 9 Trinity Square, Nottingham, had some months earlier operated from Nottingham to Newark, followed by routes to Ilkeston and Hoveringham, using two Alldays and Onion 32-seat open-top double-deckers purchased from West Bridgford Urban District Council. Claytons withdrew from the Long Eaton route shortly afterwards, then sold out to Trent some months later.

At the next Long Eaton UDC meeting in September a letter from Barton Bros Ltd was read to the chamber. This referred to the desire of one of the council members, for a publicly owned bus service, and offered Barton's buses and premises at valuation, but the offer was declined. This same offer was made to Nottingham Corporation, which made the same decision as Long Eaton.

December 19th saw the introduction of increased services on most routes, as Barton now had additional vehicles to cover its needs. The Derby service became hourly and was extended into Nottingham. Eighteen months from granting of the licence, Castle Donington was reached, with an hourly service daily, by extending the Sawley route via Shardlow cross roads, about half a mile from the village itself. Double-deckers could not be employed on this route, due to a very low bridge at Sawley Junction, adjacent to Wilsthorpe Road.

Castle Donington, with a township of over 1,100 people, is situated in North West Leicestershire, resting on a hillside to the south of Trent Valley. Textiles were its staple industry, and two bus operators were already established. Ella Bus Service of E. and H. Frakes operated to Long Eaton on Saturdays, and W. Potts, a local carrier, ran on the same route through to Nottingham (Collin Street) with one return journey on Wednesdays and Saturdays. He also ran to Derby and Loughborough on market days.

Sandiacre could now boast two daily, hourly, services — one from Nottingham and the other from Long Eaton.

Barton's registered office had been transferred to a house on High Road, Chilwell, during 1922, which was next to the main garage premises. The Company now concentrated on the heavier commercial side, dispensing with car and Mex spirit sales.

Timetables were now issued to the public, and also displayed at bus stops. On Saturday afternoons, the busiest time of the week, fares were reduced to one shilling (5 pence) for the Long Eaton to Nottingham run; this was boldly announced in local newspapers with the heading "England's Cheapest bus fares".

A further three daily services were commenced on 28th April, widening the area of operation considerably. Long Eaton-Nottingham used roads in the rural area south of the River Trent, crossing the river at Sawley, on to Kegworth, Kingston upon Soar, Gotham, Clifton, Wilford, through urban suburbs of West Bridgford and recrossing the river at Trent Bridge, finally entering Nottingham from the south. This vehicle then ran on the next route from Nottingham by the same way to Kegworth, proceeded to Hathern village and on to the Leicestershire township of Loughborough, famous for its engineering works, textile and bell making industries. The final route was a return from Loughborough to Long Eaton, by way of the villages Stanford upon Soar, Normanton upon Soar, Sutton Bonington, then to Kegworth using the earlier route from there to Long Eaton. In addition a Wednesday and Saturday service operated from Nottingham to Clifton, then on to Barton in Fabis, a village nestling by the edge of the River Trent.

With the controversy that surrounded each application to the Nottingham Corporation, Barton decided to apply in May to run in opposition to them on all routes operated by motor omnibuses. This was refused, and must be considered as a purely tactical move.

The Castle Donington service was now so popular that the local press asked if this service could not be linked to extend into Nottingham. A compromise during October was to extend to the most unlikely place — Sandiacre. This was for a short period only, soon reverting to Long Eaton.

In direct opposition, H. H. Farrer of Kegworth successfully applied to run from his village to Nottingham, through Clifton, on Wednesdays.

Greyfriar Gate terminus was restricted by the Local Authority to one vehicle standing. To overcome this two vehicles stood on adjacent land belonging to Barton in Whiterent Street. However, at times there were extra vehicles, and being aware of this, Nottingham Corporation instructed the police to enforce the regulations. Driver Harold Tuckwood recalled off loading his passengers in that period, then driving round to Carrington Street, Canal Street and back, often doing several circuits before there was space, or the policeman had moved on.

Lady conductors were still a regular sight; several who had been employed from outside the family were to remain for several years.

Daimler manufactured the majority of chassis placed in service in 1922, five being CB models with fleet numbers 24, 27, 29, 30, 31, the first three having 36-seat centre-entrance bodywork, whilst Nos. 29 and 31 had 39 and 40 seats respectively. Two of the 'Y' models, Nos. 25 and 26, received centre-entrance 35 and 36 seat bodywork, whilst No. 13 was fitted with 42-seat centre-entrance bodywork and given registration AL 4408 from the Thornycroft. A further double-decker was No. 17, with open-top bodywork again seating no less than 64, on an extended Daimler 'Y' chassis, whilst No. 28 was a mere 20-seat charabanc with the same running parts. For a short period a small second-hand Ford T bus had been allotted the number 8, but it was quickly sold, to be replaced by the largest single-decker yet to enter the fleet. This was an extended Daimler 'Y', measuring 34ft. 2in. long and having seating capacity for 60, with space for a further 40 standing in its centre-entrance bodywork. To give extra strength, steel bracings were fitted inside the body framework and passengers fell over these with amusing regularity. T. H. Barton had attached a generator to the chassis, from which sufficient current was obtained to provide an efficient lighting system throughout. Power was only produced when the engine of the bus was running, so it was necessary to keep ticking over whilst standing. It was claimed that any disadvantage was compensated for by the saving in batteries! However, the system was not generally adopted.

January 1923 saw the entry of an even longer extended Daimler 'Y' chassis, No. 10, which was 36ft. 6in. long with capacity for 66 seated passengers, and again with centre-entrance. These two juggernauts, about 10ft. longer than contemporary normal 'full-sized' buses, did not find favour with Nottingham Corporation, which is not surprising when locals recall many incidents on a typical journey between Nottingham and Derby. The road in Old Chilwell twisted around very tight bends, and when negotiated by the bus the long back end often knocked cyclists over. At the hump-backed Long Eaton canal bridge, it is rumoured either No. 8 or 10 was grounded — balanced on the top, with its wheels suspended in mid air.

Entrance to Draycott from both directions was restricted by a narrow Z bend railway bridge, in which the bus became trapped. To ease the situation both vehicles were transferred to the more open Gotham route, where the bounce from the considerable rear overhang kept the conductor busy replacing upholstered seat cushions which fell to the floor.

Four further Daimler 'Y's entered service, and these were to be the last — No. 6, a 26-seat saloon, and Nos. 38-40, which were fitted with 64-seat open-top bodies. Finally, the earlier No. 6 was rebuilt to 58-seat open-top layout and renumbered 37. When application was made for licences to Nottingham Corporation these double-deckers were referred to as NULLI SECONDUS. This was a name adopted for the LGOC-AEC NS model introduced some months earlier, meaning 'second to none', having lower floor height than usual at the time and requiring only two steps from the ground. The only resemblance between these models and the Barton product were the solid tyres and open top deck, although Barton had provided its drivers with a partly enclosed cab. On earlier models received from London, windscreens had been added, incidentally.

The original 'Y' and 'B' chassis were 22ft. 6½in. long, with 12ft. 10in. wheelbase. Barton extended this by a further 6ft. 9½in. giving an overall length of 29ft. 4in.; the width was increased by one inch to 7ft. 3in. It is noteworthy that even this more modest length was to be more than permitted for a two-axle vehicle by national regulations when they were introduced in the early 'thirties and remained so until 1950. At least two double-deckers, Nos. 38 and 39, were fitted with route number indicators though these were short-lived as service numbers were not yet in use. The fleet, although reliable, was proving very slow and ponderous in

BARTON BROS. LTD.
BEESTON. TEL. 95.

BARTON BROS.
BEST AND CHEAPEST
Road Motor Service
TO
Nottingham
Derby
Long Eaton
Loughboro'
Sandiacre
Castle Donington
Etc.

BARTON BROS., LTD., Engineers
BEESTON, NOTTS.
Telephone 95.
Time Tables on Application

The double-deckers lengthened in 1923 received bodywork from an unknown source, possibly local, seemingly with lower profile than the earlier Hickman bodies, although this may be an illusion since deeper windows were provided. More leg room would have been provided on this model as the bodywork extended over the driver's cab. Taken from a contemporary advert.

the face of competition, which was almost encouraged by the local authorities responsible for the issue of route licences. Many of these competitors were owner-operators using small, fast, pneumatic-tyred buses, often undercutting fares, rarely running to a timetable, and then diverting to other routes when there was a shortage of passengers. The only way to compete, it was thought, was to adopt a policy of 'chasing', which was rife throughout the British Isles. The idea was to place your own vehicle in front of the opposition to collect all the passengers. When it stopped, a second vehicle, which lay immediately behind, overtook the rival, to take prime place for the next stop. This form of leap-frogging continued between each terminal, in the hope of running competition into financial ruin, or into a ditch causing damage. The roaring 'twenties were very hairy days!

It was decided that faster vehicles were required to combat this opposition, and so the Italian Lancia was adopted. This Turin company had been manufacturing superior motor cars since 1906, making its introduction to the British passenger vehicle scene at the 1921 Olympia Show. Lancia was to be one of the more popular continental manufacturers during this period. Seven of the type joined Barton's fleet that year; numbers 32-36/41, they had 26-seat front-entrance bus bodywork, except No. 35, which had front and rear doorways, and No. 34, with 32-seat front-entrance bodywork on an extended chassis which was 26ft. 1in. long. Several of these and subsequent chassis were purchased from the Italian Government, or through Lancia, which had re-purchased the vehicles after army service. This is confirmed by the fact that brothers Tom, Maurice and Carl were sent to Turin to inspect the vehicles, of which they purchased 20. It would be unusual, even in the Barton fleet, to have altered a new chassis at such an early stage of its life, so it must be safe to assume they were not new.

The service from Long Eaton to Nottingham, via Gotham, was withdrawn in 1923, and Nottingham-Loughborough reduced to Wednesday and Saturday operation, but the Gotham to Nottingham section remained unaltered.

A short-lived service was commenced in April from a Repertory Theatre in Hyson Green, a Nottingham suburb, to Beeston, Chilwell and Long Eaton, on Monday, Wednesday and Friday evenings.

Road surfaces were improving gradually, although operators were having difficulty in some areas. When Barton complained to Stapleford RDC of the condition of approaches to Stapleford and Sandiacre railway stations the matter was discussed, and their reply expressed the view that tarmacadam would be an improvement, but they had no jurisdiction in the matter.

Barton was lobbying various councils at this time regarding defined bus stopping places. This was agreed by most councils to be acceptable for overcoming the problem of operators using various unauthorised thoroughfares.

In June and July voices were raised in Long Eaton UDC meetings, expressing concern at the possible dangers of racing buses which were often overcrowded. Speeds were estimated to be up to 25 mph, considered to be particularly high when the speed limit was still set at 12 mph, an inheritance from the red flag days, though widely ignored.

Competition was increased on three routes, F. Justice (Quick Transit Line) operated on Stapleford to Nottingham; Radford Mason, John Newbold, and S. Chapman between Long Eaton and Draycott; and M. Saxelby, Castle Donington to Long Eaton. All were to cease business within a few years. However, J. W. Kirkland with his Long Eaton-Sawley run was to be a thorn in the Company's side for some years to come.

Nottingham Corporation was still intent on getting into Beeston. Permission was obtained from the Ministry of Transport and Beeston UDC in 1920, enabling the Corporation to operate beyond its boundaries, but it was not until 1923 that it was decided to operate. Realising the situation, T. H. Barton again offered in June to sell the whole business to the Corporation, or certain vehicles and the Beeston service. Upon inspection of these it was decided the price was too high.

Barton also again offered Long Eaton UDC the opportunity to purchase the business, which it declined. Immediately after this, the UDC discussed running its own motor buses, as it had the previous year, again the same conclusions were reached, although it was added the fares could be double those of other operators.

Barton made an unsuccessful approach to the Ministry of Transport to stop NCT from operating to Beeston, but on 2nd August, two days before powers elapsed, they commenced operation.

This was not the end of the matter, however, for on Bank Holiday Monday, 6th August, a new bus in Barton Bros Ltd colours drew up to Nottingham Market Place in front of the NCT bus. On entry every passenger was given a voucher entitling the holder to a free ride to the Beeston boundary; those wishing to travel beyond this point were charged a penny for the remaining distance into the centre of Beeston. The vehicle carried a large board across its front boldly stating "Rate-payers rob Private Enterprise". It is stated legal action was under consideration against Barton for obstruction, as they were not licensed to operate from the Market Place.

Fares were now so cheap it was possible to travel from Long Eaton to Castle Donington, a distance of five miles, for 3d, to which the Long Eaton Advertiser commented: "It is quite probable there will be further cuts, in fact we are looking forward to free rides."

The Castle Donington-Long Eaton service was extended through to Nottingham in the same month, operating every fifteen minutes on Saturday and Sunday afternoons.

Accidents were rife in this period, sometimes virtually self-inflicted from chasing, but others did occur. A double-decker was stopping to unload in Beeston when the rear wheel caught in a gulley grate, forcing the bus to mount the kerb. The driver immediately turned out into the road, catching the rear end on a telegraph pole. Unfortunately the side rail of the top-deck hooked on to a foot plate on the pole, pulling away the upper-deck side and all the seats on that side. The seats and their eight passengers came tumbling to the ground, but amazingly not one person was seriously injured! A few days later, whilst travelling into Long Eaton, the Rev J. Brown stood up on the top-deck as the vehicle passed under Nottingham Road railway bridge. He suffered concussion from this encounter. On a lighter note, it was reported in a local newspaper that a passenger stopped a bus at Stapleford to retrieve a cigarette he had dropped from the top-deck.

A measure of agreement was now reached with NCT in that vehicles of both operators should run on the Beeston service alternately, as from 3rd January 1924. This provided a fifteen minute service, increased at peak periods, and during afternoons of Wednesday, Saturday and Sunday to 7½ minutes. Barton provided any extra journeys at holiday times. An increased fare of 4d was agreed, upon withdrawal of concessionary fares. Further consultations took place shortly afterwards and it was decided that as from 1st March NCT would take over the route completely, with ten saloons, Nos. 8, 11, 13-15, 24-7, 30, and the licences for the purchase sum of £12,000 less 5%. A protection point was, and still is, fixed at the Hop Pole, on the then boundary of Beeston UDC.

Not content with this situation, Barton overcame a clause in the agreement which it is understood stated, "their buses shall not stop to pick up passengers after the protection point on journeys into Nottingham, and not set down on return", by instructing its drivers to pick up passengers, but to keep the vehicle's wheels in motion. It is said many passengers were collected — except for old and infirm — but after much wrangling this was settled by rewriting the agreement, and an adjustment of costs. In consequence of this agreement, all Barton Beeston services were extended to Long Eaton, operating at fifteen minute intervals daily.

Long Eaton UDC was again offered the business during March, as was Stapleford RDC, both declined. It is interesting to reflect on what might have been if the councils had taken up this offer! Would Barton have withdrawn from this area completely? It is very doubtful!

The Company's engineering department made an interesting sale when they supplied lengthened prop shafts to the Blackburn firm of Lancashire Industrial Motors Ltd, known as Pendle Services, who sold out to Ribble Motor Services Ltd of Preston, two years later.

The takings for the year ending 30th September 1923 were £46,190, from which a gross profit of £6,709 was made. Buses were valued at £67,558, and it is believed the fleet consisted of 38 vehicles.

An extension of Nottingham-Castle Donington on to Ashby-de-la-Zouch, commenced on 17th October, taking in the Leicestershire villages of Isley Walton, Breedon on the Hill, then turning off the main road, to Ticknall and Smisby, operating two-hourly on a daily basis. Ashby-de-la-Zouch (population over 5,000), situated midway between Nottingham and Birmingham, provided the mainly agricultural area with market town facilities. Rather interestingly, the local line of the newly-formed LMS railway company ran from Breedon to Ashby, connecting with the Ticknall line which had been an early horse tramway opened in 1802 to feed the Ashby canal with lime and limestone. These had been inherited by the Midland Railway when it acquired Ashby canal in 1846; it rebuilt to standard gauge the Ashby to Breedon section to link with the Breedon to Peartree, Derby goods branch line, a through passenger service being inaugurated in January 1874, but only to survive until 1932, being replaced by a Trent 3A Derby-Ashby service. A second railway passenger service line served Leicester to the south and Burton-upon-Trent to the west, but a rather intriguing tramway served Burton-upon-Trent by a different route, through Swadlincote. Operating under the name Burton and Ashby Light Railway, it was opened in 1906 by the Midland Railway as an alternative to involving itself in the cost of building a branch railway line. With 20 open-top double-deck trams, it passed to the LMS, which abandoned the system in 1926.

Of the many operators appearing before Courts at this time, it is interesting to pin-point one, reported on 14th November, when Derbyshire Constabulary checked the bus service between the Derby boundary and Long Eaton. The Barton bus, driven by Harold Tuckwood, made the journey of ten miles to Long Eaton in 20 minutes, thus averaging 30 mph. On the return drive by Alan Farnsworth, the journey time, including thirteen stops, was 30 minutes. Obviously both drivers were fined, but it showed the Lancia had a fair turn of speed, again proven in October when Long Eaton UDC reported the Nottingham to Derby service with 32 stops was timetabled for 55 minutes journey time only.

Daimler No. 10, aptly known as 'Long Tom' was introduced in 1923 and remained in the fleet until the end of March 1929. Registered NN 3561, the vehicle was 36ft. 6in. long and 7ft. 2in wide. The authorities — perhaps not surprisingly — frowned on the vehicle and Barton made a concilliatory gesture; he reduced the seating from 66 to 56!

Chapter Four: The Barton gliders

A Lancia chassis, extended and with a third axle added, stands opposite Chilwell garage, before Charlie Parker drove it to the bodybuilders, probably Strachan & Brown of London. The wall behind displays large timetables of services to Ashby-Loughborough-Castle Donington-Derby and Tours.

The Lancia's suitability was reaffirmed when seven more were added to the fleet, with various types of bodywork. No. 8 was 26-seat, Nos. 2, 15, 11 and 14 were 29-seat front-entrance vehicles, whilst No. 7 received a 31-seat rear-entrance body from AEC 'B' No. 7, possibly also using its chassis frame but having Lancia running parts. The final addition to the fleet in 1924, number 12, again received its predecessor's 36-seat rear-entrance body, but this time a third axle was fitted. With the success of this vehicle, it was decided in 1925 to put into service eleven similar vehicles numbered 24, 42, 43, 46, 47, and 49, all with 39 seats, and Nos. 45 and 48 with 40 seats, all having front entrances. Bodies transferred from earlier buses Nos. 9 and 4 retained their fleet and registration numbers, and No. 52 received 39-seat bodywork and the registration number from No. 29. Of the foregoing, Nos. 42, 43 and 46 were fitted on to extended Lancia Z chassis.

These, the famous Barton Gliders, were claimed to be the first six-wheeled buses to be introduced into regular service in this country, although this configuration had run successfully both on the Continent and in the United States. The idea of producing this type of machine was to increase load capacity without exceeding the axle loadings, and, in particular at that date, the limitations of pneumatic tyres. Improved riding comfort was claimed.

To give an overall length of 29 to 30ft., (individual vehicles appear to have varied in this respect) the frame was cut between the gearbox and rear axle and extended by the insertion of an ash timber section inside the channel of the chassis. It was necessary to fit a new longer propeller shaft and lengthen the existing torque bar. A plain tubular axle was installed behind the standard Lancia driven axle, to act purely as a load-carrying member, each wheel being free to rotate independently. The two pairs of leaf springs were linked at their innermost ends. These springs were mounted on brackets outside the chassis frame, with the rear pair on the outside of those in front. Many of the chassis were fitted with 35 hp engines, on which the original tyres were 40in. by 8in. pneumatics, but on conversion 32in. by 6in. tyres were used, giving a low body line for easy access and vehicle stability.

Bodywork on many of these chassis was by Strachan and Brown of London, although Barton and other local coachbuilders did complete some. The longer bodies were divided into two for smoking and non-smoking compartments.

Smaller Lancias were also purchased, Nos. 6, 25, 26 and 30 being fitted with saloon bodywork and varying from 26 to 31 seating capacity. The bodywork and registration were transferred from No. 3, to

Rear axle layout of a Glider.

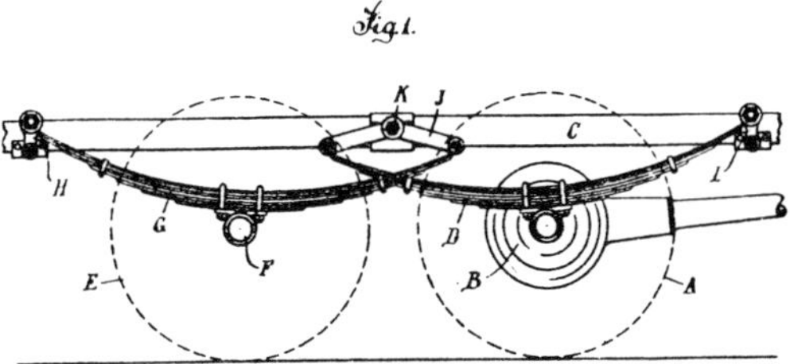

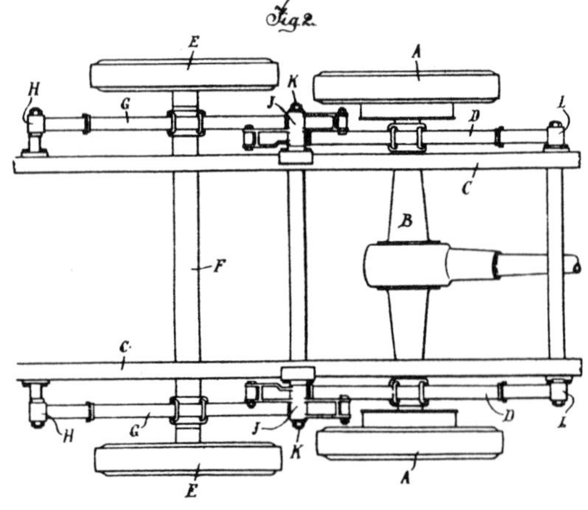

a new Lancia retaining the same number. A second-hand Lancia, No. 50, with 20-seat bodywork, was purchased, but was operated only for a short period before being used for spares.

One of the aforementioned, possibly No. 26, was converted in a different manner. To avoid extending the chassis, it was decided to convert it to forward-control and fit a separate driver's cab beside the engine, allowing a 29-seat dual-doorway Strachan and Brown body to be fitted. It was an unusual vehicle, and many remember the small cab which had no entrance door, allowing the driver's body to project outside the structure. Being fitted with 40in. rear wheels and 32in. diameter front wheels, it had a higher floor level and entrance at the rear. From photographs, the roof line appears to be level, although the chassis and waistrail lines are raised to the back. The petrol tank was placed directly behind the engine on the outside of the bulkhead; generally on normal-control Lancias these were placed directly behind the driver's seat. Karrier charabanc No. 26 was renumbered 57 upon entry into service of this vehicle.

Long Eaton UDC had advised all operators that after 31st December 1924, licences would not be granted unless vehicles were fitted with front and rear entrances. This was the reason for the production of No. 26, which joined No. 35 as a dual-entrance type. The council evidently rescinded this instruction as none of the other bus companies complied with it.

Two different marques joined the Lancias this same year. The first was No. 44, a standard Ford T with 24-seat bodywork with extended chassis. Kits were produced by Eto, Eros and Baico, which added a further 3ft. 6in. to the chassis, but it is more than likely that Barton used an older chassis carrying out alterations themselves. Standard Ford T models were normally capable of carrying only fourteen passengers.

The second stranger to the camp was a Morris one-ton chassis, usually fitted with a lorry or van body, but again this was 'Bartonised' with the addition of a trailing axle to give 24 seats in a small compact Strachan and Brown body. Fifty years later 'Motor Transport' were to remark:

> "Barton Brothers were dab hands when it came to modifying vehicles to meet their requirements. Sometimes though there is a suspicion that the mods were made more to suit the whim of one or other of the family, and this six-wheeler looks whimsicial indeed. It also has that distinctly unusual front entrance, which certainly made one-man-operation a distinct possibility, but gave the vehicle something of the air of a pre-war London taxi or hotel bus".

Two new services introduced during May of 1925 served the villages to the north of Nottingham. Starting from Greyfriar Gate they followed the City Tramways route 6 along and past its terminus on Wells Road, then joined tram service 2, following this to Mapperley. After leaving the city and the tracks, the bus followed Plains Road, giving an hourly service to the residents. From here the journeys were split into two sections, the first served Lambley (population 800), Woodborough (population 700), Calverton (population over 1,000) and Oxton (population 400). The second route continued further along Plains Road, before turning off to Woodborough by the more direct route, then on to Epperstone (population 400). None of these villages was close to the railway, and the service therefore attracted considerable custom, particularly as Woodborough was only served by a carrier, J. Leafe, on Wednesdays and Saturdays, whilst Epperstone had a daily service via Lowdham operated by W. R. Clark. Three of the Epperstone journeys were extended through to the cathedral township of Southwell (population 3,085), taking a circuitous ride through the small villages and hamlets of Lowdham, Gonalston, Hoveringham, Thurgarton, Bleasby, Hazleford Ferry, Fiskerton and Morton. This extension was short-lived being withdrawn by the end of the year, possibly due to competition from Trent and the railway.

After having their offer to run bus services within the city on behalf of NCT rejected, Barton applied to run in competition with them from Greyfriar Gate to Blue Bell Hill, following closely the route of the Epperstone service within the city, and also across into West Bridgford, but again they were not successful.

A serious fire at a cable subway at St. Anns Well Road, on 17th June 1925, cut off electric light and power in Nottingham for three days. The trams were stranded at various parts of the system, and so to cover the emergency many bus operators carried out the work for them. This involved at least two Barton double-deckers and two single-deckers.

During September NCT commenced an alternative service to Beeston, via Dunkirk and the now completed University Boulevard, allowing the tramway powers to lapse. To combat this Barton diverted many of the journeys to Long Eaton via this same route, and on 1st October added a new hourly service to Sandiacre taking this route to Beeston Square, then on to Wollaton Road, to join the existing service which was now run quarter hourly.

The Ashby service was diverted to cover the village of Wilson after Breedon, then to the small township of Melbourne, and on to Ticknall. Melbourne had two claims to fame; firstly giving its name to the Australian city, and secondly the birthplace of Thomas Cook who ran the World's first excursion, on the Midland Counties Railway line between Leicester and Loughborough and back, on 5th July 1841.

Early in December of 1925, the Oxton service was rerouted, starting from a new terminus at Parliament Street. This followed the heavily populated Mansfield Road, through Carrington and Sherwood, passing the NCT tram depot, into Daybrook beyond the city boundaries, on to the service 9 tram terminus at Arnold, and terminating at Redhill, a mile further, every hour. Every second journey proceeded to Oxton, via Calverton village with over 1,000 folks, being seven miles from Nottingham, and four and a half miles from the railway station. There was a hosiery factory in the village, which had possibly developed from Rev William Lee's invention of the stocking frame during the reign of Queen Elizabeth I. Arnold with Daybrook had a population of 12,000 involved in hosiery and mining industries. Beside the tram service, they had a regular railway run into Nottingham from Daybrook; obviously the potential was seen by other operators, with Trent operating through Daybrook to Mansfield and elsewhere. The earliest known operator from Calverton was J. Bridger, operating from 1911 with an 8-seat Armstrong until his death in 1917. For a short period in 1924-25, H. Bardill operated this service to be followed by W. E. Ward of Calverton, who was to be Barton's main competitor. The original Oxton route was cut back to Lambley to operate on Wednesdays, Saturdays and Sundays only. Epperstone was served two-hourly, except on Saturday and Sunday when an hourly service was provided. It would appear from the timetables that a vehicle was outstationed at Oxton and Epperstone from this time.

During January 1926, Barton suggested that a central bus station be erected in Nottingham, but the Corporation took no action on this. However, a sloping piece of land was acquired by Barton between Wollaton Street and Upper Parliament Street, known as the Slipway. They extended all services to it, except the Gotham and Loughborough route. The Long Eaton to Loughborough service was extended into Nottingham, and the section from Sutton Bonington rerouted via Hathern, whilst the Gotham to Loughborough journeys on Saturdays and Sundays only, were amended to operate via Rushcliffe Halt, East Leake and Stanford-on-Soar. Rushcliffe Halt was a railway station on the outskirts of East Leake, on the LNER (Great Central) Nottingham to London line, built in 1899 in competition to the then Midland Railway. A vehicle was outstationed at Gotham by this time, and when the local drivers had a day off a relief came over by rail to Rushcliffe Halt to work the day's operation, returning home by the same method. Rerouting by way of East Leake was surprisingly late, as this was the most direct route to Loughborough, and also a large village of over 1,000 people, served only by a four-times daily bus service of W. Harwood of Costock to Loughborough. Obviously the railway had a firm foothold here.

So successful was the introduction of the Nottingham-Redhill section of the Oxton route that it became half-hourly within a month of its introduction. During this period a wooden office was erected at Albert Street, the new terminus in Derby, opposite Northcliffe House. This was managed by Fred Stafford, on behalf of Barton and Phipps of Horsley Woodhouse who shared the premises. There appears to have been some sort of working relationship between the two operators, with Phipps operating Albion 'Gas Bags' in the First World War, and at least one six-wheel Chevrolet in the late 'twenties. A new service was introduced operating hourly on Saturdays and Sundays, between Old Sawley, New Sawley, Long Eaton Market Place, Derby Road, then proceeding the whole length of College Street, to Spinney Road, Long Eaton.

Earlier, reference was made to a West Bridgford application. By April of 1926, this had been introduced without consent of the local councils, using the policy adopted in Weston-super-Mare of operating from private land, with Greyfriar Gate, Nottingham and Tavistock Road, West Bridgford as termini. Fares were not taken, as the passengers purchased books of tickets — 1d to Trent Bridge and 2d to West Bridgford prior to the journey, thus creating a private contract between Barton and the passenger. The fare was 1d less than the alternative service, which involved a tram journey to Trent Bridge, then changing to West Bridgford UDC bus. By the end of the year, demand had increased sufficiently to justify a ten-minute headway, although at other times the service was operating half-hourly. After following the tram route along Arkwright Street, the bus crossed Trent Bridge into the county, taking Bridgford Road, Musters Road, Millicent Road, Henry Road, and Melton Road to its terminus in West Bridgford.

On 27th May, Wollaton Hall and Park were opened to the public, having been purchased by Nottingham Corporation for £280,000, as a public amenity. All Barton journeys passed the south gate, with the exception of one Long Eaton and a Sandiacre route. The Hall grounds were enclosed by a brick wall, alleged to have been built in 1765, by seven men and seven apprentices, taking seven years to construct, being 7ft. high and seven miles long.

On 16th July 1926, Barton Bros Ltd announced the business had changed hands. Negotiations had been proceeding between Sir Arthur Wheeler of Leicester, and Albert Parker of Long Eaton acting for Barton Bros. However, the announcement proved premature. It was stated a price had been agreed, with the entire service being purchased, as well as the patent 'Glider' feature. When interviewed, Mr Parker was not in a position to give details, but said Sir Arthur Wheeler had purchased the concern, including 60 buses.

'Glider', was a name said to be adopted from the public who had given the six-wheel buses, patented by T. A. Barton, this title, recognising the smooth fast ride given. Many of the vehicles carried a large Barton's 'Glider' legend on the side panels. It was stated on 13th August that the Barton contract had been signed, but no date fixed for the further takeover by an American syndicate from Sir Arthur Wheeler. At this time the staff were being provided with uniforms, which led to speculation of a complete takeover. In fact this never came to fruition, and nothing further was heard of this particular syndicate.

The shell filling factory at Chilwell, now known as the old Garrison, was almost completely run down, when it was rumoured the Ford Motor Co was intending to manufacture cars on this site. Ford decided against the project when the War Department required assurances of complete withdrawal in the event of war and instead subsequently set up the works at Dagenham. It was also mooted that 'Gliders' would be manufactured here, but this was not to be as T. H. Barton had purchased an engineering works from Cowens, on Beck Street, Nottingham, where he was to carry out this type of work. Mr George Cowen, the principal of the original concern, had brought the first horseless carriage to Nottingham from Coventry in 1897.

The takings for 1926 had risen to £71,344, giving a gross profit of £15,539. New Lancia 'Gliders' placed in service were numbered 31, 55, 59 and 61, with Nos. 54, 56 and 58 based on Lancia Z chassis with 39-seat front entrance bodies, 29 and 53 with one extra seat, and Nos. 33 and 60, small 26-seat versions. A further 26-seat bus on its original Lancia chassis was numbered 32, whilst three more were purchased second-hand from the same manufacturer. A small 14-seat bus, No. 51, came from Jones of Pontycymmer, South Wales, but was withdrawn within a short time for spares and rebuilding. The other two Lancias, Nos. 50 and 51, came from Autocar Co Ltd of Tunbridge Wells in the form of 20-seat vehicles.

'Long Tom', as No. 10, the 66-seat Daimler had now been affectionately named, was operating on a contract service from Long Eaton to a new housing site on the Nottingham boundary with Beeston. To be known as Lenton Abbey, this site involved the construction of 900 houses, to be served by NCT buses. 'Long Tom' was carrying workmen four and a half miles for 1½d on solid tyres, and T. H. Barton claimed this bus had made more money for him than any other vehicle.

The solid-tyred double-deckers were now only used during the weekend or peak periods. Some 26-seat Gliders, converted from Lancia models normally seating twelve to fourteen passengers, were used for high-class work, and during the industrial unrest of the General Strike, transported small bodies of police quickly from place to place.

During this period T. H. Barton had experimented with a front-wheel drive vehicle, which had been built and fitted with a body using an advanced hooped-frame principle for chassisless construction. The author is of the opinion that the front-wheel drive idea was sold to Gilford Motor Co which produced both a complete single-

In a fleet containing so many unusual vehicles one may be excused for thinking there could be no real surprises. Alfred's wry smile suggests even he might disagree this time! Note the incredibly minimal ground clearance. More photographs overleaf of this front-wheel drive vehicle.

decker and double-decker for the 1931 Olympia Show using many of the principles featured in the Barton original. There were other novel ideas such as twin engines, with two accelerators and clutches. One wonders if four-legged drivers were to be employed? The thought behind this was that the second engine would be brought into operation when climbing the very steep Derby Road hill in Nottingham, or when extra speed was needed when chasing a competitor's vehicle. To operate this contraption the driver sat centrally at the front of the vehicle, on a higher level than the passengers. Interestingly, a photograph of

The experimental front-wheel drive bus, although never completed, did venture out on to the streets, but it is understood another vehicle towed it there. The dual controls are evident in the photograph below, whilst the whole assembly is seen [right]. Standing on High Road, Chilwell, with Charlie Parker at the wheel. There seems more than a passing resemblance to an underground railway carriage.

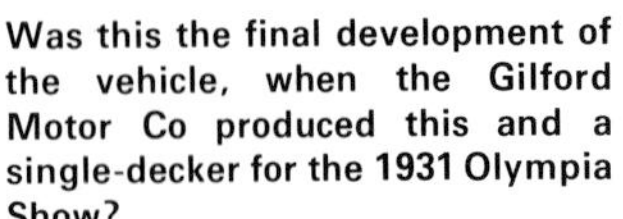

Was this the final development of the vehicle, when the Gilford Motor Co produced this and a single-decker for the 1931 Olympia Show?

this vehicle appeared in a magazine with the curious caption "being fitted with small wheels it gives the appearance of the vehicle touching the ground", in fact it was intended there should be very little ground clearance for ease of passenger access. Barton employees christened this 'The Wheels and Power Company'.

The General Strike of May 1926 briefly affected almost all industries, but Barton continued to operate through it and the whole period of the depression, sometimes with the assistance of the police.

Towards the end of 1926, route numbers were adopted for several of the services, but were not displayed on the vehicles. They were used mainly for clerical purposes, although roller-blind destination boxes were fixed to the roofs of some saloons.

Barton successfully applied for an Old Sawley to Ilkeston run which was granted in March 1927, in effect extending the Stapleford service through Trowell village. Ilkeston, colloquially known as Ilson, a very industrialised Derbyshire township, built around a hillside upon which the church and market place were situated. This was the terminus for most bus services. It was at this time occupied by two completely different types of community, those on the south being iron and steelworkers, at the Stanton Ironworks, some two miles distant, whilst those to the north were coal miners in the Erewash Valley pits.

The first bus service on this route from Ilkeston was started by Trent on 14th August 1925 as far as Sandiacre, but it was withdrawn by 1926. Next came Billingham Brothers, who operated right through to Long Eaton on 10th January 1926. Further Ilkeston operators were to join in during the next few months. June saw the arrival of E. Gregory, Edwards and Grainger Bros, and so by the time Barton had become involved, there were five operators on a very remunerative route, with more to follow. By the end of the year H. Boxall and W. Winfield were added to the foray, but Edwards had withdrawn.

Though Daimler No. 19 stands immobilised by the strikers of 1926 in this picture, Barton continued operating throughout the period. The bus had just turned out of Wollaton Street, on its journey to Sandiacre, and is standing in Theatre Square, Nottingham, with the pillars of the Theatre Royal in the background.

During April, NCT amended the Beeston route via Beeston Lane so that it proceeded along Derby Road and into Wollaton Road, trying to combat Barton's second Sandiacre service, which was still unnumbered. The main road route was now numbered 4.

Violence erupted on one occasion in May when a Barton inspector asked one of their competitors not to pick up passengers at the Co-op Arcade near to Long Eaton Market Place, on the Long Eaton-Sawley route. Obviously when approached in this manner. during times of free trading, the driver — a member of a family concern — told him to mind his own business and a fight ensued. This illustrates the passion felt by operators as they endeavoured to eke a living. The local court was not impressed, and they fined all parties concerned accordingly.

A Nottingham (Greyfriar Gate)-Coalville service started in August 1927. Using this terminus in Nottingham the route followed the normal route to Gotham on to Kingston, Kegworth and Hathern as the earlier abandoned Loughborough service, on to the small township of Shepshed, then into the Leicestershire coal mining communities of Thringstone, Whitwick and to Coalville itself (population 9,500). This was a slightly longer route than the Ashby service, being a distance of 24 miles, operating every two hours daily. Earlier that year O. C. Bishop of Coalville had successfully applied for a similar route, this time operating through Long Eaton, but it is not known if this was ever operated.

Another unsuccessful attempt was made to operate in the Mapperley area, when Barton applied for an extension of the Sandiacre service on to the Porchester Road area. This was not served by trams, although well within the city limits. This application prompted NCT to provide a service some months later, using two one-man-operated Street-bodied 26-seat Dennis buses.

With takings now rising to £87,663 for the year ending 30th September, it was decided to restructure the Company, and from 1st October it was registered as a public company to be known as Barton Transport Ltd. At a meeting on 25th November 1927 this new company acquired Barton Bros Ltd for the sum of £70,000 which included £10,666 in respect of goodwill, the sum of £20,000 paid in cash, and the balance in 180,000 cumulative participating preference shares and 10,000 deferred shares. The new public company was formed on a nominal capital of £95,000, in 280,000 eight per cent cumulative preference shares of 5 shillings (25p) each and 50,000 deferred shares at 1 shilling (5p) each. T. H. Barton was to act as Managing Director for three years with two Directors Alderman E. Huntsman (Mayor of Nottingham at this time) and E. B. Ridsell (a Director of Simms Motor Units) whilst E. L. Taylor became Company Secretary, having joined the Company a few years earlier. The purchase included Chilwell garage, Parliament Street, Nottingham Slipway or bus station; leasehold of Greyfriar Gate depot, and 75 buses valued at an average of £474 per vehicle.

The 75 buses taken into stock included the 1927 arrivals, all Lancias, but with usual variations. No. 62 was the only long-wheelbase front-entrance 39-seat six-wheeler; all the twelve remaining three-axle vehicles were 32-seat front-entrance buses numbered 63-66, 69-76. The Morris-Barton six-wheeler, No. 27, was withdrawn and its body was fitted to a standard Lancia, No. 27. Number 44 suffered the same fate, though it is believed the body passed to a new No. 44, a second-hand Lancia from an unknown source. Two second-hand 1924 Lancia Pentaiota 26-seat front-entrance buses, Nos. 67 and 68, were purchased from Pye of Heswall, Cheshire having previously operated with Richards (Busy Bee), Caernarvon and then Crosville Motor Company Ltd, Chester, as its 199 and 200. The AECs, Nos. 5 and 16, had been fitted with Daimler radiators, and were now officially classified as Daimlers by the Barton concern.

The name Barton Bros Ltd was to survive as a separate company, operating from Beck Street Works, Nottingham, with T. H. Barton and his son Alfred directing operations. Radiators were being manufactured by the company for the Lancias. These looked very similar to the originals, with the surround produced in brass, and the waterways in copper. The design was altered shortly before the changeover, when aluminium castings were used, with BARTON embossed in the top section. These generally had a more up-to-date look, similar to Gilford or Leyland radiators of that time.

During 1925 Strachan & Brown bodied No. 27, a Morris 1 ton lorry chassis, extended to allow 24 seated passengers, and incorporating the Barton patented third axle. It is seen in operation on a Saturday/Sunday only Spinney Road, Long Eaton to Old Sawley service. This was withdrawn within a few weeks to be replaced by a Long Eaton [Green] to Stapleford service via College Street and Spinney Road. It is turning out of College Street into Derby Road, Long Eaton.

Chapter five:

Neither coy or limited

To complete 1927, a further twelve Lancias entered service, albeit under the new banner. Number 82 was a 26-seat extended chassis with local registration, while No. 88 was purchased with a Glasgow registration, being put to work with its original 1925 chassis and bus body. The remaining ten were obtained from Ireland, possibly from the Irish Government, as was No. 62 earlier in the year. Harold Tuckwood distinctly remembers driving these back from Liverpool docks; several were without bodies, and no more than the size of a large car. Of these Nos. 83-4 were rebuilt immediately to 26-seat dimensions, whilst No. 81 carried two passengers fewer. All these second-hand vehicles surprisingly retained their original registration numbers, Nos. 77-81 and 85-88 also keeping their original bodies.

A temporary wooden office was erected in Derby Road, Long Eaton in close proximity of The Green stopping points, to deal with enquiries and the extensive parcels traffic which had been built up. It was replaced by a permanent building, close by, in 1928.

From the formation of Barton Transport Ltd, the Barton brothers each had definite jobs within the organisation — at least in the eyes of their father. T. A. Barton was Chief Works Engineer with afternoon and late night duties; Maurie was his assistant with early morning and afternoon shifts; Alfred was 'engineer, outdoor, on road' and Carl was Traffic Superintendent.

Although they had different nominal duties within the Company they did not regard themselves as limited to their respective posts. As one said, "We may all have different jobs but in reality we all work together on the same problems and generally help each other." They were all pleased with the formation of the 1927 company: "It was the first time we had any regular pay."

The rebuilding programme for Lancias continued during 1928. Numbers 8, 12, 35 36, and 85 were extended to become six-wheeled with 32-seat bus bodywork, while Nos. 15, 26, 51, 67, 68, 77, 80, 86, and 88 were treated in the same manner, but retained their four-wheel layout. Number 26 received the chassis from No. 50. An additional axle was fitted to No. 30, and at the same time the seating was increased from 31 to 32, whilst No. 29's seating was reduced from 40 to 32 though it retained the six-wheel layout. During these alterations the registrations of Nos. 86 and 88 were exchanged.

Varying amounts of work were carried out on each vehicle, especially as some of the earlier lengthened chassis had been prone to sagging, just behind the front axle. Some retained the extended front spring, a notable feature on Lancia chassis. The most complicated rebuild involved No. 67, which received the chassis from 68 and the body from 85, with the original body being overhauled for fitting to No. 44 the following year.

This policy, which required considerable ingenuity, was intended to ensure that the maximum use was made of all components. The Company was using its assets — technical expertise, business acumen and assorted mechanical hardware — to the full.

New Lancia-Barton six-wheelers were Nos. 9, 50, 89, 90-3, 95, 99, 100, 103-4, and 107, all 32-seat buses, together with No. 102, a slightly smaller 26-seat bus. The four-wheel version of the 32-seat bus was represented by No. 106, while No. 94

The road staff wore the Company peak caps, with chrome on brass badges produced in the workshops. Although standard uniforms were provided, they appear to be wearing their own clothes. The bus behind is No. 88, a Lancia-Barton which had received the registration XI 5768 in exchange for its original which passed to No. 86.

was a true Lancia chassis with 26 seats. Massey Brothers of Wigan supplied the bodywork on No. 107, but this was to be the final year for Strachan & Brown bodies, which were fitted to Nos. 12, 68, 35, 77, 80, 86, 88-9. 90-1. They also bodied Nos. 96-7, the first coaches to be operated, which were mounted on Lancia chassis with 26-seat coachwork typical of the time. They incorporated a front and rear entrance, and a full-length canvas roof which was folded down at the rear to give passengers full advantage of the summer sunshine. This had been derived from the charabanc design which had disappeared in the early 'twenties.

A lightweight chassis which has been extended and a third axle added to allow for a 32-seat Strachan and Brown Ltd body to be fitted. The bus is unidentified but appears to be from the last batch to be bodied in Acton during 1928.

The British manufacturers, having seen the foreign competition gaining a temporary but sizeable stronghold, were now offering sturdy machines which were not only reliable, but were, in some cases, also capable of high speeds. Barton, therefore, took the opportunity to purchase two new models. The first newcomer, No. 98, was a Commer 4PF with Challand and Ross 32-seat front-entrance body with more conventional lines. This was operated very successfully and a further example was introduced later in the year, being numbered 105, and fitted with an identical body, plus a roof rack.

The other new chassis manufacturer was Gilford. Number 101, a 1660T model, was fitted with the popular Wycombe 32-seat rear-entrance body, though this retained an imported element in its American-built Continental engine.

This was the first bus in the fleet to be fitted with luggage racks. Unlike Commer which had established its business very early in the motoring age, and had built double-decker buses as early as 1907, Gilford were 'new boys', starting manufacture of lorry chassis in 1925. Their business had been developed from the earlier practice of rebuilding British and Continental chassis after the First World War. Prior to 1926, the business had been operated under the title of E. B. Horne & Co Ltd, from Holloway Road, London. This was changed to the Gilford Motor Co Ltd on the 6th November of that year. Gilford was now enjoying a very successful period, supplying many chassis — particularly for coaches which were often fitted with bodywork by Wycombe Motor Bodies Ltd, a subsidiary of Gilford's.

Another office was now provided to keep up with the expanding business. Situated on Upper Parliament Street, Nottingham, directly opposite the 'Slipway' terminus, it opened early in 1928.

Barton was now enjoying considerable success on routes operating within NCT territory which encouraged an increase in the number of journeys to Arnold; this was achieved by extending both Sandiacre to Nottingham routes to give a daily quarter-hourly service. The original section to Oxton was further extended to reach Newark, taking in the villages of Farnsfield, Edingly and Halam, to approach Southwell from the west, in a second attempt to serve the small township. From here to Newark, the villages of Upton, Averham and Kelham were also served. During layover in Newark, and before making the return run, the opportunity was taken to operate to Balderton, an adjoining village, with some journeys extended to Claypole. Two journeys served the large Simpson works.

This extension to Newark offered passengers a choice of an additional shopping centre, for Newark was a sizeable market town situated on the Great North Road (pop. 18,000 approx.) with municipal borough status. The principal trades were in malt, flour and corn, there were three sizeable breweries, iron and brass foundries, a ball-bearing factory, steam boiler and agricultural implement works, all offering work for many of the population.

The terminus was in the shadow of the castle, which had been partially destroyed, but a considerable portion of the outer walls remained, with one side built on the River Trent banks. Newark had been well-served by the railways, with the LNER main line from London to the North bisected by the LMS line from Nottingham to Lincoln. A third line operated by the LNER ran from Newark to Melton Mowbray and Market Harborough. The Fairway Omnibus Co, Nottingham also provided a service from Nottingham to Newark, serving the villages east of the River Trent after leaving Bingham. A daily service of three to four journeys each way was provided.

With the purchase of newer vehicles during 1928 it was possible to be more ambitious and to expand the area of operation by looking towards the larger cities. This was the general trend throughout the United Kingdom, and many express services were established during this period. Application was made to operate to Birmingham, Chesterfield, Coventry, Leicester, London and Skegness, involving some extended battles with other companies and municipalities. All these services were eventually operated, with the exception of Chesterfield and Coventry.

Local services were not forgotten, and Barton endeavoured to serve Wilford village from Nottingham, but this was not

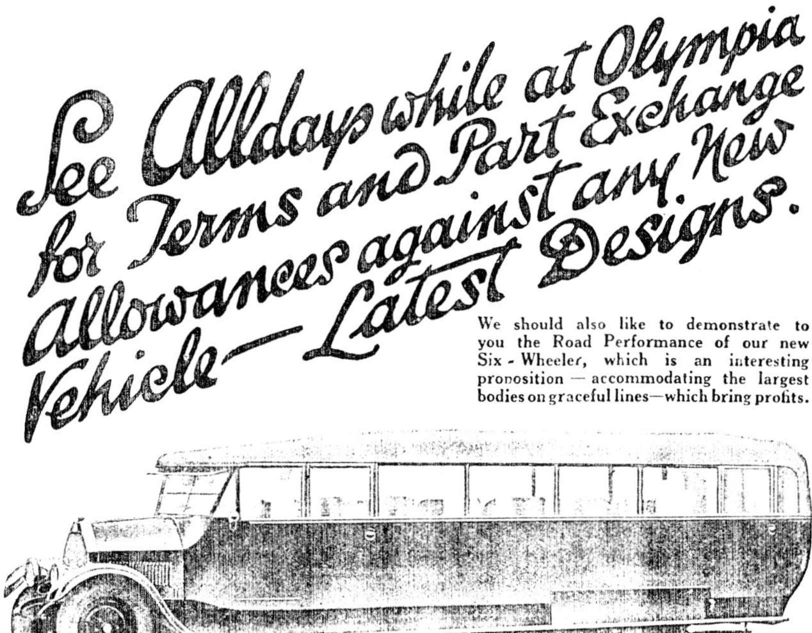

Our new Six-Wheel All-Weather Coach.

ADVANTAGES:

1. Six-cylinder engine, 38/90 b.h.p., ample power and speed.
2. Greater safety—no side skidding—brakes on six wheels.
3. 'Barton' patent springing, affording greatly increased comfort.
4. 'Dead' or 'Trailing' final axle, free of complications.
5. Ample room for latest lounge seat bodies with plenty of knee space, and lowest lines.
6. The price—£1,025 (Chassis)—real value!

At our Works during the Olympia Show, we shall have on view a range of chassis and vehicles fitted with the latest Coachwork, including:

ALLDAYS Six-wheel Passenger Chassis and 32-Seater All-weather Coach.
DENNIS 28/32-Seater All-weather Saloon Coach.
DENNIS 20-Seater Saloon Bus—on new "G" type 30-cwt. Chassis.
REO 26-Seater Saloon. MORRIS 14-Seater Saloon.
LANCIA 26-Seater All-weather Saloon Coach. (Rebuilt Chassis.)
LANCIA 20-Seater and 26-Seater Saloon Buses. (Rebuilt Chassis.)
DODGE-GRAHAM 14-Seater All-weather Coach.

A Large and Varied Range of Second-hand and Rebuilt Bargains.

Telephones: Regent 2421-2422.
Telegrams: "Aldamota, Piccy, London."

ALLDAYS
COMMERCIAL MOTORS LTD.,
78, Jermyn Street, London, S.W.1

WORKS: FARM LANE, FULHAM, S.W.6 (10 mins. only from Olympia)

PLEASE SAY YOU SAW THE ADVERTISEMENT IN "THE COMMERCIAL MOTOR." E63

This advertisement for Alldays was interesting in detailing the advantages, particularly items 3 and 4, of the six-wheeler. Barton springing is mentioned, but the author cannot trace any details; it is possible they may have misprinted as it seems more likely to be the trailing axle which was a Barton patent.

approved, although they were more successful when they were given permission to operate the Ruddington service, formerly operated by 'Ideal Bus Service'. Unfortunately this deal fell through when the company was reconstituted as Ideal Coachways (Ruddington) Ltd and recommenced operations to this large village four miles to the south of the River Trent just beyond Wilford.

A further proposal, entirely within the city of Nottingham, and which stood no chance of approval, was from Parliament Street to Hyson Green (Stockinghill Lane) via Goldsmith Street, Waverley Street, Mount Hooton Road, Noel Street, East Street and Church Street.

Passenger demand on the West Bridgford route prompted the Company to run a further service, serving the area to the east of the district. This took the same route as the original to Trent Bridge, turned on to Radcliffe Road, then followed the whole length of Trent Boulevard to its terminus. The two authorities were now losing substantial revenue and so by June they linked their journeys to provide joint through services. Under pressure, Barton withdrew by June 1928. At this time both services were operating a half-hourly daily service.

Melton Mowbray was reached early in 1928, having a three-hourly service Sunday to Friday, but hourly on Saturdays. Leaving the Fountain, buses took the normal route to Trent Bridge following the Loughborough road and Melton Road out of West Bridgford, on to Edwalton, Plumtree, Normanton-on-the-Wolds, Hickling Pastures, Upper and Nether Broughton and Ab Kettleby — all small villages situated on the main road.

The LMS line from the north of England and Nottingham ran parallel to this route, on its way to Melton Mowbray, Kettering and London. A second line from Leicester also used Melton Mowbray (Town Station) on its way to Bourne, Spalding and the East Coast. Melton Mowbray could boast a second station, (North), which was served by the previously-mentioned LNER Newark-Market Harborough line, an extravagance for a small attractive Leicestershire market town nestling on the edge of the delightful Lincolnshire Wolds and the Vale of Belvoir. The headquarters for the Quorn hunt, Melton is known countrywide for its celebrated pork pies, Christmas puddings and prime blue Stilton cheese.

M. King of Long Clawson operated a daily bus service in the Melton Mowbray area, including a route to Nottingham taking the long way through Belvoir villages, as also did A. Allen of Hose, though he ran on Saturdays only. Midland Red had reached Melton Mowbray from Leicester with its Tuesdays-only 134A service, renumbered 462 in 1925. A second Tuesday route (464), this time via Twyford, commenced in 1926, becoming route 622 in 1928, whilst 462 changed to 620. Two short runs were also made on Tuesdays to Knossington (624) and Oakham (621). Many market day services in Melton were operated by numerous small operators.

All journeys from Ilkeston were extended from Long Eaton to Sawley with Sunday departures after 3.00 pm extended to Castle Donington, as were all Saturday journeys. At weekends Castle Donington was now very well served; in addition to the competition Barton also provided a ten-minute service from Long Eaton, plus the usual service on the Nottingham to Ashby run.

The Ashby service was extended to Birmingham in September after three earlier refusals by Nottingham Corporation although it is possible Barton surmounted the problem by using private premises for the terminal and extending the existing Ashby licence through Measham, Tamworth, Fazeley, Curdworth, Minworth, Tyburn, Aston Cross to Samuelson's Garage, Bath Street, off Whittall Street, Birmingham. At this same time BMMO (Midland Red) had commenced a similar service which deviated after Tamworth through Sutton Coldfield.

Midland Red, based in Birmingham, was a member of the countrywide BET group, (of which Trent was also a member), and was spreading its tentacles to distant points, as they were also given consent to operate between Coventry and Nottingham, via Coalville. Barton immediately challenged this by applying for an extension of its Coalville service. It would appear from information available that only Midland Red operated the whole section, possibly via Ashby-de-la-Zouch and Coalville, and albeit for a few months only, before they withdrew completely. Barton's Coalville service had been rerouted earlier in June from Nottingham (Fountain) through Beeston, Chilwell, Long Eaton to Kegworth. The original section between Kegworth and Nottingham was now reduced to three journeys only on Wednesday, Thursday, Saturday and Sunday taking in Barton village between Gotham and Clifton. Barton had now expanded the Gotham to Loughborough section to operate on Thursdays, as well as Saturday and Sunday, with short journeys on these days between East Leake and Loughborough. (By June all journeys were operated daily on an hourly basis to Loughborough).

The Leicester operation was granted on the understanding that Barton would withdraw from Arnold. They did not do so until the following year, much to the annoyance of Nottingham Corporation. Barton operated services which passed over Trent Bridge from Greyfriar Gate, or Fountain as it was commonly known.

The Leicester route commenced from this point, taking the same road as the Melton Mowbray service to Plumtree, then on to Keyworth, Stanton-on-the-Wolds, Widmerpool, Willoughby-on-the-Wolds, Six Hills, following Fosse Road to Syston, Thurmaston and Belgrave then turning into Randell Road off Belgrave Road, in Leicester.

Midland Red commenced operating their 660 service from Leicester (Jubilee Road) on the 1st December 1928, taking the same route but using their normal terminus in Queen Street, close to Midland Station. Both companies operated on a three-hourly daily basis, presumably giving a 1½ hour headway. Commer Cars produced advertisements showing No. 98, and extolling its virtues, whilst operating between Nottingham and Leicester. Barton withdrew from this route (by now numbered 14) during 1929; this was probably a compromise between the two operators over this and the Coalville service.

Leicester was quite an attraction for bus operators as it had a similar population to Nottingham, and was heavily involved in hosiery and shoe manufacture, but the journey did not warrant a regular headway due to the sparsely populated intermediate area it served. Both railway companies ran to Leicester via Loughborough.

Skegness was the nearest seaside resort for Nottingham people with the LNER providing regular excursions for day trippers and holidaymakers — nevertheless the bus companies saw the opportunity of attracting a portion of the passengers by offering cheaper fares. The first known operator providing a Sunday summer service during 1919 and 1920 was Holmes

From the 'Commercial Motor' of 19th February 1929.

February 19, 1929. THE COMMERCIAL MOTOR Advts. 69

60,000 MILES

in 6½ MONTHS!

ON 21st July, 1928, this 4.P.F.-type COMMER bus was put on a daily service between Nottingham and Leicester. This vehicle—on a route involving frequent stops—runs 320 miles daily, and the Owners report that they have not experienced a single involuntary stop.

The "Right" Chassis is assuredly the

Early deliveries of Special Chassis for 14 to 51 Passengers and Goods Chassis for 1½ to 6 tons.

WRITE FOR SPECIFICATION.

CHASSIS PRICES:—

Type 4.P.N. (for 26 seats) **£820**

Type 4.P.F. (for 32 seats) **£845**

COMMER CARS LTD. - - - LUTON

Telephone: Luton 192. Telegrams: "Komerkars, Luton."

LONDON OFFICE: WILLING HOUSE, GRAY'S INN ROAD, W.C.1. Telephone: 4082 Terminus.

READERS ARE REQUESTED TO MENTION "THE COMMERCIAL MOTOR" WHEN WRITING TO ADVERTISERS. C13

Transport Ltd, Nottingham. The first year only it commenced from Long Eaton, picking up at Beeston. Trent had also ventured to this Lincolnshire resort in 1919, and by 1927 this had become a daily operation. In July 1921, A. Baker of Warsop made an unsuccessful licence application but Jacklin & Co (Elect Bus Service) had joined the exodus in 1927, with Barton following the next year. Many other concerns ran days trips from Nottingham as excursions, whilst others, such as those from Ilkeston, operated via Nottingham taking the opportunity to pick up what passengers they could.

The route chosen by Barton was more direct than that of its competitors who ran via Lincoln, but Barton vehicles turned off at Newark to operate via Sleaford and Spilsby, offering picking up points at all the intermediate villages. These were served with one journey each way daily during the summer season, being extended to Long Eaton on Saturdays. All journeys to this Lincolnshire resort terminated on the seafront opposite the Figure of Eight roller coaster, actually using the Seaview Hotel car park.

London was reached by Barton vehicles towards the latter end of 1928 using Parliament Street and Central Bus Station, Crescent Place, as terminals. The following points were served with one journey each way daily, West Bridgford, Six Hills, Leicester (Southgate Street), Market Harborough, Northampton, Newport Pagnell, Woburn, Hockliffe, Dunstable, St. Albans, Barnet and Highgate; there were fare stages between each point, even a 5d single and 10d return between Highgate and Crescent Place.

Crescent Place Bus Station, London, had opened earlier that year, attracting many of the large North of England independent operators.

Earlier operators on the London route were A. Woods of Mansfield (December 1927), Gladwyn Parlour Car Services of Nottingham, commencing from Mansfield (June 1928), Fairway Omnibus Co (June 1928) and Haxby, Tealey & Co (NE Plus Ultra) Retford, operating from Sheffield (July 1928). Many others from the north also picked up in Nottingham and Leicester, this possibly being the reason for Barton's withdrawal some twelve months later. It then became a regular excursion, retained in timetables as such until August of 1931. Again both the LNER and LMS ran express rail services to the capital by different routes.

In May 1928 petrol prices were increased and Barton forecast that it would cost them a further £8,000 per annum, increasing the petrol bill to £20,000. This of course led to discussions about increased fares with the Nottingham Bus Owners' Association; the Long Eaton and Ilkeston operators were also discussing increases.

The established operators were now pooling their ideas, and forming associations to protect their licences and to cut out needless competition. The local Ilkeston group on the Long Eaton route formed the United Bus Service so as to operate on a more organised basis.

Bank Holidays were often very busy. Twenty vehicles were required at Whitsun 1928 for an excursion to Welbeck Abbey in North Notts, and on August Bank Holiday Monday 500 people travelled from Long Eaton to Derby, whilst every available

This rear view of Commer 4PF with Challand & Ross C32F bodywork would have been identical to No. 98 save for the roof rack — a new fixture for long distance work.

bus was pressed into service for the Agricultural Show held at Kingston-upon-Soar. Half-day excursions were operated to Alton Towers, near Uttoxeter, and Matlock every Thursday and Saturday from Upper Parliament Street, Beeston and Long Eaton.

With the intensity of competition accidents were regularly reported involving all operators' vehicles, but the most unfortunate must have been the Barton driver who drove the Chief Constable of Derby off the road between Breaston and Draycott! Many bus operators were involved in taking workers to the large Celanese synthetics factory at Spondon, very often diverting from other work to do this, but Barton did not need to make any such detour as their Derby service passed the entrance at quarter-hourly intervals. Towards the end of the year, during a very foggy evening, six vehicles were involved in a nose to tail accident. Two were owned by Annison (Pride of the Road), two were Uptons, all from Long Eaton, one belonged to A. Skill of Nottingham, and the sixth was one of Barton's.

During 1928 an unsuccessful application was made to operate 'a coupled coach' There are no details available of Barton's ideas, and one can only surmise what might have been envisaged. Was Barton half-a-century ahead of its time, (for the articulated bus has still not been fully accepted fifty years later, although increasingly common elsewhere). Whatever it was, we can be sure it was to be revolutionary and competitive with the railways, for at this time T. H. Barton was interviewed by 'The Industrial World' making the following comments:

> "We are of the opinion that services, such as ours, are of the greatest possible advantage to the country at large. To open up new routes which it would be impossible for a railway to cover. We are prepared for every emergency, and you will appreciate that it is quite possible for a district to spring into popularity be heavily populated, and then fade away before ever a rail bill could be passed through Parliament. The motor bus is ready whenever it is wanted, to go where-ever needed. And there is no loss when the necessity for working the route disappears. But a railway — well, it is impossible to cope with such circumstances.
>
> The railways are gradually becoming obsolete, owing to the apathy and conceit of railway engineers, who have blinded themselves to progress, and considered their position unassailable. The locomotive and rolling stock of today is hopelessly out of date. The top heavy, dangerous build of a locomotive, we consider, is not really safe at over 40 miles per hour, except on the straightest bit of railway.
>
> If the rolling stock and permanent way was re-designed on modern engineering principles, there is no way why an express train should not make the journey from Nottingham to London, 120 miles, in the hour, and thus try to get back the business they have lost by their apathy and the false security, in which they have passed the last 20 years. Thinking their monopoly was impregnable, and they could make their own terms with the public, whom they considered were at their mercy for transport facilities."

The statutory speed limit applicable to most of the Company's vehicles was increased from 1st October 1928. Buses and coaches with pneumatic tyres were now allowed to travel at 20 mph, instead of 12 mph as previously. However, 14-seat buses had been allowed to run at 20 mph since 1921.

At the first shareholder's meeting held on the 12th December, the Chairman was able to report that it had been a year of expansion, greater than was anticipated, with the route mileage increased by more than 100 per cent, mainly in long distance services. The fleet had now increased to 100 buses. A profit of £11,847 was made out of revenue amounting to £118,447 of which £116,166 was from traffic receipts. Dividends of 8 per cent and 10 per cent were declared on preference and deferred shares. A fourth director, S. G. Chamberlain, was appointed to the Board.

During January 1929, Nottingham Corporation, as the plaintiffs, met Barton Brothers, as the defendants, in the Chancery Division of High Court. It was contended that the defendants had plied for hire in a prohibited area between Nottingham and Beeston, from which the plaintiff had asked for an injunction and damages. Under the terms agreed in court, the defendants submitted to a perpetual injunction, agreeing to pay £1,000 damages and costs. This would appear to have been an accumulation of offences before the new company was formed although they had a signed agreement.

An extension was granted on the Melton Mowbray service allowing the company to run through to Stamford and Peterborough. There is no record of this ever being operated and Barton must have regretted this decision for it was 36 years before they eventually reached these destinations, after several years of wrangles in the Traffic Courts.

It was increasingly difficult to open up new routes, as they were in most cases fully saturated by existing bus proprietors. Thus it was inevitable that business should be expanded by takeovers. The first operator to be absorbed was H. Smith of Magnet Garage, Tamworth Road, Long Eaton, who owned two vehicles, a Chevrolet and a Thornycroft. Although they never ran in service they were numbered 108/9 in Barton's fleet; this gave an extra vehicle allowance on the Long-Eaton-Ilkeston service, the Sawley and Castle Donington extension having by then been curtailed. Smith commenced operations in 1925 on the Long Eaton-Castle Donington service, but moved between other routes including Kegworth before obtaining the Long Eaton-Ilkeston route licence. The business was rather unstable so the father took over from his son, though he only survived until 1929, when he was adjudged to be bankrupt.

Within a month Barton had acquired a second business on the Ilkeston service, that of H. Boxall of Marlpool, near Heanor, together with two Reos and a Gilford. The latter was numbered 111; one of the Reos became No. 108 but it is not certain the second Reo received a fleet number — it is likely 110 would have been the number issued. This gave an allocation of three further vehicles on the Ilkeston route, allowing the operation of a quarter-hourly frequency. United Bus Service protested to Ilkeston Council, but to no avail since these had been transferred legitimately. For several months Boxall's premises at Marlpool were used to garage the three vehicles before they were transferred back to Beeston. Included in the deal was a second service which operated only on Saturday from Stanton-by-Dale, a small village near to Ilkeston, on to Sandiacre and then used the Barton route into Nottingham. This was extended through to Arnold with the Sandiacre group of services. Boxall had commenced operation in 1926 on the Stanton-by-Dale run, then on to Long Eaton-Ilkeston which was extended to Heanor for a period during 1927. Heanor was only three miles from Ilkeston, and of similar size, which of course generated a lot of business for many operators of this short section. Boxall had been a member of United Bus Service whose other members were Billingham Bros, E. Gregory, Grainger Bros, S. Pounder, and T. Winfield & Son. United had ten buses on the Ilkeston-Long Eaton service to Barton's eight, producing an overall headway of 7½ minutes.

On the journey between Sandiacre and Long Eaton, Barton was able to reduce the operating time by cutting through its own private land to connect to College Street, a distance of some 200 yards, cutting off the section through Wilsthorpe. This land had been purchased with this in mind, and many of the locals remember on rainy days buses travelling axle deep in mud. College Street also provided a lot of extra revenue, being heavily populated, whereas Wilsthorpe was open countryside.

Timetables now showed route numbers, many vehicles had roof destination boxes replaced by a sign reading "Bartons Gliders", destinations were shown on signwritten boards, or handwritten in whitewash on the windscreens. The route numbers were as detailed in 'Services Operated' (See appendix) and were the same designations as 1926, except that Nottingham-Kegworth-Loughborough, became 10 from 6, the Birmingham service taking the latter number for a short time, then became 3A and Swadlincote 3C. When the service from Ashby was continued through to Birmingham, the bus travelled from Breedon along the main road direct to Ashby, avoiding Wilson, Melbourne, Ticknall and Smisby but this was on a three-hourly basis, whereas the original had a two-hourly headway.

Rear end of Lancia-Barton No. 2, NN 8891, provides a backcloth for the male members of the Barton family. From the left:- Carl, Maurice, Tom Senior, Tom Junior, and Alfred. Note the roundel advert for BP Oil on the offside rear corner of the bus.

Buses continued to run on the original route to Ashby, retaining these timings before it was decided to divert from Ticknall to Hartshorne, Woodville, Swadlincote and Burton-on-Trent, but were only allowed to run into Swadlincote, a coal-mining town in South Derbyshire, which had been served by the previously-mentioned Burton & Ashby Tramways. Trent served a similar route from Melbourne from about the same time with their Derby 3B, although the territory was virtually monopolised by Midland Red, who had a depot in Swadlincote. Potteries Motor Traction were granted a licence from Nottingham to Burton-on-Trent, possibly via Derby, but it is doubtful if this ever operated, however, S. Bentley of Chilwell did operate but only as far as Repton; again the Burton local authority was reluctant to have opposition in its area. Bentley followed the Trent route to Borrowash and then the back road via Chellaston and Swarkestone.

The British Industries Fair opened at Tyburn near Birmingham during February 1929. Barton provided a special service during this period offering reduced terms for travellers, no doubt using the normal service bus, as the times were identical.

The Kegworth to Nottingham via Gotham service was cut back to Barton Village, extended from the Fountain to Long Eaton, number 1B, and reduced to Saturday-only working; however, it was completely withdrawn by the end of 1929.

A second service was introduced to Newark and Balderton number 7B. This was extension of the 7A to Lambley from Trinity Square, then took a similar route to the 1925 short-lived extension to Southwell, travelling by a shorter route through Lowdham, Gonalston, Thurgarton then the same route as service 8 to Newark, operating on Wednesdays and Saturdays only. Popularity of the 9 Skegness service brought about the introduction of a second daily timing, which allowed buses to run direct from Birmingham via Nottingham, returning from Skegness during the following morning. On service 10, extra journeys were provided between Kegworth and Loughborough using the same route as the main service.

J. Atkin of Park Street, Beeston was taken over in October 1929; there were no vehicles involved in the transaction, although a short service between Nottingham and Keyworth was included, being numbered 6 this came just after the withdrawal of 14 Leicester, which covered the same route as far as Keyworth. They also inherited a new Nottingham terminus in Collin Street, just off Greyfriar Gate. This was used by many of the independents who came in from south of the River Trent. Mr Atkin had gained his driving experience with Bartons, then in 1921 he purchased his own vehicle to operate in competition on the Beeston to Nottingham service, offering to sell out to NCT at the time of the Barton agreement but this was not taken up due to the poor condition of the vehicle. By the late part of 1924 he had moved on to the Keyworth run. It is understood the buses carried passengers from Beeston to Nottingham before working on Keyworth duties and the reverse procedure in the evening on their return to base. After selling to Barton, he operated local works services, tours and excursions and private hire work from Beeston before ceasing operations in March of 1933. When Barton applied to the City for the Keyworth licence they again promised to withdraw from Arnold which they did on 3rd November; the remaining journeys still operating on service 8 to Oxton, the Newark extension had been discontinued, with Sandiacre journeys cut back to Upper Parliament Street.

Perhaps the most remarkable takeover of any business was that of J. Turner 'Eagle Bus Service', Findern, Derby, on the 12th October. The deal included three Gilfords with front-entrance bus bodies, seating 20, 32 and 26 respectively and numbered 117-9. Seemingly this was a normal deal, except that the service involved was Nottingham (Trinity Square) to Derby (Cheapside) operating on the same roads as Trent service 8, using the Sandiacre road then on to Risley and Borrowash, joining Barton service 5 for the remainder of the journey into Derby. This must have caused quite a stir at Uttoxeter Road, for it is said Trent immediately threatened to run into Long Eaton from Derby using a licence they had for operating to the former town's greyhound track. It must have worked, for Barton had re-sold this service to Trent within eight days, the buses remaining in the Barton fleet. A part of the agreement included Trent's withdrawing a Risley-Nottingham service, which ran as an occasional extension from Sandiacre. Turner successfully applied to run in April 1927, providing by late 1928 a daily half-hourly service. He also had a Derby (Cheapside) to Sunnyhill Estate operation, which passed to S. O. Stevenson, Little Eaton, Derby, who also adopted the 'Eagle Bus Service' title.

A proposed service to Sutton-in-Ashfield and Mansfield from Nottingham was refused in November, this would have operated in heavily-populated, but almost completely Trent, territory. The short journeys on service 5 to Long Eaton from Nottingham were extended to Draycott, becoming 5A.

Tom Barton, senior, applied to patent his invention for fireproofing petrol tanks, which basically involved surrounding the tank with a lockable metal outer casing having air space between, making it more accessible and readily removable when damaged. The risk of fire was reduced if started from the carburettor, as it would travel along the feed pipe, but the compartment would restrict the flames' access to the tank, and also if fire broke out in the tank itself it was possible by shutting the door to prevent further combustion.

T. H. Barton's suggestion to Nottingham Corporation some three years earlier must have made an impression, for a new central bus station was opened in Millstone Lane, to be renamed Huntingdon Street two year later. Buses stood in long bays nose to tail, with a raised pavement for the passengers, and a covered area was provided on one corner of the site. A small wooden office was erected by Barton on platform three to deal with enquiries and parcels. Greyfriar Gate operations had virtually ceased now, the office being closed by 1933. All services had been transferred to the new bus station by the end of 1929. It was a half mile from Upper Parliament Street but there was an attraction for the passengers, as there was now a covered central market adjacent, which had been transferred from the Market Square in the city centre. Services 5 and 11 still continued to operate via Greyfriar Gate, all remaining services to the west operated via Derby Road, whilst the services to the south of the River Trent used the London Road thoroughfare.

Safety measures enforced by Long Eaton UDC involved the movement of bus stopping places from the area around 'The Green', a large roundabout with public conveniences in the centre. This affected delivery of parcels to Barton's Long Eaton office and although there was considerable controversy, the new stopping places were adhered to, some remaining in the same position up to the present time.

It was recommended no payment of dividend be made for year ending 30th September 1929, although the gross receipts amounted to £136,282, the nett profit was only £2,240. This may have been the result of four takeovers, and the intake of new vehicles, which consisted of seven Gilfords, three Morris, two Chevrolet, five Barton-built chassis and several Lancia rebuilds. Five of the Gilfords (32-34 and 112-113) were 166OT models fitted with open-top double-deck 56-seat bodies from Daimlers 17-21 which had been withdrawn earlier that year. However, covered tops were added to 33-4 and 112 before the end of the year; these were to a centre-gangway 'highbridge' layout, and the resulting overall height led to them being employed on Sandiacre-Arnold. The top cover on No. 112 was glazed at the front only, leaving the upper-deck sides open; it is possible all three were so treated, but No. 33 was fully-glazed by the following year. The remaining two Gilfords (Nos. 108-109) with 32-seat bodies were purchased second-hand from another operator, Sales of Netherseal, Derbys, who had only operated them for a few months. These were given fleet numbers previously allocated to acquired buses. Of the three Morris chassis purchased, Nos. 121 and 123 received Ashwood 20-seat bodies, whilst Barton fitted a similar structure to No. 122. Challand and Ross had been supplying operators all over the country with bodywork for many types of chassis, but in the main for Thornycroft, for which they were main agents in the East Midlands. Products of the Canal Street, Nottingham works were very often photographed under the rocks of Nottingham Castle, a short distance away. The association with Barton appears to have commenced during 1928, when they carried out

Moustached Jack Bloor, on the left, rests with his gang after removing bodies from chassis by means of skids and barrels. The bodies were stood on the barrels awaiting a reconditioned or new chassis.

work on Lancia-Barton Nos. 8, 9, 36, 50, 99, 92, 93, 95, 103 and 104 and Commers 98 and 105. Early in 1929 they provided 32-seat front-entrance bus bodywork for Barton chassis 110, which was fitted with a Meadows engine. An identical chassis was 120, this time with the Barton-built 32-seat bodywork. The two Chevrolet LQs, 115-116, bodied respectively by Witham and Ashwood were 20-seat buses, although this chassis type normally carried 14-seat bodywork.

Again Lancias were rebuilt during the year, those involved were Nos. 4, 49 and 59 which were reduced to 32-seat vehicles, No. 4 reverting to a four-wheeler, whilst the other two remained as six-wheeled vehicles. The two remaining chassis were Nos. 6 and 44 which, although increased to 32 seats, remained with four wheels, with No. 44 receiving the old body from No. 67. Two Lancia-Barton chassis, Nos. 114 and 124, carried registration numbers from 41 and 42 and it is thought these may have had the running parts from these original vehicles; No. 124 received a new 31-seat Ashwood body whilst No. 114 was fitted with a 32-seat body from No. 44.

It is believed Ashwood was a subsidiary of Barton Bros, and the works were situated in Long Eaton.

During the summer of 1929 and 1930, Nos. 96 and 97 were repainted cream up to the waistrail and operated under the fleetname of Cream Coaches. This appears to have been a subsidiary for the operation of tours and private hire, although No. 97 did operate the Skegness run in this guise. It may be possible that this title was taken from one of the operators taken over during the year. At 31st December 1929, the fleet strength stood at 97 buses including the five double-deckers. All Daimlers had been withdrawn from service although No. 37 had been converted to a box van for the service department.

Two new directors joined the Board when C. W. Latham succeeded E. B. Ridsell, and T. A. Barton resumed the position he held in the earlier company.

A very serious competitor on the Nottingham to Gotham route was the South Notts Bus Co Ltd, of Gotham, which had successfully applied for licences on this service in 1926, and had gained a lot of support from the local inhabitants. T. H. Barton, rather surprisingly, took the decision 'If you can't beat 'em, join 'em, so on 21st November 1929 he obtained on behalf of Barton Transport Ltd a 50 per cent share in this business, which had been incorporated as a private company having Limited added to its title on 17th January 1928. The other half of the company was owned by Mr C. T. Dabell and family who originally founded this undertaking — the family continues to run it today. Only two directors were appointed, being the head of each family, C. T. Dabell and T. H. Barton.

As from 1st January 1930, timetables showed service 1 being operated by the associated South Notts Bus Co Ltd, which at the same time took in to its fleet two vehicles from Barton, Nos. 89 and 120, the former becoming South Notts 5, although No. 120 was returned to Barton in March of 1931.

An additional service added on this same date, using route number 4 was a Sandiacre - Beeston Square - Barton Street - Ericsson service extended to Nottingham (Friar Gate). This was a drastic curtailment of the original Sandiacre - Beeston - Nottingham service possibly due to restraints imposed the previous year by the High Court described earlier. In February attempts were made to again operate an Arnold service, but this was not given consent, although all journeys on service 8 were diverted into Arnold, after a short period of operating on the main road through Daybrook.

Rather interestingly in May of the same year, a licence was granted for a Blackpool service, whilst at the same time G. V. Dennis of West Bridgford trading as 'Robin Hood Transport' who already held a Blackpool licence, was given permission to operate to Skegness. It can only be supposed, since neither ran on these routes, they had co-operated to give each other protection from other operators. Barton amended the route of the second journey to Skegness which linked with Birmingham, to serve Grantham, Sleaford, Boston, and intermediate villages. Both these summer express services used route number 9. Service 7B had been reduced to three journeys on Saturdays only, whilst the Birmingham terminus of 3A had been moved to Smithfield Garage, Digbeth, near to the Bull Ring. During October they were unsuccessful in obtaining the licence for further journeys to Keyworth held by R. Ellis of Keyworth, who in turn applied to re-establish his business and was also refused, possibly due to the route being over-bussed. Also at this time the ex-Boxall service Nottingham-Stanton-by-Dale was withdrawn.

It was publicly announced during January of 1930 that negotiations had been proceeding for almost a year, with a view to the LMS and LNER obtaining financial control of Barton Transport Ltd; fortunately this was never concluded. The two largest bus-operating combines, British Electric Traction Co Ltd and Thomas Tilling Ltd, by that time owned the majority of the major company operators in England and Wales, either directly or through the jointly-owned Tilling and British Automobile Traction Co Ltd, which had been reconstructed to administer business in which both groups had interests. The Railways had obtained general powers at this time to operate goods and passenger road vehicles, although most were already operating buses to varying extent. Late in

1928 it was decided that the railway companies should take interest in TBAT companies equal to that of the holding company, an instance being that of the Trent concern. However, to quote John Hibbs' 'The History of British Bus Services'

> "Very little progress had been made in 1929, so the railways, particularly LMS and LNER, tried to obtain control of principal independent companies and use them as a base for competitive operations against Tilling and British group. At that time there were several large independent concerns, and it would have been perfectly possible for the railways to have done this, and so to have been able to force the combine to accept a much lower price for a settlement".

Clearly Barton was seen in the same light as Crosville, which for a while was taken over by LMS, and United Automobile Services Ltd which was bought by the LNER, though both ultimately formed part of the joint TBAT and railway interests.

Far less work on rebuilding of old Lancia-Barton chassis took place during 1930, although Nos. 12, 35, 90 and 50 were converted from six wheels to four. However, No. 31 was rebuilt to six-wheel layout and 32-seat bodywork. The last newly-registered vehicle with six-wheel layout was No. 107 in 1928; at its peak in 1929 the fleet contained 53 of this type of vehicle. Several of the Lancia-Barton chassis were scrapped involving the interchange of registration numbers, no doubt including exchange of bodies, though this is not proven. Those involved were the registration of 43 to 59, the chassis and registration from 52 and 73 to 69 and 72 respectively, also No. 59 received the body of No. 80. The chassis of No. 63 had been scrapped after being involved in a head-on collision with No. 66 at Wilsthorpe crossroads, Long Eaton, when one of the vehicles had overtaken a steam lorry and his view had been obliterated by the smoke. The body of No. 63 was placed on a new chassis renumbered 66, but retaining its original registration number.

During a visit to the Shipping and Machinery Exhibition in August 1929, the two Tom Bartons, senior and junior, became very interested in an oil engine exhibited for the first time by L. Gardner & Sons Ltd of Patricroft, Manchester. The fuel used was at the time sometimes referred to as 'crude oil' to distinguish it from petrol and other lighter products, though in fact far removed from the thick fuel suggested by the name. This 4L2 engine had four cylinders, of 5.6-litre capacity and gave an output of 38 bhp, for use in marine work. Father and son decided it was adaptable for a road vehicle, but on expressing a desire to purchase for this purpose, the makers raised a number of objections, being somewhat unwilling to sell. However, the Bartons' enthusiasm overcame these objections and on 28th February 1930, 4L2 engine unit number 28423 left for Beeston. This was fitted to Lancia-Barton No. 78, using Thornycroft universal joints, a Lancia gearbox and back axle and the vehicle entered service during March operating on service 11 to Coalville, accompanied for several weeks by a Gardner representative to obtain data on operational conditions. On 30th April this vehicle was demonstrated at Nuneaton and the following press release appeared:

> "Nottingham had a direct interest in what will probably prove to be an epoch-making event in the gas industry, at Nuneaton on 30th April. In the presence of a large assembly of public officials, scientists and municipal authorities, the new low temperature carbonisation plant of the Nuneaton Gas Company was formally inaugurated. High hopes are held out for the future of this process, which not only enables gas to be produced at a considerably lower rate than was possible by the usual means, but it results in the production of valuable by-products. These include crude oil one of the chief uses of which has been demonstrated by Mr. T. H. Barton of Barton Transport Ltd. Mr Barton has now placed on the road the first crude oil bus ever constructed and yesterday he showed to the gathering at Nuneaton how practicable a form of transport he had produced, as a result of his years of research. Mr Barton's crude oil bus was driven from Nottingham to Nuneaton, where it was examined by the experts including Major Henrici, a member of the Fuel Research Board and representatives of the Institute of Gas Engineers. The crude oil bus constructed at Beeston, stood up to its tests well and showed itself to be capable of an equal performance to that of any petrol-driven bus. Mr Barton stated that the bus was averaging a minimum of 20 miles per gallon on crude oil, whereas on petrol ten miles per gallon was the normal consumption. Furthermore, crude oil

The inimitable Thomas Henry Barton, instantly recognisable by his peaked cap, holds a lighted taper in the oil spray from the Gardner 4L2 engine fitted to Lancia-Barton No. 78, demonstrating the safety of 'crude oil.' A photograph of the bus in operation is shown on page 99.

was only one third the cost of petrol, so that with the latest type of bus, he was hopeful of reducing the cost of road transport by at least one penny a mile. To prove the safety of the crude oil bus, Mr Barton held a lighted taper in the oil spray from the engine showing that it was impossible to ignite the fuel. It is expected that if the crude oil can be produced by the Nuneaton Gas Works economically, Mr Barton will use the fuel on his present crude oil bus, and in still larger quantities when he has extended the process to other buses on his services.''

During July the engine was removed, No. 78 receiving a Continental Red Seal petrol engine. The Gardner engine was modified to allow the crankshaft speed to be raised to give an output of 50 bhp at 1300 rpm, it was then fitted into newly-built Lancia-Barton No. 91 in October, running in normal service until March 1931, when it was returned to Gardners for overhaul. In less than twelve months it had run 50,000 miles, with a negligible amount of wear. G. G. Hilditch, in 'Looking at Buses', states this engine was resold again to another customer, Northern Motor Utilities, although it is known a similar engine was fitted by May 1931.

The first British oil-engined bus had been introduced during December 1928 by AEC who fitted an Acro indirect injection engine into an experimental works bus, though this was not used in public service. A Sheffield Corporation Karrier single-decker with a Mercedes-Benz engine entered service just after Barton's No. 78.

As stated in Chapter 1, T. H. Barton refused to recognise Dr Rudolf Diesel as the inventor of compression-injection engines, though use of compression-ignition engines for road vehicles was well-established in Germany before the pioneer British ventures.

All Barton vehicles that were converted carried a bold display on the roof or waist-rail stating they were a ''Bartons British crude oil bus'', the word 'fuel' being substituted for 'crude' from the second vehicle. It is noteworthy that they all indicated that Nuneaton fuel was being used. Certainly Barton's claim to have pioneered the operation of oil-engined buses in public service in Britain seems unshakable.

As usual, new vehicles were added in 1930, although the fleet was reduced to 83 by the end of the year. Newcomers included a further pair of Morris saloons (126-7) fitted with 26-seat bodies from Lancia-Barton Nos. 83 and 81. These were longer than the three already in service, and it would appear they had extended chassis. William Morris had produced his first car in 1913 at his Oxford works, going on to be one of the major producers of cars. He had ventured into the commercial market during the early 'twenties firstly with vans, then one-ton lorries which had been the basis for the bus chassis, eventually adopting the title Morris-Commercial for this side of the business. A Barton-bodied Gilford 166OT (No. 125) was the last purchased from this manufacturer, and seated 32 passengers in its front-entrance bodywork. Gilford's business was to decline rapidly in the next few years and they were bankrupt by the end of 1937. It seems possible that there was some co-operation between the two companies on the development side, notably in relation to front-wheel-drive buses, for the Barton venture in this field had some similarities to Gilford's famous though unsuccessful designs.

Using the Strachan & Brown body from No. 91, this Barton six-wheel chassis, the last of this layout to be built, retained its body's fleet number. Extolling the virtues of 'fuel oil', the waistline advertisement claims 'No Petrol No Danger'. Route number boxes are now fitted, but not yet standard. The 4L2 engine had been transferred from No. 78.

The remaining vehicles for 1930 were all on Barton chassis using various engines and running parts, which were built mainly at Chilwell, having engines in some cases fitted at Beck works. These vehicles received the following engines: Nos. 128-131 and 133 Coventry Climax; Nos. 132 and 136 Gardner 5L2 and 4L2 oil respectively; Nos. 134 and 137 Continental Red Seal, and No. 135 Sunbeam 8-cylinder. Bodywork was supplied by Witham of Long Eaton for Nos. 129, 130 and 133 being C32F/B32F and B32R respectively. Barton built 32-seat bodies in its own workshops for Nos. 131, 132 and 135 and for 24 seats on Nos. 134 and 137. The remaining two vehicles 128 and 136, received bodies from older vehicles Nos. 29 and 76, which had their chassis scrapped. Most of these were forward-control (driver beside engine), although it is known that Nos. 134 and 136-7 were normal-control types. It is said by the drivers of this time that No. 135 was one of the fastest buses ever owned, its Sunbeam engine coping adequately with any type of work. The engine is presumed to have been a 30/90 unit of 4.8-litre capacity, as used on the biggest Sunbeam cars of the period — the Sunbeam bus engine briefly made at about this period was larger, but had six cylinders. Three of the five Gilford double-deckers, Nos. 32 and 112-113, were converted to single-deckers when they received 32-seat bus bodies from Nos. 8, 64 and 36.

The vehicle colour scheme was changed from all cream above the waistrail, to red all over with a cream band along the waistrail, and completely lined out in gold leaf which had been standard for the past decade. From the inception of the new company the shorter underlined Barton title was re-adopted from the previous decade. However, there were a few variations in the early days in which the full legend was given in varying styles of design. Route indicator boxes were fitted as standard, with a few exceptions, on new and rebuilt buses from Commer No. 98 on-

Generally local authorities were issuing fewer licences for service routes, determining bus stopping places and enforcing bus operators to provide timetables in the hope of reducing chasing. This tidying-up operation was in preparation for the Road Traffic Act, 1930, which was passing through Parliament, ready for implementing early in 1931. The Bill's intentions were to protect the existing operator on established routes, but at the same time insisting on higher standards of maintenance covered by Construction and Use Regulations and backed up by regular inspection of vehicles at operators' premises. Drivers, conductors and staff hours of work and conduct were regulated, and fares were fixed to prevent undercutting. All of this came under the control of the Traffic Commissioners, who worked from eleven areas in England, Scotland and Wales. Barton was to come under the East Midlands Area based in Nottingham.

So ended an era, when mechanics sat on the plywood mudguards, adjusting the carburettor with bonnet completely removed, travelling around the streets of Beeston and Chilwell at a furious rate. Inevitably, more formal methods were soon to be adopted, making Barton's fleet look more like that of one of the big combine companies. No doubt many of the methods used in the inventive late 'twenties would have been unacceptable to the Ministry of Transport engineers whose duty was to report to the Traffic Commissioners, but who knows what bright ideas might have seen the light of day had Barton been able to continue unchecked.

Probably the World's first five-cylinder oil-engined bus was Barton's No. 132, built and bodied by the Company in 1930 and seen here with Gardner 5L2 on display at Shakespeare Street, Nottingham. Despite being predecessor to thousands of Gardner five-cylinder powered Bristol, Daimler and Guy buses of later years, it received a Commer petrol engine in June 1932.

Chapter Six: Life with the Lions

The new legislation did not greatly alter matters at first, and for a time chassis continued to be constructed at Chilwell, six entering service during 1931, with an assortment of engines:- Coventry Climax (No. 138), Leyland (No. 140), Commer (No. 144), whilst No. 139 received a Blackstone oil engine from Stamford, but this was replaced very quickly by a petrol engine from a Gilford. The afore mentioned received bodies from older scrapped Lancia-Bartons, except No. 144 which was fitted with one of Barton's own construction having a 32-seat bus layout. The two remaining chassis were short Lancia-Bartons fitted with 20-seat bodies from Nos. 115 and 116, when the Chevrolet chassis were sold off. Old registration numbers were used, possibly using running parts from these originals, also the fleet numbers allocated to the bodies were retained. A Commer (No. 141) with B32 bodywork dating from 1929 was purchased from Foster & Seddon of Pendleton, Lancs, (the forerunner of Seddon, the lorry manufacturers). The final two purchases in 1931 were very significant as they were to be the basis of a completely new fleet, being based on Leyland Lion LT2 four-cylinder petrol-engined chassis, and fitted with standard Leyland 35-seat bodies and allocated fleet numbers 142 and 143. The Lion LT-series had been introduced two years previously and was an outstanding success for Leyland Motors Ltd of Leyland, Lancs, with over 700 of the initial LT1 model being placed in service. It was fitted with a 5.1-litre four-cylinder T-type petrol engine. The revised LT2 version introduced

A long association with Leyland began with the delivery, in 1931, of a pair of Leyland-bodied LT2s. The Lion's head is clearly visible in this view of No. 143, taken in Huntingdon Street Bus Station, Nottingham, in 1934. Note the separate route number box fitted above the autovac. The next batch had the route number incorporated into the canopy.

in the Spring of 1930 incorporated more features in common with the contemporary six-cylinder Tiger model, apart from the engine and radiator; it had a wheelbase of 16ft. 6in.

The two remaining Gilford double-deckers were rebodied as single-deckers, No. 34 receiving an adapted 32-seat body from six-wheel Lancia-Barton No. 52, whilst No. 33 was sent to Witham's for a new body of the same capacity.

From 1st January the speed limit for public service vehicles was increased to 30 mph. Operators were now submitting applications for services to the newly-appointed Traffic Commissioners, but in the meantime Long Eaton UDC reduced United Bus Services' licences from thirteen to five on the Ilkeston service, at which United appealed; however, this was not resolved until the traffic courts met, which caused a delay of several months due to the number of applications involved. Barton's first hearing was during May which involved Services 2, 3-A-C, 4-A, 5-A, 6, 7-A-B, 8, 9, 10, 11, 15 plus Tours and Excursions from Nottingham, Beeston and Long Eaton and an application for a Nottingham-Spondon (British Celanese works) service which was duly introduced early in 1931, following the Derby route, except for variations around Long Eaton, and one journey following the main road via Sandiacre and Stapleford. The latter was not included in the licence as this competed with Trent and A. Skill of Nottingham. All the other licences were granted as proposed with the exception of 7B to Newark and Balderton, journeys being cut short at Lambley thus becoming part of 7A service. The Skegness service 9 operated from Nottingham, with connections from Birmingham, taking the original route via Newark.

Service 8, although granted, was immediately transferred to a new associated company, Wards Bus Service Ltd, to which Barton had appointed Carl Barton and E. L. Taylor as directors, together with Mr H. Knight and Mr W. Marshall who had been involved in the operations of Wards earlier, whilst Mr P. Smith became Manager. Originally W. E. Ward had commenced operations from his base at Calverton to Nottingham in April 1925, only to find he had competition from Barton within nine months, but he continued until late 1929, when a group of four took over operations as Wards (Arnold) Bus Service operating from Calverton Road, Arnold. The new address was the garage of S. Smith who had tried unsuccessfully to operate between Arnold and Nottingham, but he was now listed as a director together with a Mr J. Wardle and the two aforementioned. Wardle was replaced on the Board a year later by Mr S. Hammond who had premises on Mansfield Road, Daybrook, to which address the vehicles were transferred. Barton, finding it desirable to co-operate on this route, bought out S. Smith and S. Hammond from the business, changing the title of the company, retaining the Calverton Road address for the office, but moving the vehicles to Calverton, with one out-stationed at Oxton. At this time the fleet consisted of a Reo with EMCO 25-seat bus body and 28-seat Vickers-bodied Maudslay ML4 to which Barton immediately transferred number 68 from their fleet, followed by No. 50, a month later, in July 1931.

Extra journeys operated on Saturdays only between Long Eaton-Nottingham were numbered 5B, whilst Saturday and Sunday extras on Long Eaton-Castle Donington became 3B. The diversion via the Fountain on route 5 was omitted, operating instead via Derby Road.

One of the outcomes of the applications for road service licences was the condition imposed on picking up and setting down points giving Nottingham Corporation protection, although Barton did reach an agreement with NCT to convey passengers along the new Queens Road, Beeston on to Chilwell. For this purpose Barton purchased tickets from the Corporation at face value less 33 1/3 per cent to issue to passengers travelling within this area, this continued until March 1935 when NCT introduced service 5/5A to cover this district. A further agreement with NCT allowed Barton to introduce late journeys over the Beeston-Nottingham section, paying the Corporation a fixed sum per mile for the privilege.

Many of the Lancia-Barton buses received replacement Commer engines during 1931 and 1932, 'giving a more gentle pull' presumably implying a milder degree of tune and perhaps a less temperamental character, and were found to be much cheaper to maintain because, as the sons related in 'The Barton Story', their father had insisted on making so many of his spare parts for earlier engines. Number 67 was fitted with an oil engine and No. 61 chassis transferred to the body of No. 95.

The final two Barton chassis were completed in 1932, No. 145 with Barton 35-seat bodywork and Commer engine and No. 147 having Ashwood 32-seat coachwork and a Barton Bros oil engine. With the experience of operating Gardner oil engines, T. H.

Detail of the Barton oil engine.

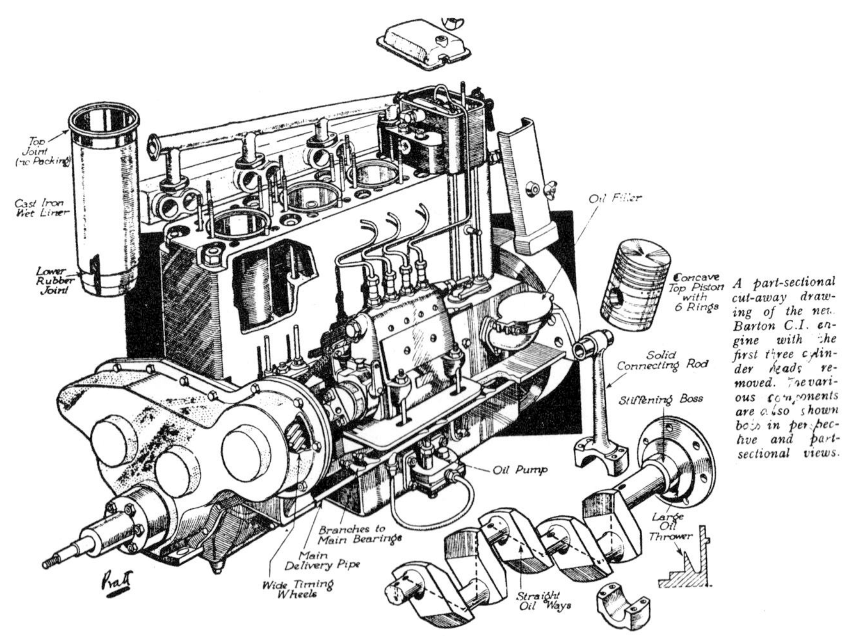

produced an engine at Beck works, under the Barton Brothers title, the following description appearing in 'Modern Diesel':

"The engine is a four-cylinder unit of 110 by 152.4 mm (5,794 cc) and everything has been done to achieve lightness, trouble-free lubrication, and easy replacement of cylinder liners.

The engine is a monobloc aluminium casting, with inserted liners and separate detachable cylinder heads with overhead push-rod operated valves. The alloy pistons are fitted with six rings with the object of preventing the transference of fuel oil into the crankcase. Considerable experimental work has been carried out by the company developing a new combustion head which combines the advantages of the open chamber, to give easy starting, with the improved combustion of the ante-chamber type. By baffling or screening one or both valves and forcing the air to meet the injected fuel, intimate mixing of the fuel and air is ensured."

The cylinder dimensions suggested derivation from Gardner practice, though the bore size was slightly increased. The aluminium construction was an advanced concept, especially for the period, and cannot have been easy for a concern with limited experimental facilities to develop.

Surprisingly, by May 1932 all oil engines were removed from buses, and the four Gardner units sold off. Engines of Barton manufacture were fitted into lorries and tug-type boats used for towing barges along the River Trent to the Humber. One, however, was sold to the Paisley Omnibus Co, who fitted this into a Crossley. The reason given was as surprising as the decision itself. It was considered the authorities did not favour the use of this type of engine in passenger service vehicles, since the type of fuel used was not at that stage taxed in the same way as petrol. This was certainly not sufficient to deter the London General Omnibus Co or Manchester Corporation in their enthusiastic adoption of oil-engined buses, to mention only two prominent operators. Moreover, Mr Barton senior preferred this form of propulsion, as the running costs after the initial outlay favoured the oil engine, although maintenance costs in those early days were found to be higher.

A double-decker (No. 148) was purchased in April 1932, being a Leyland Titan TD1 which had been a demonstrator, with the manufacturers' own 48-seat 'lowbridge' bodywork. This was to be the only two-deck vehicle in the fleet for three years, being used generally for works service and duplicate operations on the Derby service. The lowbridge layout allowed access under the previously mentioned Nottingham Road railway bridge at Long Eaton.

Although it would be frowned upon in today's safety-conscious society, this device provided electricity somewhat in the form of an early trailing lead. The inventive minds of the Barton family developed this idea of two live electric wires, on to which was hooked a lead for various attachments much in the manner used by trolleybus operators. The system was used successfully for many years. A frontal view of a similar LT5 is shown on page 104, the TD1 is the ex-Leyland demonstrator.

The effects of the Road Traffic Act were now being felt and to overcome the loss of earlier vehicles no longer considered satisfactory, twelve Lion LT5 buses (Nos. 150-161) were purchased from Leyland, again with basically standard 35-seat bodywork. This time there was a slight difference in the external appearance as they were fitted with separate route number indicators slightly deeper than the destination indicators, as well as carrying clips on the roof on both sides and the rear to accommodate white-painted boards giving destination details. The side boards were approximately 20ft. long, giving details of intermediate points and the terminals. Special staging was erected at the Chilwell garage to allow two men to lift these into position. The boards were stored in racks showing the details for easy identification. The LT5 model was 27ft. 6in. long, 18in. more than the LT2, and had fully-floating rear axles and triple servo brakes. Coach seats were fitted in Nos. 156-7 for the summer season of 1932.

An exchange of services was made with Midland Red when they took over completely the operation of the Birmingham service which they numbered X98, running three-hourly but with their X99 gave an hourly service. Barton took over operation on the same date, 22nd February 1932, of Nottingham-Leicester (Southgate Street) daily service numbered 12, taking the route of 14 withdrawn three years earlier. A register of operators was prepared by the East Midlands Traffic Commissioners, from January 1932, Barton being issued with the first, ie TER1. The initials denoted T for Traffic Commissioners E for East Midlands and R for road service licence. Each area had its own reference letters completely different to the above.

The opportunity arose during 1932 to consolidate on their services by the acquisition of other operators. During March, W. Upton (Cosy Service) of Long Eaton had been taken over with three vehicles, thus adding to the fleet Nos. 146, an ADC 426 with Hall Lewis 32-seat bus bodywork; 148, Maudslay 26-seater and 149, a 24-seat Star. The Star was sold almost immediately (during July), whilst No. 148 passed to Wards Bus Service Ltd, leaving this fleet number briefly vacant again until the ex-Leyland demonstrator Titan took it up the following month. A regular daily service was operated between Long Eaton and Sawley, and two works journeys from Long Eaton, one to Celanese works which was incorporated into their own timetable, whilst journeys to Ericssons Ltd, at Beeston came under the 4A timetable which now comprised basically works journeys, with Nottingham runs deleted. Originally A. Henson had started the Sawley run in 1926, being joined by Upton later the same year, though during 1929 Henson left the business. From 1927 up to the time of the Road Traffic Act the service had been extended to Castle Donington.

In May H. H. Farrer of Kegworth came into the fold, though it is believed that the business was operated separately until the end of June, when the small fleet of Chevrolet 14-seat buses were sold off and replaced by two Lions. Two services were involved, 10A Kegworth-Loughborough daily, most following the Barton 10 route except a few which travelled by the main road, and a Saturday and Sunday Normanton-on-Soar-Loughborough service via Zouch and Hathern. Barton continued to use Farrer's garage premises in Market Place, Kegworth. As stated earlier, Farrer commenced operations in 1922 with a short-lived Nottingham service; possibly he had run to Loughborough before this date. A service had been operated from Kegworth to Castle Donington via Lockington and a works journey to Leicester, but neither of these were involved in the purchase.

A second operator to be taken over in May, was Mrs A. Eaton of Breaston operating from Long Eaton-Draycott daily, but the transaction did not include the one bus she owned, which it is believed was a small Bedford. Her husband had commenced operation on this run in July 1925, and the service had been an embarrassment to Barton from the inception of operations.

Finally in November, Barton obtained full control of service 6 to Keyworth when Mrs N. R. Howe (Comfy) of Beeston sold this service and two buses; an ex-Nottingham Maudslay which was transferred to Wards immediately, and a Commer F4 with 32-seat bodywork which became No. 149. Mr Howe commenced operations on this service in 1925, from premises in Keyworth, his wife taking over four years later, then shortly afterwards moving to Beeston. Her son-in-law, L. W. Powney of Beeston, had also operated this route in the late 'twenties, joined Mrs Howe in February 1932, his Beeston Coachway buses being transferred to her, together with three work services in the Beeston area.

During 1933, a lunchtime-only short works service was introduced between Dennis Avenue, Beeston and the Boots Pure Drug Co Ltd works across the other side of the town. Spondon works journeys were numbered 5C for a short time before this was given to the ex-Eaton service. The number 5 Derby service had been operating via the new Chilwell by-pass for some time, except for early journeys, and since further road improvements had been made it was now possible to by-pass Beeston also, so every other journey now used this new road.

The ex-Farrer service to Normanton-on-Soar was now operated on Saturdays only, numbered 10B, whilst shorts on this ran to Hathern as 10C. The sparse section of route 10 between Sawley and Kegworth was given added traffic by diverting certain journeys from the A6 into the small villages of Hemington and Lockington. Construction work had been completed on the new Boots works, Barton now providing runs to Long Eaton, Beeston (Imperial Road), whilst the Dennis Avenue service was extended to Woodside Road. In September an entirely new service was applied for and granted to operate on Saturdays, Sundays and Bank Holidays only between Sandiacre and Bulwell, via Stapleford, Strelley, Bilborough and Cinderhill. It was not a success as it had been withdrawn by the end of the year.

Full control of Wards was obtained, and from 1st October 1933, service 8 came under Barton control again, together with five buses which became Nos. 172-6 in the fleet. Interestingly, Nos. 175 and 176 had been 148 and 68 earlier, No. 172 was the Maudslay from Howe, whilst the Reo and Maudslay became Nos. 173 and 174. Garage premises at Calverton were retained. The remaining competitor on the Long Eaton-Old Sawley service, J. W. Kirkland of Sawley, was taken over during December 1933, but his vehicles were not included in the deal. A. Annison, the other operator on this service had his licences revoked by the Commissioners in 1930, and had, therefore, ceased to operate. Kirkland commenced operations on this service in 1923, using a Ford, followed by a Lancia, two Fiats, a Guy, a Renault and finally a Commer Invader. During 1929 he was granted a licence for a Long Eaton to Shardlow evening service, with Tuesday and Saturday journeys extended to the Institute, which also passed to Barton. Shardlow, a small village a mile from the nearest point served by the Castle Donington buses, had gained considerable importance during the heyday of canals, when James Brindley made this the inland port of the Trent and Mersey Canal building an extensive system of warehousing and basins. However, as the canals lost their importance so did Shardlow, although it was situated on the London to Derby road.

The Sawley service extended on to Castle Donington for works journeys, which was incorporated into the same licence.

With a further ten new single-deckers entering service in 1933, the amount of reconditioning work on older chassis had been reduced considerably, as the Traffic Commissioners would not grant a licence for fare-paying passenger vehicles until a vehicle had a Certificate of Fitness. This was valid for five years on a new bus, but decreased to a minimum period of one year as the vehicle got older and overhaul to the required standard was not considered economic.

Eight of the 1933 delivery were LT5 (Nos. 162-9) of the same construction as the previous batch, except that rear destination and number indicators with roller blinds were fitted, a feature which was to be a Barton standard on saloons for many years. The two remaining chassis were also LT5 (Nos. 170-1) but fitted with Duple 32-seat coach bodywork, thus beginning a long association with this bodybuilder. These had external luggage racks, with access by step holes in the sides of the body, which was to a standard Duple design of the time. A transfer was affixed at the rear, showing the name of the company in a ribbon, encircling the fleet number.

A copy of the advertisement for the Barton diesel combustion head, which appeared in trade magazines of the period. In it Barton referred to diesel possibly for the only time, to give the announcement more impact, as the name was by then becoming a widely accepted term for this type of engine. This head was applied to a Commer 4PF engine, upon which tests were made but it did not run in passenger service.

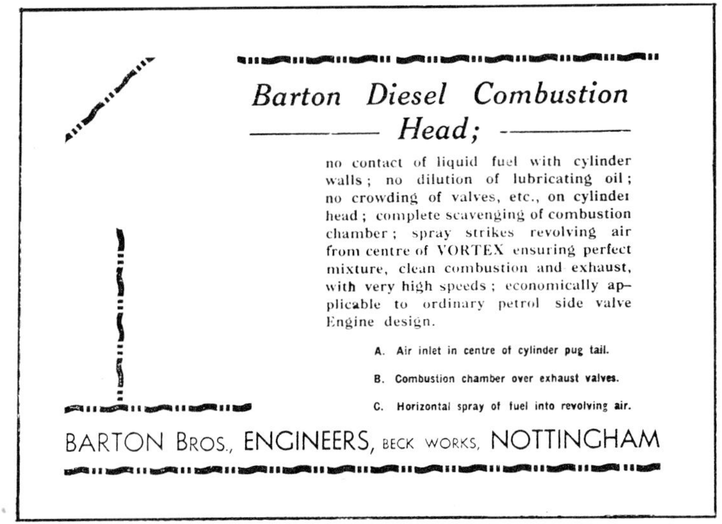

Leyland revised the Lion in 1934, reducing the bonnet length by 11¾ins., and slightly increased the wheelbase to 17ft. 7in. A new slimmer but deeper radiator was adopted greatly altering the appearance. The permitted maximum overall length of a single-deck was 27ft. 6in. at that time and the reduction of bonnet size and alteration to the position of the bulkhead behind the driver gave increased floor area. By repositioning the emergency exit from the rear to the offside, (as adopted on coach bodies), it was possible to increase the seating capacity to 38 passengers. Therefore twelve of the new LT5A model were purchased (Nos. 180-91) to this layout, this time with Brush bodywork, though in appearance they resembled the Leyland design. Although short-back seating was fitted, these were the first of many dual-purpose vehicles, suitable for stage carriage, express or even limited private hire work, in the Barton fleet. Two more LT5A's (Nos. 193-4) came towards the end of the year but these had Willowbrook bodywork with the maximum possible seating capacity of 39. This was achieved by turning the seats over the wheel arch to face forward; on the previous batch one seat had been provided on the nearside and two on the offside. The Willowbrook products were virtually coach bodies, having sliding entrance doors, standard coach fittings and internal trimmings. Thus, the standard layout for all future service-bus deliveries up to 1939 had now been achieved.

A further two Leyland-bodied LT5s arrived late in 1932. Nos. 160-1 were to replace second-hand buses acquired from operators during that year. Here we see No. 160 travelling between Sutton Bonington and Kegworth on service 10 from Loughborough, running into flood water, which is such a regular feature that footboards are provided as a permanent pavement, and are still used at the time of writing.

From 1932 it had been policy to fit curtains to the windows and a sliding roof on the coaches which were used for 'quality' work. Normally they were taken off the road during the winter and stored at Chilwell under dust sheets. The 1934 contingent comprised two LT5A (Nos. 178-9) and an AEC Regal (192), all bodied by Duple to the normal 32-seat coach layout. The LT5A coaches had radios, and illuminated panels above the windows advertising the Skegness service, as hitherto shown on the white boards described earlier. The fleetname for the side panels of coaches was a much reduced BARTON insignia enclosed in a garter in which was written Beeston, Notts, whilst at the rear the same arrangement applied as on previous deliveries, though compact BT Ltd lettering replaced the fleetnumber in the centre.These three coaches were bought principally for operation in the newly-introduced 'Road Cruises' or extended tours of the British Isles. Included in that first year's programme was a 4-day tour of Weston-super-Mare and Cheddar Gorge, no doubt influenced by the 'Guvnor', with his earlier experiences in this resort. With the driver would be a Guide or Courier, who gave a commentary on the journey, and generally helped passengers during the tour. Very often this duty was taken up by the Chief Inspector, Freddie Orton, who

These rear views show [above] the standard Leyland body for the LT5 and [below] the changed appearance when fitted with the Barton rear display indicator which became standard for the next 30 years. Note the clips for side and rear destination boards.

had held this exalted position since the late 'twenties. Other comforts for the passengers included a built-in library containing a selection of guide books, maps and travel literature. This was not the first such venture available to the people of Nottingham as Trent had operated a series of tours since 1925, when they had successfully introduced a five-day trip to North Wales operating six times during that first summer.

The acquisitions in the Long Eaton area left one remaining operator, Frakes, serving south of the Trent, and attention was turned to United Bus Services on the Ilkeston route. The first operator to come into the net was S. Pounder (Empress), of Ilkeston in March 1934, who, apart from working to Long Eaton, operated from Ilkeston, service No. 16, to Spondon (the Celanese factory) via Kirk Hallam daily, and on to Derby Football Ground during the football season, as well as having a tours and excursion licence. The Spondon service was covered by several operators and involved many journeys due to shift-work requirements. It is not certain but it would appear that Barton used Pounder's base in Station Road, Ilkeston, for a period until a new garage was built on Manor Road. Two vehicles were taken into stock, a Gilford with Strachan and Brown 26-seat bus bodywork which became No. 176 but was passed on to South Notts as their No. 18, whilst the second vehicle, a Minerva bodied by Wilton, became Barton number 177, and had previously run for J. Bloomfield of Arnold. Apparently Pounder commenced in January 1926, when he was granted a licence for two buses to operate between Ilkeston and Nottingham, but it is not known whether this was taken up.

From this time all buses were numbered chronologically, and the earlier method of re-using certain numbers ceased.

Evidently Barton were impressed by Duple Bodies and Motors Ltd, as they were to be the main suppliers of bodywork for the next five years, and indeed, apart from the later wartime years, until the end of the period covered by this volume. Mr W. E. Brown, formerly a partner in Strachan and Brown Ltd, had moved to Duple at Hendon in 1929, being responsible for the sales side, and was thus well-known to the Barton family. So for 1935, Duple supplied three 32-seat coach bodies on two LT5A (Nos. 204 and 9) and a six-cylinder Leyland Tiger TS6 (a model new to Barton), No. 210, which were similar in design to that on No. 192, the AEC. However, more interesting were thirteen (Nos. 195-203, 205-8) LT5A fitted with 39-seat dual-purpose bodies, with similar-looking design to the coaches,

T. H. Barton sits between sons Alfred [left] and Carl and surrounded by the staff of Ilkeston garage, with a Leyland Lion dual-purpose Duple-bodied bus in the background.

except that a straight waistrail was used. Clocks were now fitted in all new single-deckers, and these vehicles had the floor sloping upwards to the rear for improved passenger vision. Surprisingly radios were fitted into all new deliveries, requiring an aerial along the whole length of the roof. This was still a relatively novel feature at the time, having been fitted on coaches since Nos. 178-9, but it was unknown on service buses. It became a standard feature on single-deckers until 1940. Nos. 204-9 were converted to 39-seat dual-purpose standard vehicles within the next two years.

The latest saloons worked on the prestigious Nottingham-Derby route, before relegation to other services when new vehicles were received.

To replace acquired buses which were to enter the fleet during 1935, it was decided to purchase a further four more (Nos. 212-5) Duple LT5A 39-seaters, which arrived later in the year.

With the style of bodywork and chassis now standardised it was decided to introduce with the Duple products a revised fleet livery; the white roofs were discontinued, and maroon was added to the red and cream. For a short period the maroon was used below the waistrail but this was reversed.

The Lancia breakdown vehicle was replaced by a Leyland Bull, and a Lea Francis car rebuilt with a miniature Duple coach body, used for advertising purposes.

Considerable expansion of the Company in 1935 saw the intake of 37 buses acquired from operators that had been taken over. Five of them were from Ilkeston — firstly F. W. Charlton provided a Bedford WLB with Rainforth 20-seat bodywork which was numbered 211, plus works services from Ilkeston to Stanton Ironworks and Stapleford (Johnson & Barnes) to Cotmanhay via Ilkeston, also a tours and excursion licence from Ilkeston. Two years earlier the Midland General Omnibus Co Ltd of Langley Mill had purchased two works services from Charlton, who had commenced operations in 1928 with one small bus. After an unsuccessful attempt to operate on the Long Eaton run, he contented himself with serving the many industries around Ilkeston, and by 1930 he owned two buses to carry out these operations. W. Horsley of Awsworth operated a short daily service from Ilkeston to Sandicare taking the back road through Stanton-by-Dale, which he had purchased from E. Whittaker in September 1931. This was added to Barton's services during February, without any vehicles.

MGOC had commenced operations in May 1922, to provide feeder services for the Nottinghamshire and Derbyshire Traction Co Ltd tramway system, both concerns being members of the Balfour Beatty group. At the end of 1932, the Ilkeston town and main line tramway ceased, with MGOC running buses as replacement, until a new trolleybus system was completed a few months later. Unlike the self-contained tramway systems the trolleybuses ran between Heanor and Ilkeston. So with the development of these trolley services, the group looked to expanding bus operations, turning attention, as had Barton, to Ilkeston, which had an incredible number of small operators, many originally creaming the Ilkeston tramway of passengers. Eventually there was to be a clash on operating areas, and when MGOC purchased Billingham Brothers in January, Barton countered by taking over F. W. Chambers & Sons in February. The Billingham purchase must have been the cause of considerable concern to Barton, as this had been operating as a part of the United Bus Service on the Long Eaton service. MGOC did apply for all these services in January and licences were granted, but no-one can recall the blue Midland General vehicles running them, possibly as the Billingham fleet was retained until an agreement was made under which the services were shared, basically with Barton taking the south side and MGOC the north side of Ilkeston, plus tours and excursions, including those from Pounders and Charlton.

As from 1st August 1935, the ex-Billingham vehicles entered service in the Barton fleet as numbers 216-221, comprising a Dennis Lancet 32-seat coach plus AEC Reliance and Gilford 32-seat buses, all with Willowbrook bodies, a smaller 26-seat Gilford, followed by two Bedford WLB Duple and Willowbrook 20-seat buses. This was Billingham's complete fleet at the time; obviously Midland General did not wish to acquire non-standard vehicles. The application for licences had been made during May, resulting in the following additional works services, besides that to Long Eaton:-

Ilkeston-Sawley (Concordia Works)
Ilkeston-Spondon (Celanese)
Ilkeston-Stanton Ironworks offices

Billingham had started operation in 1925, being given permission to operate to Nottingham, although the concern evidently gave this up in favour of the Long Eaton service mentioned in Chapter 4. A short-lived Bulwell-Ilkeston service had been started in 1928, this was run by the Mark Bus Service, which was owned by Mrs Billingham, using one of the son's names for the titles. However, this concern had been absorbed by Billingham Bros, before the end of 1931. Chambers' operations were shared with MGOC on the basis of the new agreement, although it took until November to bring the matter to conclusion, when Barton took into stock two vehicles which became Nos. 236 and 237, a Leyland Lion LT5A with Brush 32-seat body and a Tilling-Stevens B10A2 with Beadle 31-seat body; again Midland General did not take any of the vehicles. Chambers had tried without luck to run to Long Eaton in September 1928; in November after taking a Mr Twigg as a partner he was again refused a licence. Nevertheless in February 1929 a grant was made for Long Eaton operating via Stanton-by-Dale, Sandiacre, Stapleford and Toton. Unfortunately this was not so lucrative as the main road service and they had withdrawn from it by 1931. Chambers' son, Bert, came in to replace Twigg, continuing his working life as a driver with Barton at Ilkeston. Services for which licences were successfully sought on the occasion of the Chambers transfer were:

Ilkeston-Derby via Spondon — Fridays
Ilkeston-New Basford — Works
Ilkeston-Spondon (Celanese) — Works
Ilkeston-New Stanton via Dale — Saturday and Sunday
Ilkeston-Stanton Road — Works
Ilkeston-Mapperley Colliery Village — Friday to Sunday
Ilkeston-Stanton Ironworks — Works
Nottingham-Stanton Ironworks — Works

At the time none of the Ilkeston area services received route numbers.

Ilkeston Area Operators Aquired during 1934-35

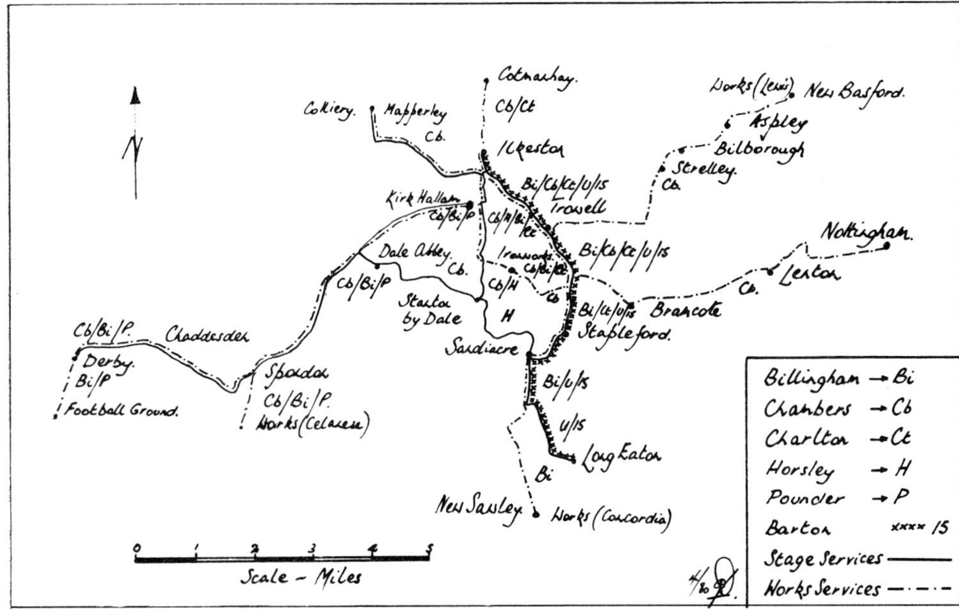

The three remaining members of United Bus Services, Blue Services [Grainger Bros] Ltd, E. Gregory [Excelsior], and T. Winfield & Son [Star] continued operation of the Ilkeston-Long Eaton service marked 'U' on the map. Grainger Bros had changed its title on becoming a limited company in 1935.

The final Ilkeston operator to be absorbed, W. H. Boam, was again shared with Midland General, who took the tours and excursion licence only. A Bedford WLB Duple 20-seat coach became Barton No. 235, and two works journeys from Ilkeston to Sandiacre (Lace Webb) and Mapperley Colliery were added to their growing list. W. H. Boam had operated a single vehicle from the inception, although he is often confused with J. T. Boam (The Ray) of Heanor, who sold his concern to MGOC in March 1931. They were not related.

Chapter seven: South of the border

Any further attempts to expand, however, were limited by other major operators, except for a triangular area to the south-east of Nottingham extending to Melton Mowbray (which was already served by Barton) and Grantham. This had been allocated by TBAT to Trent, which concern probably realised its limitations. A beautiful rural area with many small villages on the Notts and Leicestershire borders which had become better-known in more recent times because of the controversy over mining in the Vale of Belvoir running across it and broken by the Lincolnshire Edge, a band of low hills, on the border. It was possible by the purchase of two businesses to cover most of this district, so approaches were made, and successfully concluded during 1935, for King's Motor Services of Long Clawson and Allen Brothers of Hose, plus a third small concern, J. Randall of Asfordby.

Malcolm King had commenced operation in 1915, and by August 1921 was serving Nottingham (Lister Gate) on Wednesday and Saturday from Hose, Long Clawson, Hickling and Kinoulton, providing a carrier operation offering passenger facilities which continued until 1928, when Queens Road terminus was used in Nottingham. By now the service was entirely for passengers, and a second route was introduced to Long Clawson taking in other villages, whilst the original was extended through to Melton Mowbray daily. At the time of takeover on 1st August 1935, services had been considerably developed, and Barton operated the following without change:

A - Long Clawson-Nottingham via Harby, Plungar, Cropwell Bishop — Daily

B - Melton Mowbray-Nottingham via Kinoulton & Cotgrave — Daily

C - Hose-Nottingham via Kinoulton & Edwalton — Mon/Wed/Sat

D - Melton Mowbray-Oakham via Whissendine — Daily

E - Melton Mowbray-Hose via Long Clawson — Daily

F - Melton Mowbray-Wartnaby via Ab Kettleby — Tues/Sat

G - Melton Mowbray-Hickling via Nether Broughton or Long Clawson — Tuesday

H - Long Clawson-Holwell Works via Melton Mowbray-Works — Daily

J - Melton Mowbray-Asfordby — Daily

K - Melton Mowbray (Thorpe End)-Holwell Works — Mon-Sat

L - Melton Mowbray Town Service — Daily

M - Nottingham-Old Dalby via Nether Broughton and Edwalton — Wed/Sat

N - Melton Mowbray-Upper Broughton via Old Dalby and Asfordby — Tues/Sat

There were also tours and excursions from Melton Mowbray, Long Clawson and Asfordby. Since Barton were not to issue route numbers until 1938, a prefix letter is given here, purely for reference purposes. Service D took its buses into the diminutive county of Rutland and its small county town of Oakham, served also by the LMS main line from Nottingham to London, United Counties from Stamford and Uppingham, Lincolnshire Road Car Co from Grantham and Midland Red from Leicester and on Tuesdays from Melton Mowbray. They were not the sole operators on J route, for Midland Red had obtained a stake in March 1934 when they purchased E. R. Bishop of Asfordby, which included through journeys to Leicester. Also A. Farrow & Sons of Melton Mowbray ran evening journeys, but withdrew by 1939, whilst the fourth concern, J. Randall of Asfordby sold out to Barton at the same time as King, although there were no vehicles involved as they were retained for another route. King had run services

UT 3282 was a Studebaker which operated on the Melton Mowbray-Asfordby service for J. Randall of Asfordby Valley. This became a Barton service in 1935, but the deal did not include any vehicles.

M and N from May of 1934 when he had absorbed the business of P. Payne, Upper Broughton, who had run with a Ford T 14-seat bus. From the time of the takeover onwards, it can be said Asfordby and the Town service were the most lucrative of the whole system. Fourteen maroon and red buses were included in the purchase, but a Chevrolet 14-seater was broken up, so only thirteen received fleet numbers. Of these five were 20-seat Commers, Nos. 222 and 223 being Centaurs and Nos. 224-6 Invaders; four were 20-seat Bedford WLB, Nos. 227/9-30 with Duple coachwork, No. 228 with a bus body; Nos. 231-3 were Morris 18- and 14-seat buses, whilst finally a 24-seat Challand & Ross-bodied Thornycroft became No. 234. It is believed Nos. 231-3 never operated with Barton, as 20 seats appeared to be the accepted minimum capacity. Earlier vehicles in Kings fleet had included Traffic, Bean, Reo and several Chevrolets, with seating capacity from 14 to 20 seats.

All Commers and Bedfords were returned upon repainting to the former King's Melton depot at Thorpe End included in the deal. Meanwhile, the first Barton vehicle to operate on takeover day was Bedford WLB 221 on the Town Service, to be joined by Gilfords Nos. 108 and 109, Commer No. 149, Reo No. 173, Dennis Lancet No. 216 and a selection of LT5 and LT5A models.

By the time the Allen Bros of Hose vehicles were included in the fleet in November 1935, Barton buses were a familiar sight in the district. However, further interest was caused by the addition of four Allen vehicles, all of which returned for a period to the district in Barton livery. They comprised two with 20-seat Bracebridge bodies, No. 238 being a Dennis GL and No. 239 a Bedford WLB; No. 240 which was a 20-seat all-Guy bus, and No. 241, a 24-seat Reo. Earlier buses owned by Allen included two Morris, a Ford T, an earlier Reo and Dennis vehicles. In 1923, Allen was serving Melton Mowbray via Hose on Saturday only, but by the time of the Road Traffic Act the following licences were held; which were 'inherited' by Barton:

P - Hose-Nottingham via Colston Bassett & Cotgrave — Wed/Sat

Q - Hose-Melton Mowbray via Stathern & Scalford — Monday to Saturday

R - Stathern-Melton Mowbray via Hose and Long Clawson — Tues/Sat/Sun

Tours and excursions from Long Clawson, Stathern, Harby and Hose. Again the prefix used is for reference purposes. The small garage of Allens was retained at Hose, being a dormitory base of the Melton depot.

Finally, late in 1935, Barton made a successful approach for two operators on the busy Nottingham to Ruddington service, following the luckless attempt seven years earlier. Ruddington, a large village with a population of over 3,000, situated five miles south of Nottingham, with a station on the LNER line to London from Nottingham and the North, had earlier in the century developed hosiery and lace manufacturing, which was now being run down and most of the population made the short journey to Nottingham for employment. In the nineteenth century a regular horse-bus service had worked into the village from Nottingham via Wilford, and as late as 1918, a Mr Hemsley and a Mr Stevenson were both using this form of transport.

Trent had served the village from 1919, taking its Nottingham-Loughborough service via the main road, passing the lane end, later with certain journeys diverting into the centre, and from 1926 R. E. Horspool of Loughborough competed until Trent absorbed them in November 1935. Meanwhile on the route via Wilford which attracted more passengers there was a flurry of applications, with several independents trying their luck. However, by 1926 there were only three working on a regular timetable. Bilbie had commenced in January 1926, later joined by Waite, who then formed themselves into the Ideal Bus Co. Another operator was C. F. Bullivant of Ruddington, starting in 1921, but these concerns disappeared from the scene late in 1930, to be replaced by E. W. Campion and Sons of Nottingham in January 1931. H. Squires & Sons of Ruddington also operated from 1926. Therefore, Squires and Campion came into Barton control, with Squires providing vehicles that became No. 242, a Brush-bodied 38-seat Leyland Lion LT5A, two Crossleys with Willowbrook 32-seat bodies, Nos. 243 (Alpha) and 244 (Eagle); and Nos. 245/246, GMC with Willowbrook 20-seat bodywork. Interestingly, No. 243 was sent to work the remainder of its time at Melton Mowbray.

E. W. Campion had met the demands of this route by providing two double-deckers, in their orange and brown livery, which became Nos. 247-8 in the Barton fleet; both were AEC Regents, No. 247 having an attractive 52-seat front-entrance body, an unusual layout for the period, whilst No. 248 had Ransome rear-entrance bodywork of style similar to that favoured by the London General Omnibus Co. The remaining three buses were of Commer make, Nos. 249-50 being Invaders with Willowbrook 20-seat bus bodies, and a 32-seat Willowbrook-bodied Avenger, No. 251. A railway bridge at Wilford Lane, Wilford, restricted the height of double-deckers, and thus No. 247 was of lowbridge layout with sunken side gangway on the upper deck, in a manner similar to that used on No. 148, the Titan TD1, enabling the overall height to be lowered by about 12in. compared to the standard centre-gangway layout. No. 248 had been constructed with normal centre-gangway design, but the overall height was less than usual, which allowed it to pass under the bridge.

The Ruddington run became route 14, and a short-lived Nottingham-Wilford (Monday to Saturday) route from Campion's became 13, which was most unusual as it was not used again; the route blinds showed ''Barton'' between 12 and 14. The usual tours and excursion licence based on Ruddington was also taken from Campion.

The Derby service from Nottingham bypassing Beeston and Chilwell along the Queens Road became 5X, a rather fitting suffix as this letter generally denoted express routes with the group operators and in this instance did indicate the quicker route. A new bus station had been opened a year earlier in Derby to replace Albert Street and other termini around the town.

An office block was built on the front of Chilwell garage, giving a modern appearance, and vehicle access points into the works were altered to suit.

T. H. Barton was still active as an inventor, for a patent specification was accepted during April 1935; his idea for maximum car parking in limited space, by providing lift cages for three vehicles high which could be raised or lowered above or below floor level, thus stowing three cars which would normally be occupied by one. It is not known if this was put into operation practically.

At about this time Barton Brothers also developed a compression-ignition engine having only one vertical overhead valve which closed the top of a cone-shaped combustion chamber concentric with the main cylinder and with the sprayer inserted horizontally at the side. Entering a chamber above the valve and concentric with the latter was an exhaust passage around which was an annular air inlet. The valve remained open for exhaust and suction and

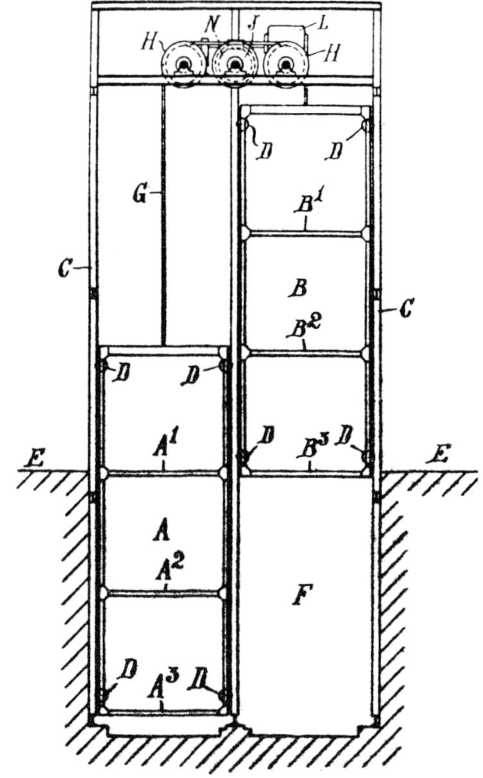

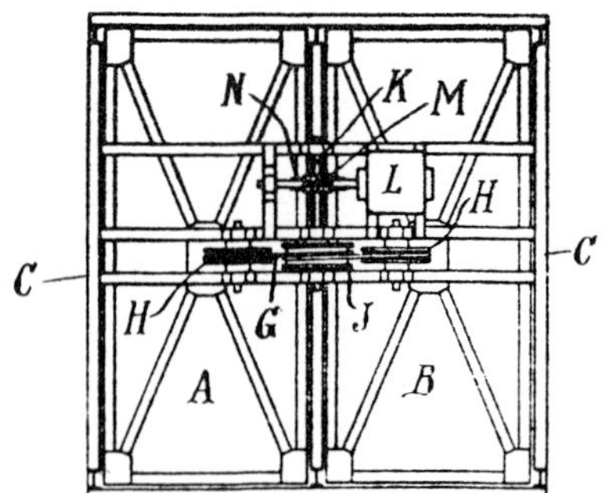

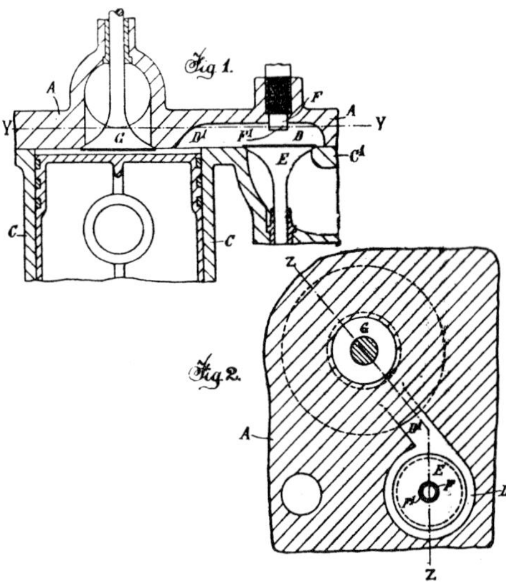

[Above] The Barton single-valve engine which is understood not to have been fully developed.

[Left] Details of the car park lift system, patented by T. H. Barton.

closed during compression and ignition. During the exhaust stroke the shape of the combustion chamber directed the burnt gases into the exhaust passage, having the effect of inducing air down the air inlet.

It is understood the patent was sold to Packard of America, who built an engine using the principle, fitting it into an aeroplane, one of the few occasions an oil engine was so used. One of the difficulties of a single valve engine was the disposal of exhaust fumes.

Tom senior did not devote all his time to business, although it could be said his leisure time was often spent with the ulterior motive of profit making, as in the case of the purchase of an area of land adjacent to Barton Ferry, where he built tea rooms for weekend visitors, who

With the hills to the south of the River Trent in the background, T. H. Barton poses with his train 'The Rocket', at Barton Ferry. Drive from the Albert engine was to the rear axle, necessitating the larger wheels. It would appear the truck's bogies were from the quarry, whilst the seats came from older buses. Smoke is being emitted from the funnel. Mr Barton's youngest sons are on the front, Henry standing and Eric with arm on head. Behind are wife Clarice and Edith. Grandson David and Gerald Nudd are on the fourth row.
The foundation of the road to the Ferry on which the train ran, was made up of old bus tyres, and for many years it was possible to see these after cars disturbed the dry stone surface.

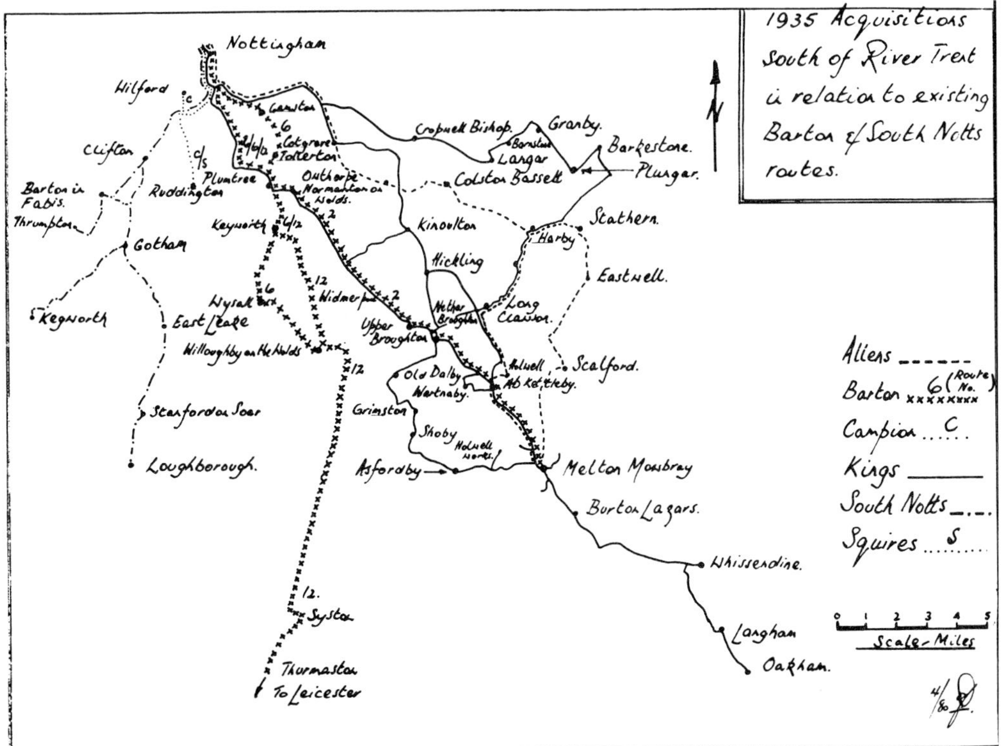

travelled from Beeston on a pleasure boat, or walked by the side of the River Trent, a popular pastime during this period. Being situated a mile from the main road at Toton, he decided to lay track, taken up from his quarry some years earlier, from the tea rooms to the Ferry Farm house some two or three hundred yards away. The engine, named 'Rocket', was powered by a petrol engine from an Albert car, having three rows of old double bus seats, as did the two carriages it pulled. The whole system had disappeared by the outbreak of war, although several bus bodies which were used for weekend homes were to remain until the early 'sixties. This whole project would probably be dignified nowadays by the phrase leisure complex.

With the fitting of vacuum-hydraulic brakes to otherwise little-altered chassis, Leyland re-designated the Lion as LT7 and the Tiger TS7, and examples of both were added to the Barton fleet during 1936. Some 28 of the LT7, with Duple 39-seat bodies of Barton's now usual dual-purpose style, arrived in three batches, Nos. 252-67, 272-5, 286-93, of which the first two batches were similar to the 1935 deliveries, except for slight alterations to side flashes, but the third delivery had a revised design at the back, giving a dipped band shape.

During the early morning of the 10th July 1936, a disastrous fire at the newly-built depot on Ashby Road, Kegworth, burnt out four vehicles believed to be three Lions dating from 1932 (Nos. 150-2) and one of the acquired second-hand buses. The rebuilt garage opened later in the year. Duple also supplied four 32-seat coach bodies, two on LT7 chassis (Nos. 268-9) and two on TS7 (Nos. 270-1), and as before the LT7s were to become dual-purpose after their short coach life. A new standard Duple coach design was adopted, the most noticeable change from the version previously chosen by Barton was the removal of the canopy over the front nearside wing.

Leyland had produced the lightweight chassis (Cub) of normal-control layout at their Kingston-on-Thames factory from 1932, of which Barton decided to buy ten examples (Nos. 276-85) of type KPZ2 with 14ft. wheelbase, a 4.7-litre light-six petrol engine, and capable of carrying 20 passengers. Brush provided the bodywork for these, adopting a style which was close to the Duple design, with full coach seating. The Cubs and the coaches were finished in large areas of cream below the waistrail with red lining and roof. Most of these operated the Belvoir area services from Nottingham, Melton Mowbray or Hose, replacing the majority of the second-hand smaller vehicles, although at the end of 1936 beside Leylands they were using in regular service a Gilford (No. 219), Commer (No. 251), five Bedfords (Nos. 221/7/9/30/9), TSM (Nos. 237), and three AEC (Nos. 192, 247-8), whilst others were delicensed until the summer season including two Gilfords (Nos. 33, 125).

Acquisition activities were rather subdued in 1936 as only one operator was purchased, when the services only of I. W. Coy of Harby were taken over in December, these were:

S - Langar-Melton Mowbray via Colston Bassett, Long Clawson — Tuesday only

T - Stathern-Melton Mowbray via Harby and Long Clawson — Tuesday only

U - Stathern-Nottingham via Harby and Cotgrave — Daily

plus tours and excursions from Harby and Stathern.

William Coy started a service to Melton Mowbray during 1925, reaching Nottingham on Wednesdays and Saturdays in June 1927; ownership passed to Isaac in 1930, who had purchased G. E. Wood of Stathern in September 1936 including the tours licence from Stathern, but the application for his Tuesday only Barkeston-Le-Vale to Melton Mowbray via Stathern and Scalford route was not acceded to. Wood had used a small 14-seat Ford T, then a similar-sized Chevrolet which passed to Coy, who had owned a Commer Centaur 20-seat bus, and at the time of the takeover two Bedford WLB models, one being retained for use on private hire work, whilst the second, a 26-seat bus, was sold to Hudson of Horncastle.

An hourly service from Nottingham-Bramcote (Old Church) daily commenced in July 1936, operating via Beeston, to Charlton Arms, Chilwell, whereupon it turned into School Lane and on to Bramcote Lane. Basically this was to provide a service to the newly-erected Hillman Estate about half a mile from Bramcote. The Friday only Ilkeston-Derby ex-Chambers was withdrawn in the same month, as alterna-

Although nicknamed the 'Pig', the road staff were appreciative of this electric starter motor, which cut out a lot of strenuous work involved in manually winding starting handles. It doubtless prevented many broken wrists. Again the wall opposite Chilwell Garage is used as the backcloth, a new form of advertising is now apparent, and T. H. Barton's house erected a few years earlier is visible in the background. M. Mellors has connected the starter by means of a square spigot to vehicle 148.

tives were offered by Trent and Felix Bus Service of Stanley.

Hand starting of buses was a laborious and sometimes hazardous job, which the Company realised when they produced a portable electric engine starter of their own design, though similar units had been used by many larger operators since the 'twenties, and this was used in most of their garages. Provision on the vehicle involved welding a square spigot to the starting handle shaft to which the starter was attached.

After two years operation of 'Road Cruises', the natural progression was to the Continent — as with many other operators at this time there was a growing demand for this type of holiday. This was not a new venture, some operators had operated extended tours to the France and Flanders battlefields immediately after the First World War. To feel their way the Company made an inaugural trip which left Huntingdon Street, Nottingham on 4th October 1936, using one of the new Tiger coaches, No. 270. Driver Jack Taylor had nineteen passengers on board, including Mr and Mrs Carl Barton. Several passengers had travelled some distance to join the coach, two of them coming from Arrochar, Argyll.

E. L. Taylor accompanied them as far as Dover, acting as guide, but once the coach had been cradle-loaded by crane, R. Rickett took over for the continental section. The route taken from Calais was to Ypres, Ghent and Brussels in Belgium, on to Germany through Aachen, Cologne, following the Rhine to Heidelberg on the Danube, touching Lake Constance at Lindau close to the Austrian border, returning through the Black Forest, Baden Baden, back into France and to return to Calais via Rheims. It can only be concluded this was a success, as the following year the holiday brochure listed ten departures of the previously-mentioned thirteen-day tour at a cost of 23 guineas (£24.15 pence) and one new departure, a sixteen-day tour to Roman France, Riviera and Paris. Barton had exclusive rights for Continental tours from Nottingham. A full programme of departures on the British tours left regularly for Devon and Cornwall, Weston-Super-Mare and the South-West Country, South Coast and London, Scotland, Lake District, North Wales, Portsmouth and West Sussex, also a four-day Christmas tour to Weston-Super-Mare, Cheddar and Wells.

The cream and red livery was adopted for 1937 deliveries, which coincided with the Coronation of King George VI. The vehicles all Duple-bodied Leylands, consisted of six 32-seat coaches, Nos. 294-7 on TS7 chassis and Nos. 298-9 on LT7, four 20-seat KPZ2 coaches, Nos. 312-5, plus the usual Lion 39-seaters similar to the late 1936 batch, of which six arrived, numbered 306-11. Later in the year an order was placed for a further fifteen LT7 Duple 39-seat saloons, reverting to the normal livery, but now using the coach-type fleetname on the sides. Again some details differed on this batch, with the actual deliveries spreading into 1938, Nos. 316-26 being received before the end of 1937 with Nos. 327-30 coming early the following year.

The Thorpe End garage was closed, upon completion of new premises built at the corner of Wilton Road, Melton Mowbray, close to the Car Park bus station. Maurie Barton had by now become a director and Works Manager, Carl was Traffic Manager and Alfred was responsible for the outside depots.

Some little ceremony, long-forgotten and unrecorded, took place alongside Leyland KPZ2 Cub No. 314 before it departed for Germany on a Road Cruise.

On the 1st March 1937, the Ilkeston concern of E. Gregory was taken over in a deal adding six vehicles to the fleet. A Minerva, with a 25-seat all-weather coach body, was numbered 300 but did not operate; Nos. 301/3 were allocated to two Gilford 168OT Willowbrook 32-seat buses, whilst No. 302 had the same chassis but Duple bodywork. The two remaining chassis were Dennis, No. 304, a Lancet Willowbrook 32-seat coach and No. 305, an example of the recently-introduced Lancet II with Willowbrook 39-seat dual-purpose body. It provided further journeys on the 15 and 16 services, and Cotmanhay-Mapperley Colliery Works, with MGOC in the usual deal taking tours and excursion, and two Derby County football specials.

Mrs Howe (Comfy) decided to sell the remainder of the business she had established when moving to Beeston and the following passed to Barton:

Nottingham (Bath Street)-Beeston (Ericsson Works)
Beeston (Dennison Street)-Beeston (Ericsson Works)
Beeston (Imperial Road)-Beeston Boiler Works
Beeston (Imperial Road)-Nottingham (Boots - Station Street)
Tours and excursions from Beeston.

She owned two AEC Regal and a Leyland Tiger TS1 although these were not included in the deal.

G. Cook of Barrow-on-Soar sold his business, involving a Tuesday-only Barrow-on-Soar to Melton Mowbray service to Barton during November 1937. It ran via Burton-Le-Wolds, Wymeswold, Six Hills, Ragdale, Hoby and Asfordby, operating two journeys on Tuesdays also on the occasion of Christmas Fat Stock Market, before and after Christmas Market days. This had originally run from Loughborough, when Cook took over from Mrs L. Green in June 1932; her Nottingham-Loughborough service was taken over by Trent at the same time. A small 14-seat GMC from Green had carried out the work for Cook, but was not transferred to Barton.

Early in 1937, the ex-Horsley service from Ilkeston was extended from Sandiacre to Long Eaton and Old Sawley via Stapleford and Toton, as operated by Chambers prior to the Road Traffic Act. This again was extended in November to include the ex-Kirkland service to Shardlow, operating on a daily hourly basis.

A second new hourly service was commenced at this time from Beeston Rylands (Trafalgar Road) to Ilkeston, via Beeston Square, Chilwell (School Lane), Hillman Estate, Bramcote and Trowell.

Driver Bert Chambers, who had transferred to Barton when his father sold the business in February, 1935. With one bottle in hand, the other stands on the filler cap of No. 330. Ah, those long hot summers!

The all-weather Minerva seen below, registered RB 2274, was acquired with the business of E. Gregory of Ilkeston on 1st March, 1937. It was allocated number 300 in the Barton fleet but never operated by them.

The Melton Mowbray town service, which had operated along three legs lost the section from the town centre to Belvoir Street, which was added to service J from Asfordby. The town service L, now became a through service from Welby Lane to Burton Hill (cut back from Colles Hall), via the Times Office, Nottingham St, with certain journeys diverted via Warwick Road in lieu of Ankle Hill.

One new service was introduced in 1938, taking workers from Ilkeston to Beeston (Nether Street) via Stapleford, whilst a numbering system for certain Melton Mowbray area services was introduced as follows:

A - 23	D - 25
B - 24	J - 20
C - 22	L - 21
	M - 26

Employees of the Company had regularly entered floats in the local carnivals, and in this spirit the Company converted ex-King Thornycroft No. 234 to accommodate the Carnival Queen and her attendants, being used regularly throughout the summer. So popular was this vehicle, that the Company purchased a similar type from Ericsson Ltd, on a Bedford chassis.

Barton now had a very modern fleet of single-deckers and two double-deckers (No. 248, the Ransomes-bodied Regent having been sold) and so the requirement for 1938 was limited to just four 32-seat Duple coaches, Nos. 331-2 on LT7 chassis and Nos. 333-4 on TS8. The latter was the latest version of the Tiger, with minor changes from the TS7, notably in frame design. A corresponding revision to the Lion was designated LT8, but the first Barton examples did not arrive until the following year.

The Heanor District Omnibus Co Ltd, of Ilkeston was registered on 30th May 1934, being an amalgamation of licences held by J. Aldred, T. Brough and Mrs L. Saxton, all of Heanor, and E. Buxton of West Hallam, resulting in a varied fleet of buses, many purchased second-hand, consisting mainly of Leyland Lion PLSC together with several other makes. Four years later Barton, MGOC and Trent combined to make a joint offer for the business, which had now moved to Derby Road, Heanor; coincidentally, it also accommodated the offices for United Bus Services, from which Barton received two works journeys to Spondon Celanese, from Smalley via Morley, on Monday-Saturday and Smalley via Stanley Common, Mapperley Village, West Hallam and Stanley Village, daily. MGOC and Trent did take vehicles from Heanor and District, although none was operated. The big three took control from 1st May 1938.

Barton joined with Lincolnshire Road Car Co Ltd in the purchase of the Waltham-on-the-Wolds bus operation of Watson Brothers, on the Leicestershire-Lincolnshire border. An application was made for the licences of their services during October 1938, of which Barton were granted permission to operate the following:

V - Melton Mowbray-Knipton via Scalford Brickyard Eastwell, Eaton — Daily but only to Eaton on Saturday, additionally via Thorpe Arnold and Waltham to Eastwell — Tuesday and Saturday only.

W - Melton Mowbray-Great Yarmouth via Bourne, Spalding, Kings Lynn and Norwich — Express Saturday only during July and August.

Tours and excursions from Melton Mowbray and Waltham.

Journeys via Waltham were diverted via Scalford some years later, as Waltham was served by Lincolnshire, which gained three services from Melton Mowbray to Stonesby daily, Freeby on Saturday, and Skegness express on Thursday, Saturday and Sunday during July and August. Watson had started operations by 1928 using a Chevrolet with 14 seats, followed by a Gilford, a Reo, and three AJS Pilots. At the time of the takeover, one AJS remained which passed to Barton, together with a more modern Duple-bodied Bedford WTB, neither of which were taken into stock. LRCC took the second Bedford WTB Duple 26-seat coach, which was numbered 569 in their fleet.

A large housing estate had been developed to the south of Beeston, below the railway station, and this was penetrated early in 1939 when Barton ran an Ashfield Avenue-Beeston Square service on Saturdays only, allocated route number 1. However, it was withdrawn by August in favour of a daily 1A which ran on to Nottingham hourly. At last they again were operating a Beeston-Nottingham service, albeit from the outskirts, and the normal restrictions applied.

Route numbers were given to the following services:

3A Long Eaton-Sawley
5A Long Eaton-Draycott (formerly 5C)
5C Nottingham-Spondon (Celanese)
17 Ilkeston-Shardlow
18 Ilkeston-Beeston Rylands
19 Ilkeston-Mapperley Village
29 Melton-Barrow-on-Soar
32 Nottingham-Bramcote via Beeston
35 Ilkeston-Dale Abbey

Melton also received the numbers 28 and 31 respectively allocated to the routes designated V and N in this account.

Shorts on services 20 to Asfordby Hill became 20A, Whissendine 25A, and service 26 was renumbered 30. Meanwhile, certain of the services in this same area were recast for more economical operation thus:

22 Nottingham-Redmile-Hose, basically as old service 23 with journeys extended to Redmile from Barkstone; 23 was renumbered from 22, virtually as before, but operating every two hours daily and excluding Normanton village. 24 Nottingham-

Stathern — Daily via Cotgrave, Lime Kiln Inn, Owthorpe, Colston Bassett and Harby, this being the amalgamation of 24/P/U routes.

To replace the King/Allen/Coy services to Melton from Belvoir the following were introduced:

26 Melton-Stathern via Eastwell and Scalford — School days only.

27 Melton-Plungar via Long Clawson, Hose, Harby and Stathern with the following variations between Melton Mowbray and Long Clawson.

27 Via Scalford Road and Holwell.

27A via Ab Kettleby and Nether Broughton

27B via Ab Kettleby

This gave an overall hourly service every day.

The opening of an Ordnance Factory at Nottingham during the re-armament programme of 1938-39 was served by Barton from Long Eaton from April 1939 by way of Chilwell, Beeston, Dunkirk, Castle Boulevard and Wilford Road, daily.

During August the 32 service was extended from Bramcote to Hemlock Stone Balloon Houses, Strelley and on to Bulwell. Now a suburb of Nottingham, Bulwell could boast its own market, being well served by the NCT buses and trolleybuses direct from the city centre.

Finally, a joint Long Eaton town service with Blue Services (Grainger Bros) Ltd, (renamed in 1935) and T. Winfield & Son was introduced between Manor Park and Briar Gate via High Street, Derby Road, Bennett Street and Canal Street. Numbered 33, it ran daily giving a half-hourly service.

Vehicles were transferred from Chilwell to a new garage on Huntingdon Street, Nottingham, thus reducing dead mileage. These new premises, although small, had a very modern office and enquiry complex, and were adjacent to the garage of Robin Hood Coaches Ltd and Trent's enquiry office.

Before war broke out in September 1939, Barton received the normal supply of 39-seat Duple saloons Nos. 335-343, this time on Leyland LT8 chassis. The bodywork had a tidier, smart appearance, although still based on the 1935 designs. A new-style side fleetname was produced, using the basic format but the name and the surround were in polished metal, producing a 'streamlined' style in the manner fashionable at the time, of which Barton was a leading protaganist among major bus operators. This was used for all new deliveries until the 'fifties.

The Company found they required a further four double-deckers on the Ruddington route, so Nos. 346-9 on Leyland Titan TD5 chassis, and having the first oil engines added to the fleet since 1932, were purchased with Duple 53-seat lowbridge front-entrance bodywork. The distinctive design set the pattern for Barton's subsequent double-deckers for the remainder of the period covered by this volume. They were fitted with illuminated fleetname panels, and destination indicators at front and rear. A high finish of coachwork internally included Clayton heaters upstairs and down, fabric and panelling to the ceilings, plus a clock, and

Nottingham was unique in having three operators running front-entrance double-deckers, into the city. The Trent and Midland General designs were not as stylish as Barton's Leyland TD5s with Duple lowbridge layout portrayed by No. 349 at Huntingdon Street, on service 7 to Epperstone.

for the only time in double-deckers in Barton's or possibly any other fleet, radios were provided. The author fondly remembers regularly travelling on these to and from school some years later; particularly outstanding was the vivid red and white upholstery used also on the 1939 saloons. Electro-pneumatically operated sliding doors were a feature used on the double-deckers, and also successfully operated on the dual-purpose saloons, becoming a future standard. Two TS8 Duple 32-seat coaches, Nos. 344-5, of similar design to their predecessors, arrived just before the summer season. Unfortunately No. 344 was to have a short life with the Company, remaining in the fleet for just over six months, then being taken over by the War Department and never returned. It may have been this coach Harold Tuckwood drove on the last German Road Cruise late in August 1939. He could clearly remember forty years later, driving over a bridge to the border to leave Germany, to be suddenly confronted by an armed soldier of the Third Reich — an anxious moment. One can only contemplate the passengers' thoughts as they made the journey homewards, but within days the terrible holocaust of the 1939-45 war had begun.

This splendid night scene at Huntingdon Street, shows Nos. 142/168 and to the side 188, being LT2/LT5 and LT5A respectively. A real pride of Lions!

Easy does it as Duple-bodied No. 294, a Leyland TS7, negotiates the very tight bridge on Dartmoor, under the close scrutiny of the courier and an AA patrol man, dressed in regulation Sam Browne and puttees. This was part of the journey covered regularly during the summer months on Road Cruise 4 to Devon and Cornwall, taking six full days at the fully inclusive fare of £7.17.6d. [£7.87½]

Chapter eight: Barton in the blackout

On 1st September 1939, with air raids imminent, a blackout was imposed by the Government, forbidding anyone from showing a light visible from the air during the hours of darkness. This necessitated the use of sidelights with, at first, only a single hooded headlamp giving a feeble glow; street lights were switched off, or showed a very dim light on corners. To help distinguish vehicles in the gloom, white bands were painted around the edges of mudguards. Of Barton's drivers, 44 who were reservists were called up for military service and within two days war was declared upon Germany and her Allies. The staff at the outbreak of war was 440, 420 male and 20 female.

During October fuel began to be rationed and mileage was cut by 30 per cent, this involved the withdrawal completely of services from Nottingham to Beeston Rylands (Roy Avenue) 1A, Skegness 9 and Old Dalby 30, and also 29 Melton-Barrow-on-Soar, the 33 Long Eaton town service (Manor Park-Briar Gate) and Beeston-Sandiacre and Ilkeston. The 1A had only been in operation just over six months but the 18 Beeston Rylands-Ilkeston service still gave the district contact with Beeston. Shardlow was deleted from all journeys on the 17 from Ilkeston, with the exception of Institute requirements on Tuesdays, all remaining workings terminated at Long Eaton or Sawley Church.

Some 21 saloons were impressed by the H.M. Forces, the RAF taking the Tiger coaches. The impressment officers were always keen to take the best they could find. The Army took a collection of Lions.

This carefully angled photograph, taken from Barton's headquarters, shows Billingham's sweetshop [which was being run by daughter Kate] neatly framed between two gasbags. Note the Barton touch in the sign "Sweets for sweet lovers". To the left, out of the picture, was T. H. Barton's house. Its wall, which remains today, was built from discarded white lithographic printing stones. The vehicles are T. H. Barton's Wolseley and an LT8 Lion, No. 336, with Duple dual-purpose bodywork. Note the rear overhang of the gasbag on the bus — it was removed shortly afterwards.

As in the First World War, it was decided to convert vehicles to run on town gas, using basically the same principles, but a petrol tap was fitted on the Autovac. However, the structures for the gas bags were more sophisticated; to prevent the containers sagging over the sides a 5in. x 1in. timber base was fitted to the roof of the saloons, often using brackets which had been in use for roof-mounted side destination boards. From this base 2in. x 1in. framing approximately 5ft. high was erected and covered with plywood. T. H. Barton's Wolseley car DAU 347 was the first to be converted, together with Lion LT8 No. 336, which had the framework carried down the back, giving a 5ft. extension, making the overall length of 32ft. 6in. This did not meet approval by the Traffic Commissioners, even though some concessions on overall dimensions were allowed for gas-powered vehicles, as accidents were occurring when cornering and reversing. Originally 30 vehicles were earmarked for conversion, but only 28 were completed. Two Morris 10-cwt vans, Nos. 4 and 5, received similar conversions to the Wolseley. The gas undertaking provided metered points for fuelling, these being situated at the Head Office in Chilwell, Dorothy Avenue, Sandiacre; Melton Mowbray garage, and Station Street (Gas Department) Nottingham, vehicles making a detour on inward journeys to refill.

The Guv'nor then decided to experiment with a gas-bag trailer, constructed in steel

conduit, covered externally with sealed canvas, which measured approximately 20ft. in length, 7ft. wide, 8ft. high. One of the difficulties encountered was finding a suitable ratchet for the handbrake; after some thought he found an old sawblade, which served the purpose perfectly. Originally the trailer was fitted to Lion LT8 No. 350, but he decided to add another 4ft. to the height and converted the Regent double-decker No. 247 accordingly. However, this was very short-lived, as the trailer was very unstable, particularly in high winds, when it blew over at regular intervals.

After a lapse of six years, Brush supplied dual-purpose single-deck 39-seat bodies on four Leyland Lion LT8 and fourteen Leyland Cheetah LZ5 models, Nos. 350-3 and 354-367 respectively. The bodywork was based on the earlier Duple coach design, having dispensed with the full-width canopy, which had been a standard for saloons since delivery of the first half-cab vehicles. It is thought the original order was for all Lions, but availability may have influenced the inclusion of the Cheetah models. This lightweight chassis was officially restricted in gross weight to a limit which was liable to be exceeded, particularly with wartime overloads. When they were put into service, on the 5 Nottingham-Derby service, the rear end was found to touch the roadway at times when fully loaded. To overcome this, it was decided to take 6in. off the rear panels, and slope the skirt panels upwards from the rear axle to suit. The final five

Alfred [Peggy] connects the hose from the mains to the filler point adjacent to the autovac on No. 336 [opposite]. The small boy appears to be more interested than the trilby-hatted Freddie Orton. They were photographed outside the main entrance to Chilwell garage.

A rear view of the 'Gas Bag' trailer fitted to the ex-Campion Regent No. 247. The spoked spare wheel appears to be of Morris manufacture. Further views of this vehicle appear on page 115.

in this batch were not delivered until the early part of 1940 and these were closely followed by Nos. 368-376, nine Leyland Titan TD7 diesel-engined double-deckers, bodied again at Loughborough, but this time by Willowbrook, with 54-seat lowbridge front-entrance bodies of very similar design to Nos. 346-9, and again with a high standard of interior design and finish. A further order for ten TD7 chassis was never delivered.

During January a great frost cloaked the whole of the country, and for three weeks drivers suffered great discomfort, especially in the blackout. On the 16th, Hilda Baldock became the second conductress to be employed, Nellie Goodson had been on the staff from 1919, and was for many years the only female on the road staff. Although fuel was rationed, Government policy encouraged a restricted programme of recreational traffic and a few holiday tours operated until June.

Several Leyland Tigers in RAF colours were lost in the Battle of France, and although it will never be known whose vehicles they were, it is know that No. 270, dating from 1936, was driven off the quayside into the sea at Dunkirk, to avoid capture by the enemy. Several other similar vehicles were burnt on the quayside at the same time.

A further rival on the 15 Long Eaton-Ilkeston service, T. Winfield & Son, 'The Star' of 21 The Lane, Awsworth, was taken over on the 17th June, together with two vehicles, a Gilford Hera 32-seat Wycombe coach and a Commer 26-seat Grose front-entrance coach, becoming Nos. 377-378 respectively. A works service Awsworth-Sandiacre (Factories) was also taken over, but the remainder of the business was retained, ultimately passing to Midland General Omnibus Co during May 1948. No. 379 was a Leyland LT5A purchased from a London operator, R. Calcraft.

During July radios were prohibited in all vehicles, and these were removed, as were all interior clocks, which were blanked over. A fleet of 40 saloons with volunteer drivers were sent off together at two hours notice, on indefinite hire to the Army to meet the urgent need for transport for the troops back from France. Some of these men who had no idea where they were going, were away from home for months and upon their return, Commanding Officers sent several letters of thanks to the Company.

On 30th August, Chilwell had its own little blitz, as enemy bombers searched for the Central Ordnance Depot. Not one bomb reached this target and there were no casualties, although several homes were flattened in the district.

Twelve Lion LT5A buses Nos. 180-191, 193-4 dating from 1934 were withdrawn, their Brush and Willowbrook bodies being removed and sold for static homes, hen houses, etc. After renovation the chassis were sent to Hendon, to receive Duple 39-seat dual-purpose bodies, similar to those on the Cheetahs from Brush.

Service 31 Upper Broughton-Melton Mowbray was revived and became a Tuesday only circular, operating one journey each way from Melton Mowbray via Ab Kettleby, Nether Broughton, Old Dalby, Shoby and Grimston. Further reductions were made to all routes, to save on fuel, and late-evening journeys were withdrawn, as were all service 5 journeys via Wollaton Park, and extra market-day operations on other routes.

However, the early morning and early evening demands were increasing as workers were transported to factories involved in the war effort, at Rolls-Royce in Derby, Stanton Ironworks, Boots at Nottingham and Beeston, Ericsson at Beeston, the Royal Ordnance Factories at Nottingham, Old Dalby and the huge complex at Chilwell, which had been built from the old munitions plant. This was beyond the limited resources of the Company's fleet, and a search was made around the country for second-hand vehicles. Before the end of 1940 ten Leyland TD1 double-deckers dating from 1928-30 were obtained. These retained their original bodies, some with open staircases, operating in an all-grey drab livery, with the fleetname in chalk and numbered 380-389, these were from Chatham and District (5), Cleethorpes (4) and Todmorden JOC (1).

In November it was decided to publish at monthly intervals a newsletter for the primary benefit of Barton staff in H.M. Forces, entitled 'The Gasbag'. This was edited by Edward Newton, assisted by Zoe Rollinshaw, to be produced throughout the war years, but not always as regularly as originally hoped. During November the East Midlands Traffic Commissioners granted a concession to allow the Company to pick up inward passengers into Nottingham at double the Nottingham City Transport fare, using Corporation tickets and waybills — in effect a return to the pre-1924 days! All through these dark days the staff kept up with the job, so much so the following extract appeared in Nottingham Evening News on Thursday 26th September:

(overleaf)

[Above] Leyland LT5A with Brush dual-purpose body acquired with Squires of Ruddington business. ARR 582, No. 242, ran from 1935 to July 1940, being then impressed by the War Department.

[Below] The LZ5 Cheetahs received identical Brush bodywork to the LT8s, and No. 356 is seen on Tamworth Road, Sawley, during the 1947 flooding, on its works journey from Spondon [Celanese Works].

COUNTRY CAMEO

When a man puts his heart into his job what a job he can make of it. Travelling by a gas-driven bus into the countryside I saw a rubicund smiling conductor who seemed to be a friend of all.

Everyone knew him along the country lanes, and no service was too much for him. Two heavy cases delayed him at one point, and to make matters worse the people were out, so he had to leave them in an outhouse.

More parcels, more smiles, more helping old ladies and young children in and out of the bus, but the finest act of all to my mind was when this model conductor ran along a garden path armed with a bottle of medicine which the old fellow for whom it was intended seized tremulously and so gratefully.

As we sped away, the driver putting on a spurt as his part in this act of grace, we could see the white-headed old man scanning the label ("Three times a day, in water, after meals") and his life companion gently arming him along out of the cool breeze and night air.

(Note - 'Country Cameo' refers to the conductor of the Nottingham-Stathern bus, W. Bailey-Brown, M15).

A further nine TD1's, Nos. 390-4/6-9 of the same vintage, were purchased from London Transport (1), Southern National (1), Chatham and District (1), Tyneside Tramways (2), and Western SMT (4), plus a 1929 TS1 from Hirst of Ripponden (395).

During the early part of 1941, all these were stripped of bodies and overhauls carried out. Some were not in the least roadworthy, as exemplified in the following prose, written by one of the staff, after collecting vehicles from Western SMT:

THE GARAGE GOES TO SCOTLAND

The Boys set sail on the Scottish cruise
With heaps of wheels, and showers of screws;
With a certain foreman in command,
Who'd sixty quid grasped in his hand.

When miles from home the poor little "Cub"
Conked beside a village pub.
Harry jumped out for a diagnosis,
The boys' ideas were different to this.

They scrambled out from among the parts
And dashed in the pub for a game of darts.
"What are you drinking?" the barman enquired.
So Ken and Joe promptly replied:

"I think we'll partake of a drop of port
At the expense of Barton Transport."
"It's a good drop of port," said Ken to Joe,
"On account of the Masters providing the dough".

When in dashed Harry with a furrowed brow,
Saying "How yer going on wi' it now?"
There sat Briggy, who'd had many ales,
Looking harassed and twiddling his nails.

They cruised into Glasgow at dead of the night.
But to start work at that time was far from right.
They located the buses; assessed the repairs
By the aid of lamps and parachute flares.

But the buses they found there they might as well be
On the scrap heap at Beeston with old number three,
Or another more fitting place would be
Where the Heinkels and Junkers go down in the sea.

C. ROBERTS

Two of these elderly Titans were in such a sorry state that they were transported by rail, back to Chilwell. Another problem arose when one of the Lions with gas bag conversion caught fire on Upper Broughton Hill, but little damage was caused.

Overcrowding was still a problem, so to overcome this special dispensation was given to operators allowing repositioning of the seating from saloons to a layout with most seats placed longitudinally facing inwards around the perimeter of the bodywork. This gave seating for 30, and space for 30 standing passengers. The LT5s were of low seating capacity, making them ideal candidates for conversions and Nos. 153/5/9, 166/7/9 were so altered. Although they were not the most comfortable vehicles, they remained in service with this arrangement throughout the war years.

A further batch of fifteen Lions, this time LT7s Nos. 197-207/9, 212-3/5 and two more LT5A, No. 236 (ex-Chambers) and No. 379 (ex-Calcraft) were rebodied by Duple to the 1940 design. Vehicles in this group which were not included were away with H.M. Forces at the time. These rebuilds, though identical to the previous batch externally, were more utilitarian within, having no mirrors or clock and with wartime lighting fittings.

The fleet was strengthened by the addition of four coaches, No. 400, a TS7 from Hartley, Manchester; No. 401, an unusual six-wheeled TS6 from Webster of Wigan, and Nos. 402 and 403, Smith of Wigan LZ2 Cheetahs, Santus 32-seat coaches. The roofs on these last two vehicles were canvas, which had been capable of being folded back during balmy summer days of the 'thirties.

The final six TD1s Nos. 404, 409-13 were stripped of their bodies immediately upon arrival from Western SMT, Birkenhead, Tyneside Tramways and London Passenger Transport Board (3), one of which it is said was a reclaimed hen house. To keep pace with demand, vehicles were hired on a daily basis from the Nottingham City Transport. Two Park Royal-bodied AEC Regents stayed on loan for several months during 1941 for the Chilwell Ordnance Depot services, being painted in a two-tone grey. This was the livery for all second-hand vehicles that were not to be retained, and for vehicles returned from the Government. The Nottingham buses were numbered 405 and 406, and as they had highbridge bodies, it was impossible for them to enter Chilwell garage, so they were parked up at the side entrance of the premises each evening.

Two further TS7 coaches, Nos. 407-8, were purchased from Happiways of Oldham and Harris, Grays, Essex, both 32-seat; No. 408 had a centre-entrance, spending most of its life on works services, and private hire.

The conveyance of workers to Chilwell was one of the Company's biggest headaches, but the additions to the fleet of second-hand vehicles had eased the situation considerably. Now another problem was the control of the passengers boarding, as of course no unauthorised vehicle could gain admittance to a military establishment; all workers were set down and picked up at Depot Corner approximately a quarter of a mile away. A large and imposing shelter was built, complete with a canopy clock, to keep passengers in order, although one of the Inspectors suggested a machine-gun would be more effective!

On 19th March 1941, Mr W. W. Latham, a Director from 1928, passed away in his 72nd year, being replaced by Alfred Barton on the Company's Board.

One of the Company's drivers now in the RASC wrote to say he had been given a relief coach for a divisional concert party, this turned out to be 327 or 328, complete with window stickers "why not take a British or Continental Road Cruise this year". Mr Hetley Towlson became the 200th man to join the armed forces. This represented a high proportion in relation to the pre-war staff of just over 400. However, there were now almost a hundred conductresses, also women cleaners, some of whom worked nights in the blacked-out garages; there were regular reports of casualties, not from enemy action, but from falling into the pits.

Again the area, in particular Nottingham, received a very heavy air raid on 8th May, but the Company escaped without any serious damage, with the exception of one broken plate glass window at the Head Office.

A group of the female staff beside No. 320 [fitted with 'Gas Bag'], shortly after joining the Company. Several ladies were transferred from other industries, as transport was considered priority work.

By June, 25 million cu. ft. of gas had been consumed, representing a saving of 75,000 gallons of petrol, which would otherwise have had to be imported.

The Prime Minister, Mr Winston Churchill issued a statement asking the country to help the war effort by 'Digging for Victory' in gardens and allotments to grow more food; the Company responded to this by breaking up land at Kegworth, Calverton, Melton Mowbray and Queens Road, Chilwell.

The garage floor was lowered by 3ft. at Chilwell, to allow for over-night storage and maintenance of double-deckers, and to prevent gas bags being damaged on the roof trusses. The contractor involved in this work operated with a horse and cart, and it is said that it was chased around the premises by over-zealous mechanics with bucket and shovel doubtless with food production from allotments in mind. Steel helmets were issued to the employees; painted in maroon, they were emblazoned with the Company monogram.

Certain journeys were reinstated, with the 5 Nottingham-Derby again travelling via Wollaton Park; early-morning travellers were well catered-for but there was no relaxation on evening services. Service 31 was replaced by two routes, Melton Mowbray circular, via Asfordby, Hoby, Ragdale, Old Dalby, Grimston, Shoby and Asfordby, one journey each way on Tuesday, but Hoby and Ragdale deleted on Saturday. The other Melton Mowbray-Old Dalby route ran Monday to Saturday, via Ab Kettleby and Nether Broughton with certain times via Wartnaby and Grimston.

The 25 second-hand Titan TD1s and one TS1 Nos. 380-99, 404, 409-13 and the original demonstrator 148, were rebodied during 1941 and 1942, Duple again provided 55-seat front-entrance bodies to the design of the TD5s Nos. 346-9, and with none of the 'utility' characteristics then beginning to appear on new vehicles. They even had clocks on the lower saloon bulkhead. They could now boast a fleet of 41 double-deckers, finished to a very high standard, entirely of front-entrance layout, ten bodied by Willowbrook and 31 by Duple.

On 5th October 1941, Barton obtained complete monopoly of route 15 for the first time in thirteen years, when the Company acquired the business of Blue Services (Grainger Bros) Ltd, Park Road Garage, Ilkeston, the final member of United Bus Service group. Seven vehicles were included in the sale, the numbers 414-6 being allocated to Dennis Lancet I, 417 to Bedford WLB, 418-9, Bedford WTB1 and 420 to an AEC Regal II-Willowbrook 32-seat coach. Also involved were various additional works licences, to Stanton Ironworks, from Ilkeston, Long Eaton and Sandiacre.

Towards the end of 1941, a system of priority passes was introduced for work people who travelled before nine o'clock in the morning and during evening peak hours. On this subject Mr T. H. Barton wrote to his staff in the H.M. Forces:-

"Mr Orton is overwhelmed with bus rationing (The passengers are not trying to eat buses, but fuel economy and the loss of your help has caused overloading at peak hours, so priority tickets are being issued to workers of national importance)".

The war savings group had saved £4,800 by the end of 1941.

With the acquisition of Winfield and Blue Services (Graingers), and an increase in traffic to Stanton Ironworks, Ilkeston depot had to be extended to cope with the additional vehicles.

Grainger Bros [Royal Blue] of Ilkeston, operated this Chevrolet, though it had long-since disappeared from the fleet when Barton acquired that company in 1941. The company title was changed to Blue Services [Grainger Bros] Ltd, when the limited company was formed in 1935.

A driving and training unit of the newly-established Home Guard was formed, also a Fire Guard, Chilwell becoming the headquarters. During January 1942, five buses reappeared during Army service for a day, all looking worse for wear, one or two having odd pieces of canvas adorning the windows, where glass had been removed and illuminated internally with a single lamp. All of the buses were identified as Barton's own vehicles, unfortunately there is no record of the actual vehicles involved, but they were recognisable by a square spigot which had been welded on to the starting handle, mentioned earlier.

From 9th November, what amounted to a curfew on late evening bus services was imposed by the Government, all being withdrawn after 9pm. A technical fault at a sub-station reduced numbers of trolleybuses on the Nottingham Road and Wollaton Park sections of Nottingham City Transport network, so buses were hired from Barton and West Bridgford UDC for one day. By the end of 1942, 100,000 gallons of petrol had been saved by using town gas. However, eighteen buses were returned from the Army.

Ministry of War Transport was now responsible for the allocation of a limited supply of new buses. Although an operator could state a preference for a particular model, its availability could not be guaranteed, nor could the make of body be specified. So the first vehicles Barton received were two unfrozen AEC Regents, Nos. 421-2, with 7.7-litre engines and Northern Coach Builders lowbridge, 55-seat rear-entrance utility bodywork, joining fellow Regent No. 247. The term 'unfrozen' was given to chassis such as these which were in the course of construction or for which parts were in stock when the Government had imposed a complete stoppage on all production, for Britain had to sacrifice all but essentials to the task of defence in the dark days of 1940-41. However, transport for war workers was an obvious essential, as mentioned before, and it was subsequently decided to release all available stocks, hence 'unfrozen', for priority services. Standard 'utility' specifications for single and double-deck bodywork were laid down in 1941. Double-deckers were to be of composite (wood framed) construction, rear-entrance layout, with five windows a side between bulkhead and seating 27 upstairs and 28 down for lowbridge. Austerity features were a limit on opening windows to one on each side of each deck, together with hinged vents at front, and destination indicators to front only. The single-deck specification was similar to the double-decker, but the entrance to be at the front and seating for 36. Two vehicles to this specification were earmarked for the Company; only one was supplied, No. 424, an 'unfrozen' Leyland Tiger TS11 diesel-engined Willowbrook vehicle, the second vehicle, a Dennis Lancet II with Strachans body was allotted No. 423 (FVO 324), but was diverted to Boyer of Rothley, Leics, and reregistered CNR 516.

Three Guy Arab Mark I 5LW-engined Brush-bodied lowbridge double-deckers, Nos. 425-7, followed shortly afterwards. The registration number FVO 324 intended for the Dennis was reallocated to 426. It is interesting to note that these were to be the last orders placed with Brush. They had supplied coachwork on 33 vehicles during the past decade, and continued to flourish, though concentrating on railway work from 1951, after being involved in the

This side view of No. 421 or 422, an unfrozen AEC Regent with Northern Coachbuilders bodywork, shows the austere outlines adopted on utility bodywork. The grey livery does nothing to improve the appearance.

industry for almost half a century.

Guy Motors Ltd had surprisingly been selected as the principal manufacturer of wartime double-deck bus chassis. In the late 'thirties, this concern had concentrated on medium-weight goods and military vehicles and trolleybuses; bus production had virtually ceased in 1935. The Gardner 5LW diesel engine was the standard unit, except that, mainly for hilly districts, a small proportion of 6LW units was made available.

Several of the gas bag buses were converted back to normal use, and Jack Billingham recalled the following story:

It is told of one of our senior drivers that he was issued one day with a gas bag bus from which the gas bag had been removed. Now this is a man who lives a quiet and peaceful life deep in the countryside, because he dislikes tumult and noise. On those occasions when his duties take him and his bus into the great city his one anxiety is to return to his rustic retreat with the least possible delay.

Well, the down pipe from the gas bag had been taken off at the point where it joins the tap in the cab, but the continuing pipe to the carburettor had been left in position against the replacement of the gas bag, and what he failed to notice was that the tap itself had been left wide open.

In preparation for his homeward journey he pressed the starter with his hand, and the pedal with his foot, and as sometimes happens the engine took this the wrong way, back-firing up the pipe into the cab with a report like a naval gun. So when he recovered consciousness and collected his thoughts he decided as a first step to close the tap forthwith.

The Eastern National Omnibus Co Ltd had successfully operated producer gas trailers since 1941, and the Ministry of War Transport told 57 large provincial operators, who had more than 150 buses, that they would have to convert 10 per cent of their fleet to gas operation. The Bristol Tramways and Carriage Co Ltd manufactured these for the Ministry, of which Barton were supplied with their quota, these were fitted to LT7s and TD1 double-deckers as producer gas offered a greater saving on petrol-engined vehicles. This method of propulsion involved the heating of anthracite and water to produce a gas to drive the engine. Though petrol was required for initial ignition, the bus could run on gas for eighty miles or more before refuelling with anthracite. The foreman mechanic was sent on a practical experience course; operators were advised to avoid using producer gas buses in hilly districts, and select those which ended in a turning circle. Services from Nottingham Huntingdon Street to Ruddington and Keyworth, were chosen for this reason. However, they proved a dismal failure. The engine wear was incredibly high, new pistons and liners being required every month. The two-wheel trailers were narrower than the buses, and drivers were unaware when they had flat tyres, often running them to shreds or turning over. Operation of this type of vehicle also brought unfavourable comments from passengers as illustrated by the following article:

SOFT ANSWER

As you all know by now we are operating a number of buses on producer gas and many and varied have been the comments of both staff and passengers on the performance. The appearance of those large double-deckers with a contrivance like a chestnut roaster on tow at the back which have been operated on some of the flatter routes, because the engine is a little faint-hearted, as compared with the power developed on the more orthodox fuel. The misapprehension is not now commonly held that the producer is pushing the bus.

Well, one of the chosen routes is Ruddington to Nottingham and it is said that on one of those morning journeys into town which make a tour by way of the Midland Station there was a gentleman who displayed a measure of impatience with the somewhat sluggish progress. Looking at his watch repeatedly with an anxious expression and standing first on one foot and then on the other.

It was a long time before he burst into speech but when he did he said "Look here, conductor, I have a train to catch and please could you not proceed a little faster" and the conductor replied "Oh yes, sir, I could but I am not allowed to leave the bus".

The Guv'nor tried his own hand at a gas producer, fitting a trailer of his design to the Wolseley car.

The 'Guv'nors' version of the producer gas trailer, attached to the 'Gas Bag' Wolseley. Old silencer boxes from bus exhaust systems have been adapted into chimneys. Sid Nudd, later a partner in Nudd Bros and Lockyer, his son-in-law, gives a helping hand.

A further three Guys, Nos. 428-30 arrived in the early part of 1943, one with Roe bodywork and two with Northern Counties, these being of all-metal construction as this bodybuilder had received dispensation to retain this. Number 428 was allocated to Melton Mowbray, being the first double-decker to operate directly from this depot, although they had run on service 2 Nottingham-Melton Mowbray since 1939. Five Duple-bodied vehicles Nos. 431-5 followed from the same chassis maker, but this time they were on Mark II chassis, with the projecting radiator which had now become standard. Originally the projection had been necessary to accommodate the longer Gardner 6LW six-cylinder engine where available, but all these wartime Arabs supplied to Barton were to be five-cylinder Gardner-engined lowbridge vehicles, which coped very adequately with loads, pulling up Derby Road hill, Nottingham at peak period quite competently, if somewhat slowly.

[Upper] One of the two Northern Counties-bodied Guy Arab Mark Is, No. 430, seen at Huntingdon Street. The short bonnet identifies the Mk1 model, indicating the 5LW engine was fitted. The photograph was taken in the 'fifties when advertisements were providing additional revenue.

[Lower] Several detail differences can be seen in the lower illustration which shows the Roe-bodied Guy Arab I, No. 428, in Melton Mowbray bus station. The Roe waistrail can be discerned below the lower-deck windows, whilst the beading between decks does little for the advert, though it is for 'sliced' Condor!

A very proud old man — T. H. Barton displays his OBE on his lapel.

Among the local names included in the King's Birthday Honours List in June, was that of the Guv'nor — Mr Thomas Henry Barton, appointed Officer of the most Excellent Order of the British Empire, for services to the passenger transport industry. The Company Secretary, Mr E. L. Taylor was appointed to the Council of the new Public Transport Association, formed by successful merger of the Omnibus Owners Association and the Public Service Transport Association, bringing together company and municipal undertakings operating nearly 40,000 vehicles; membership also included the principal manufacturers.

Huntingdon Street bus station, Nottingham, was operating beyond its intended capacity, and the local authority acted swiftly, erecting a new bus station at Mount Street, close to the General Hospital; this was opened in 3rd October, with three platforms on a slightly curved, head to tail arrangement, with rounded asbestos sheeting forming the roof and part of the back, this was something of a utilitarian design, but served its purpose surprisingly well for over 25 years. All services radiating to the west of Nottingham, north of the River Trent were transferred, Midland General Omnibus Co Ltd taking platform 4, together with a small extra corner piece for parking, Barton had platform 5, while number 6 was allocated to Trent Motor Traction, with Midland Red's X99 Birmingham service at the head.

Ten saloons were returned from the Army by the end of the year and war savings now amounted to £20,900. Only two Guys with Roe bodywork were supplied in 1944, these being numbered 436-7. Rather surprisingly, during January AEC Regent No. 247 was withdrawn and sold to G. H. Austin and Son Ltd, of Stafford; for several years until the arrival of the two unfrozen Regent in 1942 this had been the only Southall product in an almost standard fleet.

The only two deliveries in 1944 were a pair of Roe-bodied Guy Arab IIs. These were the longer bonneted version — capable of taking either the 5LW or longer 6LW engine. Number 436 was photographed at Mount Street, Nottingham.

On 27th January 1944, 150 people attended a dinner at the British Restaurant at Chilwell Memorial Institute upon the occasion of the presentation to Mr T. H. Barton of a portait painted in oils by Mr Norman Hepple to the order of employees in commemoration of his appointment as an OBE. The funds to pay for it had been the surplus from the club and canteen which they had run until the Company built new premises and took over the running of it in 1935; this was earmarked as a nucleus of a fund to pay for the painting. This was mentioned to him, but being modest, they were unable to further the proposal, until the opportunity arrived to mention this again, when the King's Birthday Honours List contained his name. Reluctant consent was then given. It was mentioned in one of the speeches during the evening, that the gas bag buses had now travelled 893,000 miles and saved 162,000 gallons of fuel. Twelve LT7 models dating from 1935, Nos. 253-6/9, 261-7, were in desperate need of body repairs. Some of these had just returned from the forces, so it was decided to recondition the chassis, which were sent to Blackpool, where Burlingham fitted standard utility 36-seat front-entrance bus bodywork, using seats from the original bodies.

The war in Europe was now turning in the Allies' favour, and relaxations included the dim-out in place of blackout, easing the drivers lot considerably, although times were still very hard.

For easy identification of depot allocations, a system of colour coding was devised, each vehicle displaying a 6in. x 1in. coloured strip directly beneath fleet numbers at front and rear.

The following colours were selected:

Chilwell - Black and white check
Nottingham - Blue
Melton Mowbray - Brown
Ilkeston - Green

Twelve of the 1935 LT7s from the 252-67 series were rebodied with Utility single-deck bodywork. The MoS specification bodies were built by Burlingham of Blackpool. No. 254 is seen at Mount Street off loading passengers before running into the bus station proper.

Calverton - Yellow
Kegworth - Pink
Spare (usually for Chilwell) - Grey

Parliament Street offices were closed, being transferred to Mount Street, Nottingham, with a large parking area for vehicles on layover, this was in close proximity of the new bus station.

The timetable booklet issued in October showed a separate entry for works services for the first time, these being numbered from 1 to 35 in the Beeston/Ilkeston area, but seven were still unnumbered, while the Spondon (Celanese works), 5C Nottingham and 16 Ilkeston remained in the normal numbering scheme. Note that it has never been the practice to show the destinations (except for 'Spondon') on workers' journeys, the blinds displaying WORKS SERVICE. In future for reference purposes and ease of identification these journey numbers will be shown with a 'W' prefix, as they duplicate the normal service scheme. Although there were service to Chilwell C.O.D. from Nottingham (W1), Castle Donington (W2) and Ilkeston (W3), no details were given, due to national security; however, the Old Dalby Ordnance Factory now had journeys detailed from Stathern and Colston Bassett, and a new route from Melton Mowbray, via Asfordby and Shoby. The other route via Ab Kettleby had now been given service number 31, and the circular route operated on Tuesdays only. In the Long Eaton area, services 3A to Old Sawley had been withdrawn, as had the 5B from Nottingham, which was replaced by 5X cut back from Derby.

The business of E. & H. Frakes of 66 Station Road, Castle Donington was acquired on 13th November, the takeover included two Bedford WLB and WTB buses which were never operated, the timings covered by the licence for the service from Castle Donington to Long Eaton were embodied in Barton's 3B timetable. It is interesting to note that certain Frakes journeys diverted in Long Eaton to Manor Park, and for many years after the takeover, these were denoted in timetables by 'F'. This business had commenced on 30th May 1912, the proprietors Johnson and Frakes operating a Vulcan on Saturdays only, with three journeys each way; Castle Donington to Long Eaton, with four journeys to Sawley, two extended to Old Sawley. By 1921 the business was operated under the name 'Ella' Bus Service, the Christian name of Herbert's wife.

Normal headlamps were restored on all vehicles during December, and a further two buses were returned from the Army during the year.

The weather during January 1945 deteriorated, with very heavy snow, ice and fog, between 18 and 23°F of frost was recorded. However, all services were maintained, but the utility vehicles supplied from mid-1943 onwards were fitted with wooden slatted seats, providing very uncomfortable rides on the frozen snow-rutted roads, so much so that one passenger was heard to remark "my corns are so bad; I don't know whether to stand or sit down".

Two Guys, Nos. 438-9, with Strachans lowbridge 55-seat rear-entrance utility bodywork arrived during the early part of the year. With the ending of dim-out, there was a relaxation of restrictions on most routes allowing later evening journeys to be implemented; route 3B Long Eaton-Castle Donington was withdrawn, all journeys being extended into Nottingham on route 3, giving a basic half-hourly service with 3C.

Strachans again supplied 55-seat lowbridge bodywork for a further ten Guy Arab Mark II 5LW buses, Nos. 440-9, but this time they were to the more relaxed utility design, which was by then permitted, having rounded rear domes and upholstered seats in Nos. 442-9. No. 326, a Leyland LT7 dating from 1937, was found at Rena, some 40 miles from Lubeck, Germany, still in running order. It had been fitted with an extra entrance on the rear nearside but the emergency door had been removed, for use on the local town service. After being captured at Dunkirk it was driven across France by the retreating forces, then abandoned in Rena, where it was adopted for their use.

Between the end of the war in Europe and the surrender of Japan, the operator A. E. Hubbard of Eaton, Leicestershire, sold out on 1st June, with ACT 765, a Bedford OWB Duple 'utility' (which was sold immediately to Banfield of Newcastle) and the Eaton-Melton Mowbray service via Eastwell, Goadby Marwood and Scalford on Tuesday and Saturday. This was a similar route to the 28 service from Watson Bros, except for the deviation to Goadby Marwood.

By the time of the surrender of Japan on 15th August, war savings held through the Company's scheme amounted to £47,500, and there were 535 male and 246 female employees, an increase of 360 (almost double) in six years. The fleet now consisted of 68 double-deckers and 118 single-deckers, with the immense increase of 62 double-deckers during the span of the war period. Coach number 400 toured the district suitably decorated for Thanksgiving week. The female staff was not always accepted by the men in those days, and many tales are told of their inexperience, so with the rapid growth of the Company, the Barton family were not always recognised, as depicted by the following:
"After waiting for all the other passengers to board, there was just room for one of the 'bosses' on the bottom step, and at the next stop everyone removed their bodies to allow a passenger to alight, and when the boss and the new conductress were left to remount the following conversation took place "After you, miss," "No, its all right chum, after you, I am more used to it than you."

Six of the wartime Guys stand in Huntingdon Street parking area, with a TD7 breaking the sequence. From left to right they are Nos. 439/374/442/441/434/445/432. Hardly distinguishable among the Guys are Nos. 434/432 which have Duple, rather than Strachan bodywork.

Chapter nine : Passengers in plenty

In this Huntingdon Street, Nottingham, view of the 8.30am Saturday departure for Skegness in the late 'forties at least five of the Duple-bodied PD1s, quite new at the time, can be seen. Passengers still waiting will fill another couple. Nottingham's No. 33, FTO 616, a 1939 Regent, looks a little weary, unusually in this fleet, though few operators had yet been able to restore normal standards to all their war-weary stock.

With the return of peace, many former employees returned to their old duties, while many of the conductresses and female cleaning staff left to take up their previous employment, or returned to domestic bliss. Although there was still rationing of many commodities, supplies of paint became more readily available, enabling buses to be improved externally. But wartime restrictions and staff shortages had taken their toll on many of the vehicles, and bodywork had deteriorated, due to lack of materials. Coachbuilders, joiners and shop-fitters, were engaged throughout the area to carry out refurbishing work, as did Barton's own workshops, as well as over-hauling mechanical items.

One coachbuilder to become widely known in the industry in the early 'fifties, Nudd Bros and Lockyer Ltd, commenced operations from premises at the corner of Cator Lane, Chilwell, repairing bodywork on at least two of Barton's double-deckers. One of the directors, S. Nudd, was son-in-law to T. H. Barton, marrying his youngest daughter, Mabel.

On 1st January 1946, two operators were acquired; however, although vehicles were purchased, these were not operated or given fleet numbers. The older-established of these was Lewis Motor Services Ltd, of Cotgrave, starting operations in 1912 as Alfred Lewis Carriers, with a return journey to Nottingham via Holme House on Wednesdays and Saturdays. During 1922 a second service was commenced between Shelford and Nottingham, again on Wednesdays and Saturdays, carrying both goods and passengers. This passed to T. A. Lewis on April 1926. In 1929 Cotgrave was being served by a daily two-hourly service via Holme House or Bassingfield Lane. A haulage side had also been developed during the early days, with goods delivery throughout Belvoir district, and a milk collection service. By 1931 Mr F. N. Lawrence was proprietor of the business, which was operating under its present title. He had successfully applied for a second route via Tollerton and Gamston during 1933. It seemed rather fitting for this small operator to become a part of Barton's empire after the latter's close involvement in the development of Lewis operations, particularly during the formative years. Two Commer Commander buses, and a Bedford WTB with Duple Hendonian coach body, dating from 1932/4/7 respectively, were sold almost immediately upon takeover, all three passing to Hunts of Alford, Lincolnshire.

The second acquistion, W. Randell, of The Cross, Bottesford, Leics, operating as Vale of Belvoir Bus Service, was a joint purchase with Lincolnshire Road Car Co Ltd. The latter took over the following routes:- Bottesford-Grantham via Woolsthorpe on schooldays; Stathern-Grantham, Saturdays only, with shorts on Thursdays and Fridays from Bottesford; Bottesford-Newark, Wednesdays only. These were given route numbers 33A, 33, 33B respectively. The tours and excursion licence was shared with Barton, which also obtained Muston-Melton Mowbray, Tuesdays only service, operating via Bottesford, Redmile, Barkstone, Plungar, Stathern, then as route 26, to Eastwell and Scalford. Randell had commenced operations by 1927, using two Chevrolet 14-seat buses, and in 1930 bought a 20-seat saloon on a GMC chassis. Bedford became standard throughout the ensuing years, with one WLB and six WTB coaches, until finally, in 1943, a Bedford OWB with Duple utility 32-seat bus bodywork arrived.

Barton's next orders were placed with Duple for 40 double-deck and 15 coach bodies, to be fitted on two completely new models from Leyland. These were the Titan PD1 and Tiger PS1, both fitted with 7.4-litre engines. The demands being made upon manufacturers by operators throughout the United Kingdom were so great that it was inevitable orders could not be fulfilled promptly. The only new vehicles received during 1946 were four Tiger PS1/1 with Duple A1-type 33-seat coach bodies, Nos. 480-3, which were to the maker's standard design, with an addition of fluted aluminium strips, 12in. above the guard rail.

However, limited deliveries from the manufacturers enabled other operators to release older stock. Thus three Leyland TD2 Roe highbridge double-deckers arrived from Leeds City Transport, as well as five former Leicester City Transport TD2 models with Brush highbridge bodywork, respectively numbered 450-2, 457-61. These highbridge vehicles and three identical TD1s, 475-7, stayed in operation for almost five years presenting certain problems, as Chilwell's entrance doors were not high enough, so for maintenance purposes they were driven into the garage on flat tyres, or rims. Ilkeston depot, which was to become something of a Cinderella with regard to fleet allocation, received the majority of these vehicles. Some years later one of Ilkeston's conductors, Mr Eddie Harrison, related an interesting event.

During bank holidays, the majority of Ilkeston's workings were suspended, as these covered a high proportion of works journeys. Road staff and vehicles were then redeployed on duplicates for holiday traffic, several vehicles working service 12, Nottingham to Leicester. On this particular occasion, using one of the old Leicester 'deckers, they were proceeding down Belgrave Street, Leicester, when an almighty clattering noise arose from the rear end. The driver asked Eddie to look at the rear wheels, and upon leaning out of the rear platform, he could see the wheel protruding six inches from the wheel arch! After driving cautiously into St. Margaret's bus station, the situation was discussed with the resident Inspector. It was decided to try the City Transport depot, a few hundred yards away. Mr Harrison said "You should have seen one of their mechanics when we arrived. Holding an oil can in one hand, his mouth dropped open in disbelief; he then shouted into the depot for the rest of the staff to view the return of one of their veterans." Unfortunately the authority had disposed of spares for this type of vehicle, which had to be towed back to headquarters.

Leyland PS1 No. 482, with Duple C33F bodywork, stands on the quayside at Southampton with the Queen Mary in the background. It is understood the coach was collecting Canadians for the newly-formed Nottingham Panthers ice hockey team. Barton were to provide all coach facilities until 1958 when the team and the league were disbanded.

Vehicles were returned from the Military and Government Departments over a long period. Operators had the responsibility of tracing their old buses, which were stored at various sites throughout the United Kingdom. This was made very difficult as original registration plates had been removed. However, this task was simplified in Barton's case, as a ready means of identification was the square spigot on starting handles, mentioned earlier, quite apart from distinctive bodywork in many cases.

These were halcyon days for passenger transport operators, but unfortunately this was to last for less than a decade. Frequency was increased on the majority of routes to cater for increasing demands of the travelling public, who were now looking for evening entertainment, in particular in cinemas which were now doing big business. Suspended services were reinstated; 1A, Nottingham-Beeston Rylands and 9, Long Eaton-Skegness, while service 17 was again extended to Shardlow.

New services were introduced from Beeston (Boots) to Ilkeston (Market), a works service operating Monday to Friday, plus a daily two-hourly service 20A Melton Mowbray-Loughborough via Asfordby, Shoby, Six Hills and Burton-on-the-Wolds. The old 20A service to Asfordby Hill journeys were extended to The Bell, and included in route 20. Service 5X was extended from Long Eaton to Draycott by embodying all 5A journeys. 7A extended from Lambley to Woodborough (Four Bells) on to Calverton (Pit Lane).

On 1st December 1946, a Loughborough-Melbourne hourly daily route was introduced, virtually replacing 10A to Kegworth, but on Saturdays provided additional journeys. This passed the site of Castle Donington airfield which now housed fully-developed coachbuilders Nudd Bros, and Lockyer Ltd, undertaking work for Midland Red, Edinburgh City Transport, and other large operators, but not Barton. This airfield was to receive a new lease of life in the 'sixties, to be recounted in Volume 2. From here the journey passed Diseworth Cross Road, on to Isley Walton, and close to Donington Park at Wilson Lane End.

Two journeys deviated into COD, Donington Park. Route number 37 was allotted for all journeys including those via West Leake Lane End, which omitted Sutton Bonington.

Barton's bus park in Mount Street, Nottingham, is the location for this delightful selection of TD1s and a TD2, awaiting further duties. All chassis are second-hand, and from left to right No. 389 [ex-Chatham & District], No. 476 [ex-Leicester], No. 399 [ex-Western SMT], and No. 478 [ex-Chesterfield], the TD2. Nos. 389 and 399 had been products of the 'purchase and rebody' policy of 1940-41, having Duple bodies to Barton design, whereas the other two, purchased in 1946-47 retained their original Brush and Leyland bodies. The body of No. 389 was transferred to PD1 470 shortly afterwards.

Journeys on service 10 not operated via Hemington and Lockington villages diverted into Kingston-on-Soar, instead of Kegworth Station.

The excursion and tours licence from Arnold of C. W. Shelton, Edwin Street, Daybrook, Nottingham, were taken over on 3rd July. This small operator had sold two works service licences to Nottingham City Transport, on 6th November 1939, together with two Thurgood-bodied coaches, a Crossley Alpha and Dennis Lancet, which were immediately sold to other operators. The excursion licence remained unused through the wartime period until taken up by Barton.

The previous year there had been a change of Government and the Labour Party were now in power. They had a mandate to nationalise various industries, including passenger transport. In July Barton's Managing Director sent out a personal letter to all employees, which typified the Company's approach:

A MESSAGE FROM THE GUV'NOR

He cannot get around amongst you as he would like, or as he used to do.

He asks that you should

READ IT

"Whatever happens always let goodwill towards all men prevail".

HEAD OFFICE
BEESTON, NOTTS.

July, 1946

Dear Fellow Workers,

I want to make this special appeal to all engaged in running our great business, to build up at this critical time a new standard of Service beyond anything we have achieved in the past, however good that may have been. We are passing through a difficult period of transition, and transport is in the public eye more than ever before; we should look on this as a great opportunity. The public, who are so quick to complain, are also quick to appreciate really good Service; that is how the goodwill of this Company was established, and that goodwill made the strength and prosperity of the firm, which, as you know, is your prosperity too.

I need not go into details. If I suggest that we should give every passenger that individual courtesy and attention which makes all the difference; that we should drive and conduct our buses with full consideration not only for our passengers but for all other road users; and that those of us who work behind the scenes should always act on our old slogan "The Service comes First" — these are just pointers along the road you know so well.

You all know just what needs to be done. You have done it before. Go ahead and do it again now.

T. H. BARTON, O.B.E.

Managing Director

T. H. Barton never knew the outcome of his letter, for on 26th July, he passed away at a local nursing home, aged eighty. The following editorial appeared in Beeston Gazette and Echo, on Saturday 3rd August.

Tribute To 'The Guv'nor'

"Mr T. H. Barton — 'The Guv'nor' to his workpeople — is dead, and his biography reads almost like fiction. Physically Mr Barton was never robust, and an outdoor life was suggested to him when he was a young man. Only twelve months ago he was taken to the Pay Bed Block at Nottingham, but despite these setbacks he lived four score years during which he rarely spent an idle moment. He showed what could be done by private enterprise, by industry, perseverance, skill and grit. From the lowest class of labourer to managing director of one of the largest private passenger transport companies in the country he never altered in outlook or attire. He detested official red tape and clashed frequently with authorities stifling enterprise by restrictions. He was no respecter of persons, and two typical examples of this characteristic come to mind. In the days when Barton's had a garage at the junction of Greyfriar Gate and Castle Boulevard, Nottingham, two commercial travellers, in black coats and striped trousers, waited upon Mr Barton. But he was just leaving for Beeston in his Ford car — an open tourer with ripped hood flying like streamers in the wind. He beckoned to the travellers to board this stilted veteran which could only be coaxed to start after Mr Barton had adjusted the mechanism from a prone position in the muddy roadway. The last I saw was a decrepit flivver shrouded in a cloud of smoke, cracking like a gatling gun, proceeding along Castle Boulevard with two immaculately dressed travellers seated in the rear seats, and muddy Mr Barton acting as chauffeur. A more recent incident was when Mr Barton visited London with barristers and solicitors in connection with some transport conference. During the interval, lunch at Simpson's was suggested. For the uninitiated Simpson's, in pre-war days, was the most exclusive restaurant in the country, and it was somewhat of a shock to the assembled company when Mr Barton ordered bread and milk. The well-trained and imperturbable waiter, however, asked whether he would like it in a glass, and the guv'nor selected a basin. That was typical of Mr Barton, always ordinary, homely and a lovable genius who will be greatly missed and long remembered".

It should be added that he had been deaf for several years, probably from working in a corrugated steel shed at Beck works, testing and running engines. Up to the time of his death, he had been working on an idea of detaching mechanical running parts, including the driver's cab, from the main bodywork. This was based on the theory that it would be easier for maintenance, taking up less garage space, and the passenger section would still be operational, with the easy fitting of a spare running unit. It would have been rigidly linked, with twin axle steering. Unfortunately, his idea had only reached the stage of cutting the chassis members. He had been twice married, having four daughters and five sons by his first wife, and two sons by his second.

The funeral cortege was headed by a new PS1 chassis, conveying the coffin, upon which was placed his renowned peaked cap.

After a period of dairy farming at Inham Nook, Chilwell, T. A. Barton returned to the business to succeed his father as Managing Director.

Barton's milk floats had regularly served the districts but now the land was sold off for a very large council housing development.

The other sons retained the positions within the Company they had held since 1937, with Carl succeeding his father on the Board.

The Nottingham to Cropwell Bishop via Holme House, Stragglethorpe and Cropwell Butler, Wednesdays, Saturdays and Sundays service of J. H. Starbuck, of Church Street, Cropwell Bishop, was acquired on 1st September. Tours and excursions from the village were included, together with a surprising addition to the fleet of a 1932 Bedford WLB, with 20-seat dual-purpose Bracebridge body, numbered 479. Mr Starbuck commenced operations during the early 'twenties, with a Seldon, followed by a Ford, then a Chevrolet.

Barton operated a very small programme of extended tours in Britain at this time, all seats being sold out within a few days.

Plans were approved, and work commenced on a new depot situated in Midland Terrace, Long Eaton. This site had previously been used as a hard standing for vehicles during layover. The building was opened during 1947, relieving Chilwell of many duties in the area, and buses being transferred accordingly, eliminating the dead mileage previously involved. Vehicles based at Long Eaton were identified by black and yellow check colour code strips. The enquiry office was transferred to a large house adjacent to the new garage, the old premises in The Green being closed.

Five further PS1/1s (Nos. 484/6-9) arrived in January, followed in spring by the final six outstanding from the initial post-war order (Nos. 491/3-7). From No. 487 onwards they were fitted with rear roof-mounted destination and route number indicators, reverting to pre-war practice.

This year the seating capacity of the new PS1-Duple coaches taken into stock was raised to 35. However, four further PS1/1 (Nos. 485/92/8-9) appeared fitted with Brush DP39F bodies transferred from Cheetahs (Nos. 358/4/62/1), the chassis being modified in front-end layout to allow the transfer. Another similar PS1/1 chassis was receiving Barton-built bodywork to a rather startling design of American style, fitted with much shallower windows than usual in this country, although these were arranged to slide horizontally to give adequate ventilation. Numbered 490 it was painted with a cream flash surround to the side windows.

The attractive appearance of the Brush dual-purpose bodies from the Cheetahs was unfortunately marred somewhat by the disjointed line of the cab front, when transferred to the PS1/1 Tigers. Number 492 was working from Melton Mowbray to Knipton on route 28.

The body shop, under the charge of Lance Taylor, also removed the five-year-old Duple lowbridge front-entrance bodies from two TD1 chassis, placing them on the new Leyland PD1 chassis Nos. 455/70, slight adjustments being made to fit the cab to suit the differently-dimensioned chassis and producing a slanting windscreen. These two spent most of their working days at Calverton.

Six of the long-awaited PD1s complete with new bodywork arrived at various intervals during the year, numbered 463/5/54/74/67/71. The fleet numbering allocations were based on chassis numbers, which gave haphazard registration numbering, as the chassis had been stored at the rear of Long Eaton Fire Station, and were not drawn from stock in sequence. The Duple lowbridge front-entrance bodies were based on the pre-war design, updated externally by addition of fluted strips, as used on the single-deckers, and other details included air-operated double doors, first-aid and mechanical-aid kits displayed very clearly at the back. As before, the interior was to a very high standard of finish, with flower-pattern moquette conventional seating on the lower deck, but upstairs the four-in-a-row seats were of the high-back coach type. Although it was standard practice to fit clocks on all single-deck deliveries, they were also fitted to the lower-deck staircase panelling on several of these vehicles. This was to be the full development of this classic design of bodywork, although Duple were to build rear-entrance bodies of somewhat similar outline for Red and White Motor Services Ltd, in 1949 and 1950. Three were also built for Skills Motor Coaches Ltd of Nottingham. Mounted on Daimler CVD6 chassis, two were sold before entry into service to W. Gash and Son Ltd of Elston, near Newark. Obviously Duple bodywork must have impressed Nottingham-area operators. Generally, undertakings were purchasing rear-entrance double-deckers to a more spartan finish. The only other operator besides Barton to favour the front-entrance layout in the early post-1945 era was Birch Bros Ltd, Kentish Town, who were building front-entrance bodies for their own operation, later followed by some Willowbrook products of the same layout but with fully-fronted cabs.

An official view of No. 465, the Duple styling having outlines of the pre-war Titan bodies, with finer details and embellishments added. The fleetname was refitted in the bottom panelling, to allow for advertising in 1950.

January and February 1947 were very cold, with severe snowstorms, causing chaotic conditions for bus operation, and the ensuing flood swept away Cavendish Bridge which crossed the River Trent at Shardlow. Service 17 operated over a single-line Bailey Bridge controlled by traffic lights for many years, before a new bypass and crossing was erected. Many roads in the Trent Valley were flooded, difficulty being experienced at Wilford, Kegworth and Sawley where the river was crossed for North West Leicestershire townships. Services were maintained where possible by attaching long lengths of tubing to the exhaust, preventing water from entering the system and thereby stalling the engines.

Two carnival floats had been disposed of during the war, and so an ex-RAF Crossley chassis was used for the replacement.

A time-consuming operation each evening was the checking of engine oil on every bus. So Maurie Barton decided to experiment, and produced an oil-replenishing system which allowed the checking to be reduced to a once-a-week operation. This consisted of a three gallon engine oil

[Above left] The test model of the oil replenisher. The square tank on the bottom right represents the engine sump. Adjacent to this is the reservoir [three gallon] with the slave servo on its left, feeding up to the main servo on the right. The long lever represents the footbrake.

Heavy snowfalls in 1947 caused havoc, and No. 193 is seen caught in a drift on its journey from Ilkeston on the outskirts of Shardlow. This was followed by a rapid thaw, causing severe flooding, clearly shown on the lower picture of a submerged Duple-bodied double-decker. It is believed to be No. 347, which was rebuilt with metal frame members, suggesting this may have been necessary due to water affecting body timbers!

tank, to which was fitted a 5in. diameter vacuum servo unit. A pipe was tapped into the vacuum servo operating the footbrake, which was coupled up to the slave cylinder unit. Operation of the footbrake caused the piston in the slave cylinder to be pulled back; this drew oil from the reservoir via a non-return valve, filling the slave valve chamber. When the footbrake was released, the non-return valve closed and the engine oil was pushed through another non-return valve situated in the outlet, piped to the engine base. To ensure the correct level was maintained a second pipe was tapped into the engine base, allowing any excess to flow back into the reservoir by gravity feed. It is understood one of the 1937 series LT7s was the first to be converted together with a double-decker in the 345-9 group. The system was successful enough for several of the PS1/1s to be fitted with it.

The Bailey Bridge which replaced the original Cavendish Bridge at Shardlow after the latter was swept away by the floods. This was a remarkable structure which remained for many years before a by-pass replaced the road. Being situated on the A6 London Road, it was a hazard to traffic as single line working was in force, controlled by traffic lights. LT7 No. 207 demonstrates this.

Eight Bedford OB 29-seat Duple-bodied coaches (Nos. 520-7) were put into service in this same year to replace Leyland Cubs, and one of these vehicles was used to operate a Continental Road Cruise. Company Secretary Mr E. L. Taylor recalled the difficulties involved in setting up this tour when giving his Presidential address to the Omnibus Society in 1963:

"Getting coaches in motion again on extended tours in a world of rationing and chronic shortages was a formidable task. Many hotels that had been taken over for military and other warlike purposes took a long time to release and still longer to recondition. Controls of all kinds, as always, took far longer to relax than impose. At the same time the demand from a war-weary public was tremendous, and when, in 1946, after great efforts and against some tricky hazards, we managed to put out some sort of programme, all the seats we could offer were sold out in a few days. I do not think anyone succeeded in transhipping a coach to the Continent in that year. In 1947 there was a small improvement in this country, and some expansion in operation, and we did succeed, by curious means, in shipping a coach across to Calais, by way of a freight train ferry, which was the continuance of an operation instituted in the latter part of the war. It had to be a small one — on a Bedford petrol-engined chassis — and it had to stay in France for the whole season, but with the blessing of the French authorities it accomplished a season of fourteen-day 'circular tours' to the Riviera with great success — to everybody's slight surprise. In fact, the official French attitude was far more welcoming and benign than it has become in these sophisticated days; we had more difficulty in persuading the Bank of England to let us have the francs we needed for operating costs. At that time, tourists going into Europe could claim a foreign currency allowance of £75 plus the return railway fare. I well remember a long argument in Threadneedle Street early in 1947 based on the calculations that 28 passengers to Nice, and return by train would involve a total sterling outlay of about £480, whereas we could perform the same operation by motor coach for a quarter of that sum. And when at last we had convinced our masters on this point, we had to start all over again with a campaign in favour of the genuine necessity of the journey two of us must make, in order to complete the detailed accommodation arrangements. We succeeded with about 36 hours to spare".

Later in 1947 Mr Taylor left the Company to join Sheffield United Tours Ltd, part of the BET group; he was to become Chairman not only of SUT but also of several other BET companies in later years. He was succeeded as Barton's Secretary by Frank Broomfield.

Seven further Titans were obtained from municipal operators; Nos. 500-5 came from Wigan Corporation and had Leyland lowbridge bodies, as had No. 478 which had served Chesterfield Corporation for the previous fifteen years.

Applications were granted for three

The driver, and conductor Eddie Harrison stand in front of ex-Wigan TD1 No. 501 at Spondon Celanese Works before journeying back to Ilkeston.

Bedford OB No. 523, with Duple 29-seat coachwork, is typical of vehicles supplied to numerous operators at this period. Numbers 520-3 remained in the fleet for only a short time. Of those remaining, most had their seating reduced to give added comfort for Road Cruise passengers, and one-man operated routes.

services, the first being the 29, Melton Mowbray-Muston running hourly daily as far as Bottesford, with two journeys on Tuesdays extended to Muston. This was an amalgamation of Hubbard's route via Scalford, Wycomb, Goadby Marwood, Eastwell, and Eaton, then as Randell's service for the remainder of the route; journeys on service 26 were also covered. It amounted to quite a development from two market-day and schoolday operations.

Service 33, Nottingham (Mount Street)-Chilwell (Hallams Lane top), was to be the most successful of the new routes, being from the outset daily on an hourly headway, to Beeston Square, Devonshire Avenue, to Bramcote Avenue serving the Hillman Estate, then on to Bramcote Lane. Service 18 to Ilkeston now operated from Beeston to Hillman Estate by the same route giving a half-hour service, with the 32 to Bulwell again serving this Estate via Cator Lane. A new service 26, Nottingham-Kinoulton, operated on Monday to Saturday via Cotgrave and Owthorpe village, was mainly a peak-period timetable, except for Saturday extras. Redmile became the terminus of all 22 service journeys from Nottingham, which included the former Starbuck and Lewis Motor Services licences via Tollerton and Gamston, on a daily hourly headway. So also was 24 service Nottingham-Stathern which incorporated Lewis's other operation from Cotgrave. Finally in 1947, Melton Mowbray-Great Yarmouth recommenced after wartime suspension, being given route number 36 a year later.

During 1948, delivery of new vehicles came at quite a pace. A further fifteen Leyland Tiger PS1/1 Duple 35-seat coaches, (Nos. 535-49), four Bedford OB (Nos. 528-31) 29-seat Duple coaches, the earlier examples of this type being modified for stage services, and 26 more of the PD1 double-deckers (Nos. 453/6/62/4/6/8-9/72-3/506-19/572-4) arrived at varying times. All the surviving pre-war Cheetahs, Tigers and Cubs were withdrawn.

A significant event occurring in 1948 marked an improvement in relations with the Trent Motor Traction Company. For the first time interavailability of tickets allowed passengers to return on the other operator's vehicle.

The main changes in route development took place in the Vale of Belvoir, services 27, 27A and 27B being recast due to duplication on 29 introduced late the previous year. Scalford, Stathern and Plungar were deleted from the route which was extended from Harby to Langar and Bingham, all journeys commencing from Melton Mowbray under the common number 27, including variations via Wartnaby or Holwell. This was again a daily hourly service, providing links with many villages and hamlets by a system of connecting services to Nottingham or Melton Mowbray, 22/29 linking at Plungar, 24/27 at Harby, and Stathern 24/28/29.

Once again Old Sawley to Long Eaton was, for a short period, detached from 15 to Ilkeston, and extended from the Market Place through the main shopping street to Manor Park, as Frake's old route. A ten-minute headway was adopted Monday to Saturday, and 20 minutes on Sunday, with four journeys on weekdays extended from Old Sawley to Draycott, the service then continuing to Derby by the normal route, all being given service number 39. On alternate Fridays a 38 service was provided from Chilwell (Married Quarters) to Beeston Square. A Melton Mowbray local, 40, RAF Station (Dependents Mess)-Nottingham Street-Holwell Works operated Monday to Friday works journeys.

A very successful daily express summer service, 34, Nottingham-Llandudno, was launched serving Long Eaton, Derby, Uttoxeter, Newcastle-under-Lyme, Chester, Rhyl, Colwyn Bay and many intermediate points. Summer Saturday loadings on express services were phenomenal, up to 40 coaches being provided, and on the Skegness run PD1A double-deckers were regularly used; on one occasion over twenty were required. Seating was lost to provide luggage space, but even so fifty pasengers were carried. To cope

Shelters were being erected at Huntingdon St, when Geoff Atkins took this night shot of platforms 2 and 3. Two Duple-bodied PD1s await their passengers.

with this demand many of the older LT5s were retained, being licensed during the summer season only for use on local stage carriage runs. August Bank Holiday Monday was perhaps the peak day, operating tours and excursions to many points, with the main attraction of a show in the grounds of Lord Belper's residence at Kingston-upon-Soar. Up to 50 vehicles supplemented the 10 service between Nottingham and Loughborough, including double-deckers mainly from Ilkeston garage. To avoid low bridges at Sawley and Kingston, they were re-routed via Breaston and Kegworth station, using large portable signs indicating 'Deckers this way'. However, at least two double-deckers were 'beheaded' despite these precautions.

Increase in Belvoir area services necessitated additional vehicles being allocated in the district. Hose depot was too small and could not be extended, so a large area of land was purchased at Boyer's Orchard, Harby. A temporary hard-standing for six vehicles was provided, adjacent to a wooden shed provided for storage facilities. It was intended to build covered premises but these never materialised. Hose depot was closed shortly afterwards, being in a dilapidated condition.

A further order was placed with Duple for 20 A1-type bodies, this time modified to provide seating for 39 passengers, a return to prewar practice! This was achieved by fitting more upright steering columns to the PS1/1 chassis, and the back of the driver's seat became part of the bulkhead panel. Nineteen of this order were delivered towards the end of the year and in the early part of 1949, being numbered 550-68; the remaining chassis was sold to W. & B. Coaches of Chilwell, a small business in which the Company had an interest as a safeguard against nationalisation. Two coaches were operated by this concern, the second, a Bedford Duple OB, and both were sold in the early 'fifties, when the business was wound up. The remaining body was fitted to No. 484, a 1947 PS1/1 chassis after the latter had been adapted, whilst No. 484's original body was fitted to Leyland TS11 (No. 424). These additions allowed the sale of PS1/1 numbers 480-3 with their low 33-seat capacity. Eight of the LT7s were stripped of Burlingham utility bodies, and received Duple bodies to the same design as the PS1/1s, retaining fleet numbers 253-4/6/8-9/61-2/7. They had been bodied three times in thirteen years! The final eight PD1s (Nos. 570-1/5-80) had arrived by February 1949; it had taken almost two years to complete this order. Three Bedford OB coaches (Nos. 532-4) completed Duple's quota for that year. However, 1949 was to see the beginning of a large influx of second-hand vehicles, the first arrivals travelling down from Yorkshire, being surplus to requirements at West Riding Automobile Co Ltd, of Wakefield. They were of lowbridge rear-entrance design, Nos. 581-5 being TD5s and Nos. 587-8 TD4 with Roe bodywork, and No. 586, a TD5 which had been rebodied to utility standards in 1943 by NCB. Numbers 581-5 had their seating capacity increased from 48 to 55 before entering service.

Only three additional services were introduced in 1949. They were 38, Chilwell (Married Quarters) to Long Eaton, operated on alternate Fridays to the Beeston service; W2, from Long Eaton (Green) to Derby (Rolls Royce) following the usual route, and 46, Loughborough to Melton Mowbray, a Tuesday service which also operated on odd days as the pre-war 39, and took a similar route from Barrow-on-Soar to Wymeswold, but then went on to Willoughby, Upper/Nether Broughton and Ab Kettleby. Three Melton area works journeys to Old Dalby were numbered 41, from Melton Mowbray; 42, Scalford and 44, Colston Bassett. Certain 17 journeys now ran on from Shardlow to Aston-on-Trent. Services 10B/C were discontinued, and route 37 was renumbered 10B with diversions to West Leake Lane End becoming 10C.

Successful operation of summer express services saw further applications being made to the Traffic Commissioners, but they were not granted. Two were proposed from Leicester to Llandudno and Scarborough, but the third would have been very adventurous for the time, running from Nottingham, Leicester and Northampton to Nice in the South of France, via Dover, every Saturday, and returning Thursday throughout the year. It was to be almost 25 years later before operators undertook this type of journey on a regular express basis. A possible compromise may have been the introduction of a weekly winter sports cruise to Switzerland.

Many second-hand vehicles were now being purchased and stored at the rear of Chilwell garage for re-use and re-building in the most extraordinary fashion, but that is a story which will be told in Volume 2. The Barton business had come a long way and an impressive fleet had been built up, but the family's willingness to adopt unorthodox ideas was by no means at an end.

One of the eight ex-West Riding Titans which arrived in 1949, was No. 584, a TD5 dating from 1939, photographed at Tollerton village on its journey to Stathern on route 24. This double-decker was only ten years old when taken into stock.

A pictorial survey of the Barton fleet

[Above] This London-registered Scott Stirling, LE 8000, was Barton's second single-decker in the Beeston area. The driver sat over the engine.

[Below] Another vehicle operating from Beeston by late 1909 was this single-decker, believed to have been an Argyll, and to previously have been operated by the Herne Bay & Canterbury Motor Service Company Ltd. The wooden structure on the right was Barton's Ellis Grove workshops.

[Top] One of the first Ryknields to receive a Barton body. Though somewhat crude it appears to be functional, providing seating for 28. The appearance of the wheels suggests they may have used the patent adjustment for fitting solid tyres to the wheel rims.

[Above] A further development of this type of body is seen where seats have been fitted for three passengers over each front wing! At least the feet would be kept warm by the engine even though the rest of the body was exposed to the elements. Note the title 'Progress Motor Services Ltd', this being the only known photograph to show this wording.

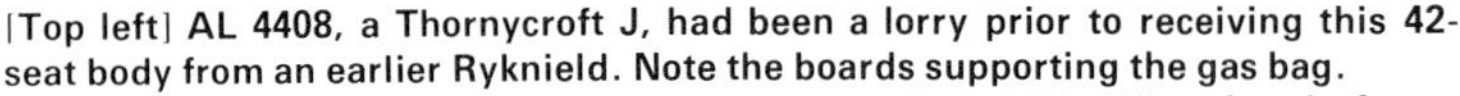

[Top left] AL 4408, a Thornycroft J, had been a lorry prior to receiving this 42-seat body from an earlier Ryknield. Note the boards supporting the gas bag.
[Lower left] The final stage of alterations to the Ryknields. The chassis frame had been extended by inserting a section between the axles. Various members of the family and garage staff are seated on the nearside, indicating that a seating capacity of 40 had been achieved. The ornate canopy came from Clayton's of Lincoln. It was intended for a steam vehicle!
[Top right] An extended Ryknield, fitted with the Barton patent Gas Bag. The group gathered round the engine may be receiving instruction on the change over from petrol to gas after the initial starting of the engine. From 1916 to 1920 this vehicle ran for Lewis of Cotgrave.
[Lower right] Lewis Motor Service Ltd had very close associations with Barton during its formative years, operating several of their lorries, buses and vans, including this gas-operated Berna, AL 4297, from July 1920 until June 1921. At the time of this photograph, gas was being taken direct from the mains to the bag, at Barton's Greyfriar Gate, Nottingham, depot. The bus is laden with typical carriers goods.

Early double-deckers

[Upper left] One of twenty Lacoste-Battman double-decker buses, purchased in 1911 for £50 each following the liquidation of a London bus company. Twelve were immediately resold to a Bedford operator and the remainder dispersed to other outlets, except for AL 68 shown here, which remained in this guise for only a short time before conversion to a paraffin-carrying lorry.

[Above]
The Clarkson steam bus seen on page 8 is now seen operating for Barton from the Ellis Grove, Beeston, base. The coat of arms on the panel is all that remains of the Herne Bay and Canterbury Motor Service Co Ltd signwriting.

[Lower left] Daimler Y, LE 9696, is not what it seems. It was originally registered as a Leyland when entering service with London Central in 1912. It passed to London General who sold it to Barton in 1920, when it probably changed its guise. The windscreen has been added by Barton, who gave it fleet numbers 5, 23 then 37. The fleet name style shown was not used again until 1927, becoming a standard design from then onwards. The line-up from the left includes Charlie Parker, T. A. Barton, Jack Bloor, Jack Billingham, Maurice Barton and John Grimdich. This view was taken at the side of the new Chilwell garage. The vehicle was rebuilt in 1921 with a 64-seat body.

Eight of the double-deckers, introduced into the fleet 1919-20, were stripped of their 32-36 seat bodies, the chassis extended, and rebodied to give seating for 58-64 passengers. This brought them into line with the high-capacity single-deck buses.

[Above] This rear view of rebodied AEC 'B' AL 9410 was taken in Market Square, Nottingham, in June 1925. The vehicle, along with others, had been hired by the Corporation during a three day electricity failure following a fire in a cable subway. In the background is Moot Hall which was destroyed during the Second World War.

[Top right] Three, if not more, received Hickman bodies including No. 16, LF 8351, an AEC B ex-LGOC B1575, purchased through the War Department. It is seen at Chilwell Road, Beeston, with Australian-style destination board.

[Right] From late 1921 chassis were extended on purchase, mainly from the War Department, and rebodied as 64-seat double-deckers. Two extended and newly-rebodied Daimlers, Nos. 38 and 39, NN 5823-4, which entered service towards the end of 1923 are seen.

Extended chassis

[Above] 'Long Tom', the Daimler Y, seen at Loughborough Rushes. It was of similar length to a present day 11-metre coach, though not so comfortable! Not identified it appears to be No. 10, NN 3561, unfortunately No. 8 was never photographed.

[Top] By contrast, this 3-axle Morris 1-ton chassis — also extended and given an additional axle by Barton — seated only 24 passengers in its Strachan & Brown body. Number 27 was photographed at Strachan's London premises.

[Above] Following the 1925 Lancia-Barton 39-seat buses came this 1926 model, bodied by Strachan & Brown. Number 55, RR 4157, photographed in Nottingham, displays the GLIDER title on its panelling. The name had been coined by the public in recognition of the smooth ride given by these machines.

[Left] Another, similar, vehicle seen heading for Derby. Number 24 carries its fleet number above the windscreen. The Lancia was a very popular chassis in the 'twenties.

Another view of 'Long Tom', No. 10, NN 3561, outside the headquarters at Chilwell in the same position as the Seldon lorry on page 18.

[Above] Number 31, RR 3074, standing at Hanley Street, Nottingham, shows the new style radiator. Note also the destination box fitted on the nearside windscreen. The filler for the petrol tank, which was located in the driver's cab, can be seen projecting below the half window behind the driver.
[Upper right] Lancia-Barton No. 64, RR 5562, was fitted out to a more comfortable standard with 32 seats. Photographed opposite Chilwell garage, its body passed to Gilford 112 in 1930.
[Right] Both Nos. 63 and 64 [upper right] can be seen to display 'Bartons Glider' above the destination. It was obviously a selling point with the travelling public. Number 63 is seen at Lady Bay [Trent Boulevard] West Bridgford. Following an accident both body and registration were transferred to the chassis of No. 66 during June 1930.

The Italian job

[Lower left and right] A high style of bodywork is fitted to Lancia No. 35, NN 5011, built to Long Eaton UDC regulations which required a dual entrance. Very few operators complied with this legislation, but Barton did introduce a second bus to this layout two years later in 1925, as seen in the adjacent picture of a Barton-converted forward-control Lancia, with Strachan & Brown Ltd 29-seat dual-entrance bodywork. There are several interesting features:- the upright steering column; petrol tank between engine and bulkhead; larger diameter rear wheels than front; rear entrance door but open front. [Captions continued opposite].

The new company's four - wheelers

[Above] 'Barton's British crude oil-engined bus' entered service in March 1930. It incorporated a Gardner 4L2 engine in the Barton-Lancia chassis, which carried its Irish registration, XI 6375. T. H. Barton gazes at the camera from the saloon. Sheffield Corporation placed its first oil-engined bus — a Mercedes-engined Karrier — in service on 9th March 1930, but Barton's was the first with a British oil engine, and claimed to be the first in service.

[Right] Challand Ross built the attractive body on Barton-chassied No. 110, VO 994. A Meadows petrol engine was fitted.

[Lower right] Barton's smartly dressed conductor exemplifies the spirit of bus travel in the late 'twenties. Number 106 was a Lancia-Barton, registered VO 167.

[CAPTIONS CONTINUED FROM OPPOSITE PAGE]

[Upper left] A long way from home is the ex-Autocar Services Ltd of Tunbridge Wells, Lancia seen standing in Wollaton Street, Nottingham. It ran in its original livery, retaining the fleet name, but part had been obliterated below the title. This was either number 50 or 51 in the Barton fleet, but within two years the body was removed, and in the case of No. 50 the chassis was extended and fitted with a 32-seat bus body from No. 26, keeping this as its fleet number.
[Upper right] The Lancia, with pneumatic tyres and lighter chassis, represented the new generation of passenger transport from Italy. Number 34, NN 4514, was the first of many to be operated, arriving immediately after Long Tom 10. Note the crude roller blind destination indicator on the roof and white disc on the radiator which reads 'Barton Bros'.
[Centre right] Number 2, NN 8891, shows the destination indicator fixed off-centre towards the nearside, to allow the conductor to be able to change this from the entrance step. Driver Alun Farnsworth and conductor Dennis Wain, stand close to evidence which shows the horseless carriage does not yet dominate the road!

[Above] Number 67 was not what it seemed when photographed in Nottingham in the early 1930s. The registration number was all that remained of a Lancia, one of a pair, which had been new in 1924 to Busy Bee of Caernarvon. Both passed to Pye of Heswall after a brief spell with Crosville. They became Barton's 67 and 68. Later No. 68's chassis passed to 67, and then the extended body from No. 85 was fitted to this chassis. In March 1931 an oil engine was fitted, to be replaced in June 1932 by a Commer petrol unit.

The new company's six-wheelers

[Above] An official Challand and Ross photograph taken under Nottingham Castle Rock, a short distance from the works and regularly used for publicity shots. Unfortunately the vehicle carries neither fleet nor registration numbers. The differing lettering styles can be compared on the two photographs on this page.

[Below] A hot sunny day and the canvas hood has been rolled back on No. 97 [RR 9323]. A Lancia Pentaiota/Strachan and Brown coach, it was one of a pair taken into the fleet in 1928. It ran only during the summer months in its latter days, eventually being sold to Squires of Barrow on Soar in 1935 with its sister. Glider 107, VO 256, behind, is a Lancia Pentaiota converted to six-wheel layout. It retains the original radiator but carries Massey Bros 32-seat front-entrance bodywork. Note the lettering on the roof panels, also the roof rack.

Forward-control buses

[Top left] The chassis on No. 130 was a Barton construction using Gilford running units and a Coventry Climax engine. Registered VO 4904, it carried Witham 32-seat bodywork suitable for longer distance work.

[Above] another Barton chassis, but this time with bodywork from a normal-control Lancia-Barton [No. 65] modified in Barton's workshops. The bus was photographed at the Stamford works of Messrs Blackstone, following the fitment of one of their oil engines. It was soon replaced by an ex-Gilford 6-cylinder petrol Lycoming unit. Numbered 139 it was registered VO 5439.

[Right] VO 4296, No. 132, often alleged to be a Gilford, was an all-Barton product. Fitted with a Gardner 5L2 engine, it was an attractive vehicle and carried 32 passengers. A fascinating selection of rears can be seen in the shed behind No. 132. Facing on to High Road, Chilwell, this was the front of the garage prior to the building of the head office block [see also page 48].

[Above] Number 98, RR 9501, was a forward-control Commer 4PF with Challand and Ross bodywork. It is seen in Huntingdon Street bus station.

Gilford single-deckers

Driver Harold Tuckwood proudly stands beside Coalville-bound No. 111, RA 5758, a Gilford acquired with the business of H. Boxall, Marlpool, in 1929. A Barton nameplate covers the manufacturer's badge.

[Top left] The first Gilford to enter the fleet was RR 9800, No. 101, a model 166OT with Wycombe 32-seat bodywork. It is posed against the Wollaton Park boundary wall, Adams Hill, Derby Road, Nottingham. The black lettering on white background is an unusual feature of the destination display. It entered service in 1928.

[Lower left] Another Gilford, No. 125, VO 2390, this time with bodywork constructed in Barton's own workshops and dating from 1930. It was sold in 1937 to J. R. Morley of Whittlesey, Cambridgeshire. The chassis is of the 168OT type which incorporated an early form of air suspension as indicated by the Gruss air springs each side of the radiator.

Gilford double-deckers

Five Gilford chassis purchased in 1929 were fitted with open-top double-deck bodies from old solid-tyred Daimler Ys. Tops were added to three a short time afterwards, but by 1931 they had all been rebodied as single-deckers. These vehicles were not quite unique as Gilford did make three attempts at producing a double-decker before bankruptcy.

[Upper left] An artist's impression of No. 33, modelled in clay, the product of Charles Forster Studios. Note the advert for the Arnold-Sandiacre service, which these vehicles operated.

[Upper centre] A front nearside view of No. 112 before entry into service, parked on the junction of Glebe Street and Bramcote Road, Beeston. This was an unusual choice of location as these roads were not served by buses until 1947. The chassis chosen for these vehicles were 166OT type, basically the standard single-decker of the period.

[Above right] The incredible covered-top fitted to Gilford No. 112, VO 1376. It was glazed at the front but open to the elements along the side. The Hickman body had been transferred from Daimler Y No. 19.

[Lower left] Another view of No. 33, this time with conventional covered-top, photographed at the back of Chilwell garage. Due to the lowbridge at Long Eaton, this version had a limited life, since other routes did not warrant double-deckers, and by now the Arnold-Nottingham section of the Sandiacre route had been withdrawn.

Enter the Leylands

The implementation of the Road Traffic Act in early 1931 put a stop to the more adventurous Barton exploits. Instead of converting, rebuilding, or extending chassis, and exchanging engines and so on, Barton now bought standard vehicles 'off the peg' — and found them very satisfactory. Following the success of the LT2 Lions delivered in 1931 an ex-Leyland TD1 demonstrator was purchased. Registered by Leyland as TE 9520 it was numbered 148 in the Barton fleet and carried a standard 48-seat lowbridge body by the chassis manufacturer. The demonstrator's livery was slightly modified with white roof and gold lining, thus matching the current single-deckers as seen below. Number 162, an LT5, carried the standard Leyland 35-seat body. [See also pages 51 and 55.]

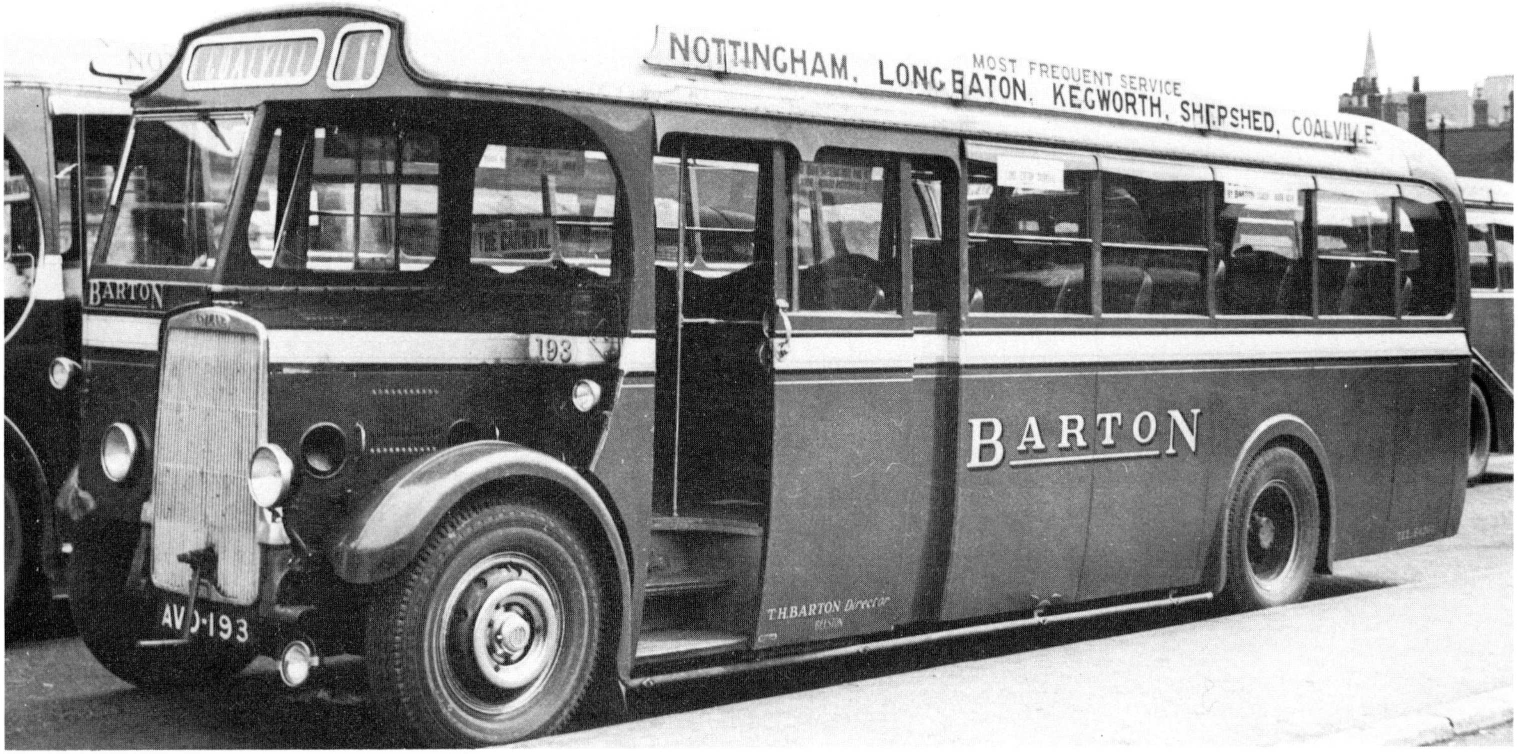

Pride of Lions 1

Following the all-Leyland single-deck buses a similar body style but built by Brush was introduced in 1934 on LT5A chassis with its more compact front-end, allowing the seating capacity to be increased to 38. The repositioning of the emergency exit door was the most visible alteration. These formed the basis of the dual-purpose buses taken into stock until 1940 though there were various restyling details with each delivery.

[Right] No. 180, the first of the batch, will be seen to be severe in appearance. Such was the need for vehicles to cover Easter requirements in 1934 that the vehicle was operated in primer, being returned to Brush for final painting shortly afterwards.
[Above] Number 193 was one of a pair of 39-seat Willowbrook saloons with more flowing lines and introducing the sliding entrance door. Both vehicles were rebodied in1940 to the style shown on page 117.

Pride of Lions 2

[Above] Lions on parade! Three Barton and, far left, a South Notts vehicle, respectively from right to left Nos. 207, 257, 213 and 20, all LT7s. The Barton vehicles were Duple-bodied, the South Notts Willowbrook-bodied.

[Below] Following the delivery of thirteen LT7 Duple-bodied saloons in 1935, four more arrived later in the year. Numbered 212-5 they were of identical design, and the last of the batch is seen working route 4 to Sandiacre.

[Above] The first delivery of Duple bodies in 1936, fitted to sixteen Lion chassis, were almost identical to the 1935 design save for the revised side flash. Number 254 received Burlingham utility bodywork, then later Duple coachwork.

[Below] The second batch of dual-purpose buses for 1936 incorporated a straight fluted waistrail. Number 274 is seen in broadside ready to work the Leicester service. Connoisseurs will recognise the Geoff Atkins touch in these pictures.

Pride of Lions 3

Duple were adept at keeping ahead of the competition when it came to design. By slightly lowering the waistrail, fitting sliding doors, revising the window pillar arrangements and adjusting the trim, they updated the appearance without losing the basic continuity of style. All versions had recognisable Duple characteristics though very few other operators were supplied with these exact styles. Number 289, on LT7 in Coronation livery is seen [above left] whilst No. 330, [above right], shows the effect of further minor changes to the 1937-38 batch. The vehicle looks well turned out and had not long been in service. The ribbon style fleet name on the side panel had been produced in a bright metal finish.

The official view [left] of No. 339, on an LT8 chassis, shows the subtle front end changes including removal of the visor. Note that the sliding door is now fitted to operate internally, being electro-pneumatically powered. The metal streamlined fleetname was introduced on this model.

Acquired in the 'thirties 1

The intake of acquired operators' vehicles adds variety to any fleet. Even the Barton menagerie was enlivened in this way and on the next pages we see some of the vehicles acquired.

Five vehicles of King's Motor Services stand in Long Clawson before leaving on what appears to be a private hire working. Nearest the camera is Commer Centaur JU 729 [later Barton 222], then Commer Invader UT 7721 [Barton 226]. The remainder are unidentifiable although the fourth may be Commer Centaur JU 730 [Barton 223].

[Upper right] Wilton-bodied Belgian Minerva No. 177 seated 26 passengers. It joined Barton's fleet in May 1934 from S. Pounder of Ilkeston. New to J. Bloomfield of Arnold, it had operated in competition with Barton, Ward and Nottingham City Transport on the Arnold-Nottingham service. The building behind the bus is the ex-Dutton Bros garage which was taken over by Trent in 1935.

[Lower right] The cobbled market place in Long Eaton is the location for No. 173, a Reo with EMCO 25-seat bodywork. Originally with Ward of Calverton it passed to Barton's subsidiary, Wards Bus Service Ltd, and then to the main fleet in 1933.

Acquired in the 'thirties 2

[Upper left] Commer Centaur JU 730 is seen here in its original King's Motor Services livery. The fleet No. 20 is just discernible, it became Barton No. 223.

[Centre and lower left] Two of the five buses taken into stock from H. Squires & Sons of Ruddington, in 1935, are shown in original livery. VO 7051 was a Willowbrook-bodied Crossley Alpha which ran as Barton No. 243 for less than two years. Two GMC 20-seat buses were included in the deal and No. 246 is shown with Rainforth bodywork. It lasted less than a year with Barton, eventually passing to United Counties as their No. 545.

[Upper right and above] E. W. Campion & Sons of Nottingham worked to Ruddington jointly with Squires. Two of their vehicles are seen at Ruddington Church. The 20-seat Willowbrook-bodied Commer Invader became No. 249, whilst the Avenger with 32-seat bodywork, also by Willowbrook, became No. 251.

Acquired in the 'thirties 3

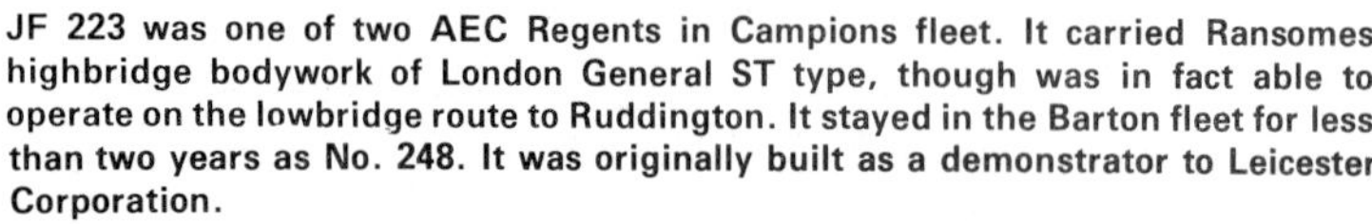
JF 223 was one of two AEC Regents in Campions fleet. It carried Ransomes highbridge bodywork of London General ST type, though was in fact able to operate on the lowbridge route to Ruddington. It stayed in the Barton fleet for less than two years as No. 248. It was originally built as a demonstrator to Leicester Corporation.

Five vehicles came with the business of E. Gregory [Excelsior] of Ilkeston, and two are shown [top right and centre right]. Number 303 was a Gilford 168OT with Willowbrook 32-seat bodywork. Also Willowbrook-bodied was ANU 739 [centre], a Dennis Lancet I. It became No. 304 and was identical to 216, ex-Billingham, registered ANU 740.

[Right] One of the few acquired buses to survive in the Barton fleet for any length of time was No. 236, a Leyland LT5A with Brush 32-seat coach body. New to F. W. Chambers & Son, Ilkeston, it was obviously of a type popular in Barton's own fleet and was converted to 38 seats as a dual-purpose vehicle upon acquisition. It was rebodied by Duple in 1941.

Coaching in the 'thirties 1

The first true coaches to be purchased new were a pair of Duple-bodied Leyland Lion LT5 models. Numbered 170 and 171 they seated 32 passengers and here we see the former turning off the Roman Bank at Skegness on its return to Nottingham. Both coaches had relatively short lives with Barton, being sold during 1938. Number 170 eventually became Lincolnshire Road Car No. 77 whilst No. 171 operated in South Wales.
Shortly after this photograph was taken the Ship Hotel, left, was rebuilt on the opposite corner where the lamp post and road signs can be seen.

Coaching in the 'thirties 2

[Above and below] ARR 178 was one of a pair of Leyland LT5A coaches. The rear view, taken at Huntingdon Street, Nottingham, shows the original 32-seat Duple body, new in 1934.

In 1938 Chappell of Waddington purchased the coach from Barton. It subsequently passed to Lincolnshire Road Car Co Ltd and was numbered 613 by that company. It was fitted with Willowbrook utility bodywork.

[Above] Number 192 was a solitary AEC Regal fitted with Duple coachwork. It was painted in almost all-over red and carried the garter fleet name used only on coaches. The coach was used primarily for the then recently introduced British Road Cruises and extended tours.

[Below] The famous clock tower identifies the location as the Sandbeck Hotel car park, Skegness. Number 179 and 194 await return to Nottingham on service 9.

The 1937 coach fleet intake included four Leyland Tigers, Nos. 294-7, [CVO 10-3]. Number 294 operated a tour in May of the same year to Devon and Cornwall, and is seen amongst the bunting for the Coronation at Lyme Regis following an overnight stop. A full frontal view of No. 294 is shown on page 67.

[Lower left] One of four Leyland KPZ2 Cubs with Duple luxury 20-seat bodywork for Continental Road Cruises, purchased in 1937, and numbered 312-5 [DRR 564-7] is seen below. The overall styling was used on the full-size 1938 coaches. During the war period the seating capacity was increased to take 25 passengers.

[Lower right] Only two coaches were ordered in 1939. Both on Leyland TS8 chassis they were bodied by Duple and numbered 345-6. Number 345 survived until November 1948 and is shown at Mount Street, Nottingham, shortly before being sold to Lees of Worksop. The second vehicle was drafted into service with HM Forces, and like No. 270 was driven into the sea at Dunkirk, in 1940, to prevent capture by the enemy.

Brush with Leyland

[Above] Ten Leyland Cubs were purchased in 1936 and fitted with Brush 20-seat coach bodies for use mainly in the Melton Mowbray area. No. 280 [CRR 815] had been sold to Leversley, Fulbeck, Lincs when this photograph was taken.

Leyland Lion No. 353 [FNN 664] carried one of eighteen Brush dual-purpose bodies fitted in 1939 to four LT8 and fourteen LZ5 chassis. The styling was based on the Duple coach designs supplied during that period. A Cheetah is shown on page 71.

[Top left] Leyland LT5A/Brush coach ARR 459, No. 379, was originally operated by Robin Hood Transport, West Bridgford, being sold to R. Calcraft, London, before returning to Nottingham when Barton purchased it in July 1940. It was rebodied by Duple to the design on page 117 during 1941-42.

[Lower left] A typical mid-'thirties interior, in this case by Brush. The Duple bodies were very similar for dual-purpose use, which offered a high degree of comfort for stage work.

Front-entrance 'deckers of the 'thirties

[Above] Willowbrook provided the lowbridge bodies for the 1940 batch of TD7s and No. 368 is shown when new. The styling is very similar to the Duple batch.

[Below] The ex-Campion Regent, No. 247, was posed for publicity purposes in Parliament Street, Nottingham, complete with wartime gas bag trailer. The vehicle dated from 1934 and its Willowbrook front-entrance body, very modern-looking for that date, seems to have inspired the general style of Barton's Titans of 1939 onwards.

Four Leyland TD5s arrived in 1939, all with Duple lowbridge 53-seat bodywork. They were oil-engined, the first for nearly a decade. Number 347 is seen [above] in wartime guise at the Nook, Ruddington, on service 14. The top-deck interior view [below], shows the excellent finish and the layout of the seats. These vehicles seated 26 upstairs but subsequent deliveries increased this in stages to 29 on the 1947 PD1s.

The rebodied TDIs

In addition to various single-deckers rebodied for Barton during 1940-41, Duple produced some 27 further front-entrance lowbridge bodies to the style established in 1939, maintaining the high standards of trim and finish during a period when thoughts were turning to the utility era. They were fitted on 26 Titan TD1 and one Tiger TS1 chassis dating from 1928-31, all but one being second-hand, and almost trebled Barton's double-deck fleet.

KR 6407, No. 392, [left] was formerly with Chatham & District. It received a TD7 radiator and is seen with wartime masks and markings.

GC 1210, No. 409, [lower left] fitted with a Cov-Rad radiator, had originally been fitted with a coach body when operated by Premier Line of London. It passed to Green Line, operating for them until the end of the 'thirties.

KO 7358, No. 396, [below], was originally fitted with a Short Bros body when operating with Maidstone & District and then Western SMT. The 1928 chassis had received a radiator of the type used on slightly later models. The background on the metal fleet name was finished in cream on these double-deckers.

Rebodied in wartime

It would be difficult to imagine a greater contrast than the bodies shown on this page. The Lion shown below, No. 181, was rebodied by Duple with dual-purpose bodywork similar to the earlier Brush bodies. Not long afterwards all normal construction ceased for the duration and utility bodies became the order of the day. Only one new single-deck chassis in the Barton fleet received utility bodywork — No. 424, a TS11 oil-engined Tiger, seen far right. The bodywork was by Willowbrook. On its left is LT7 No. 261 rebodied in 1944 by Burlingham and fitted with 36 upholstered seats from the original body. Both were rebodied after the war, with Duple coach bodies. Number 424 is seen on page 125.

Imported Assistance 1

Following reduction of the operating fleet due to Ministry demands it was necessary to import assistance for other operations. Fortunately it was possible to purchase Leylands, but with bodywork which was unfamiliar in the Barton fleet. The first four arrived during December 1940, from Lancashire coach operators.

[Upper left] CNB 215, a TS7 from Hartley of Manchester, was perhaps the most attractive [it certainly was to the schoolboys of Chilwell] with its Harrington 32-seat front-entrance coachwork. This model incorporated the bodybuilder's Dorsal Fin rear-end treatment, which was part of the ventilation system. Number 400 operated for a short period with a gas producer trailer. It was photographed at the end of the war displaying Thanksgiving posters.

[Below] Santus-bodied Leyland Cheetah LZ2, JP 2189/91 ex-Smith of Wigan, were altered from coaches to dual-purpose machines, giving extra needed seats. Numbers 402-3 were retained for eight years, then sold to Olive, Billinghay, Lincs, for further duty.

[Below] This Leyland TS6T, JP 622, with Burlingham coachwork had previously worked for Webster of Wigan. With its third axle it would have been at home in the fleet ten years earlier! Converted to dual-purpose 39-seat layout, No. 401 had a short life with Barton being sold to Beeline, West Hartlepool, in 1944.

Imported Assistance 2

[Upper left] This Leyland TS7 with Mulliner coach body, originally operated by Happiways of Oldham, became No. 407 in the Barton fleet.

[Lower left] The sixth and final second-hand single-deck purchase of the wartime period was this TS6 fitted with Burlingham centre-entrance coachwork. Under the fleet number, 408, on the Autovac, is the black and white chequer garage code of Chilwell.

[Below] Nottingham C. T. loaned a pair of Regents for seven months during 1941. Number 110, [allocated number 405 in Barton's fleet] is seen in familiar surroundings at Nottingham Old Market Place some years later. The rather upright bodywork is by Park Royal.

Utility 'deckers

The wartime allocation introduced more, if somewhat stark, variety to the fleet. A pair of unfrozen AEC Regents with NCB utility bodywork, Nos. 421-2, delivered in 1942 showed what was to follow. [upper left and see also page 75]. Twenty-five Guy Arabs with utility bodywork from various manufacturers, each slightly different in detail, but all to MoS specification, were delivered over the next four years. [For the full story of wartime production see TPC's 'Best of British Buses No. 8, The Utilities'.]

[Centre left] GAL 224, No. 427, was one of three 1942-built Brush-bodied Arab I buses, the first true utilities to arrive in the fleet. [Above] GAL 390, No. 435, was one of five Mark II chassis bodied by Duple and purchased in 1943.
[Lower left] Shortly before the end of the war Strachan bodies, perhaps the least attractive of the variants, joined the ranks. Number 438 shows the full austere outline of the first two.
[Below] The remainder were to the relaxed specification and the final eight had upholstered seats. Number 441 was thus the last with wooden slatted seats, as shown. Note the differing indicator display arrangements.

Rebuilt for further service

Following the end of the war many vehicles were rebuilt, the amount of work undertaken varying considerably. The Leyland body on No. 162 [above] had its character changed by the addition of revised flashes following rebuilding. It is parked in Mount Street, as also is No. 498, [below] a PS1 carrying the Brush body from a pre-war Cheetah. The upward sweep of the body behind the rear axle had been introduced by Barton to give increased clearance with the original chassis. Note the wooden enquiry office advertising a return fare of 3 shillings [15p] to Leicester.

The pre-war style Duple bodies from the rebodied TD1 Titans were transferred to PD1s 455/470. They had a distinctive appearance even though the adjustment to the cab front area did little for the flowing lines of the earlier combination. Number 455 is seen [above] at Huntingdon Street in June 1949, on service 8 to Oxton.

Some bodies were sent away for rebuilding and No. 214, [below] was an example handled by Yeates of Loughborough. Although the original Duple outline is unchanged, revised flashes and top sliding windows have altered its appearance considerably.

Strangers in the camp

[Upper left] Former Leeds City Transport No. 15, UG 1053, a Leyland TD2 with Roe body, became No. 450 in the Barton fleet. The staircase window had been painted over when this photograph was taken on Granby Street opposite Barton's bus park at Mount Street, Nottingham.

Further second-hand double-deckers arrived from Leicester City Transport, this time in the shape of TD1 and TD2 models with Brush bodies dating from 1931-32.

[Below] Number 475 is seen on Granby Street, Nottingham, completely lacking any destination blinds.

[Lower left] JF 2710 was built a year later and is seen on Mount Street. When built the vehicles carried a spare wheel under the staircase, but with external access. This had been blanked over when the vehicle joined the Barton fleet. Note the lamps mounted on swivel brackets and the trumpet horn extending through the cab. No. 461 was a TD2 from a batch of five purchased from Leicester.

Barton body and conversion

The first body to be constructed at Chilwell for nearly twenty years was this splendid effort on a Leyland PS1/1 chassis. Number 490 seated 39 passengers, a figure achieved by fitting an upright steering column. The finished product could in no way be regarded as a copy of other manufacturers, although the small fully sliding windows were reminiscent of American design of that period.

[Top left] Number 490 under construction at Chilwell, with an interior shot just before completion, [lower left]. [Top right] The finished product outside Chilwell garage, with No. 14, the AEC Matador breakdown truck alongside. [Bottom right] A rear view of 490, showing its interesting and clear lines.

Post-war Duple

This splendid photograph does full justice to the classic Duple lowbridge PD1 model so popular with staff, passengers and enthusiasts alike. HVO 134, No. 454, awaits its passengers before leaving Melton Mowbray for Nottingham on service 2.

[Above] Without a doubt the most elegant half-cab coach produced, a classic in its day, was the Duple A-type. Barton's styling enhanced an already crisp-looking design. Number 555, a Leyland PS1/1, was photographed before delivery to Barton and was fitted with 39 coach seats. The upright steering column and shortened cab is clearly shown.

[Below left] The design did not marry up quite so well with the Leyland TS11 chassis and some adjustment to the front wheelarches was necessary when 484's body was fitted to No. 424 as shown.

[Below right] Duple rebodied eight 1936 Leyland LT7s with this body but no adaptation was needed to achieve the 39-seat capacity. These were the third bodies fitted to the Lions. Number 259 loses something with its painted radiator.

Strangers in the camp 2

Seven Leyland Titans with Leyland lowbridge bodies were obtained from municipal operators in 1947, Chesterfield provided No. 478 [illustrated on page 83] and from Wigan Nos. 500-5. Of these No. 500 surived for three months, following a collision with the low railway bridge at Sawley and it is understood that No. 504 never entered service with Barton.

[Upper] Parked at the rear of Chilwell garage is No. 502, formerly Wigan No. 69, with an interior shot of the same vehicle [lower right] showing the reduced window height on the offside to accommodate the upper floor passageway.

[Lower left] The offside view of No. 503, EK 8110, at Mount Street parking ground; note the small fleetname on the side of the vehicle, usually fixed to the front or rear. Parked behind is Leyland PD1/Duple, No. 468 [JRR 751].

Rows of Roes

[Upper] The bare bones of the Roe body on TD5 No. 584 at Chilwell in April 1960. It was photographed as it was in the process of being broken up for spares and scrap.

[Below] TD4 No. 587, with Roe body showing earlier style of cab front, approaches Harby in the heart of Belvoir country on its journey to Stathern, on route 24, which is not correctly displayed.

Barton was fortunate to obtain former West Riding Automobile Co Ltd of Wakefield double-deckers, which were built just prior to the war. The first eight with lowbridge bodies on Leyland Titan chassis arrived in 1949, being numbered 581-8.

[Above] A utility Northern Coachbuilders body dating from 1943 had been fitted to this 1938 TD5 chassis, which became Barton No. 586. Number 606 a 1938 TD5/Roe was delivered in 1950 and will be described in Volume 2.

[Below] Owthorpe Lane, Cropwell Bishop, is the terminus for No. 588, a TD4 with Roe body with the fleet name from a 1937-8 saloon. This service was taken over in 1950 and will be detailed in the next volume.

FLEET LIST see page 134 for abbreviations and other notes

Motor bus fleet list, comprising of known vehicles from 1897 operated by T. H. Barton, Andrew Barton by 1909, Andrew Barton Brothers by 1910, Progress Motor Services Ltd, from 24.1.13, Barton Brothers Ltd, from 1.12.20 and Barton Transport Ltd, from 1.10.27.

Year	Fleet No.	Registration No.	Chassis	Bodywork	Type	Date New	Notes
1897			Benz 11 hp	Wagonette	11		
1900			Daimler Granville	Wagonette	10		
1906			Durham Churchill		Ch20		
1908		W 963	Durham Churchill		Ch28F		Obtained from Scarborough operator
1909		LE 8000	Scott Stirling		B18F		From unknown operator
			Clarkson		018/16ROS		Ex-East Kent & Herne Bay Co.Herne Bay 7.09
		AL 1141	Argyll		Ch		? Ex-East Kent & Herne Bay Co. Herne Bay 7.09?
1911		AL 68	Lacoste-Battman		018/16ROS		]Part purchase 20 vehicles from London operator,believed AL 68
		AL 1895	Lacoste-Battman		Ch		]AL 68 became paraffin lorry and fire engine
1912		R6/AL1700/2360	Ryknield 4 cylinder		Ch		]Part purchase 20 vehicles after Ryknield bankruptcy
1913		AL 2653/2986	Ryknield 4 cylinder		Ch		]As above. AL 2653 sold to Lewis,Cotgrave[15.10.16,ret.25.7.20]
			Thames 40 hp				Transferred to haulage fleet, possibly re-registered
1914		AL 3365	Ryknield				
		AL 2986	Durham Churchill				Transferred to haulage fleet, possibly re-registered
1916	17	AL 4297	Berna				Sold to Lewis,Cotgrave,25.7.20.Returned as No.17, 6.21
			Dorman-Ryknield?				
		AL 1700	Dorman-Ryknield?		Ch40		
	?13	AL 4408	Thornycroft J	Todd	B42D	1915	Body from Ryknield,reftd to Daimler 13,1922.Chassis from lorry fleet
1918	?12	AL 2360	Thornycroft J		B31R		Trans. from haulage fleet.Fitted Ryknield body later to Daimler 12, 1921
1919	11	AL 5872	AEC	Todd	B42C		Sold to Nottingham City Transport with Beeston route 1.3.24
	?14	AL 6870	Karrier		Ch35		Renumbered 26 then 57.[Passed to Barton Transport Ltd 1.10.27]
	?15	AL 7028	Daimler Y		018/16ROS		Chassis ext.1921. Rebod 034/30ROS,renum.5,then 23 [to BTL]
1920		AL 3365	Maudslay		45		Chassis from haulage fleet,body & regn. from Ryknield
	5	LE 9696	Daimler Y		018/18ROS	1912	Ex-LGOC,ext/reb 1921 034/30ROS,renum 23 then 37 [to BTL]
	16/6?	LF 8351/8424	AEC B	LGOC	018/16ROS	1912	Ex-LGOC B1575/1645.Ext/reb as o/top ROS6?renum 37,then 5 [to BTL]
	3	LC 7379	Daimler Y		018/18ROS	1906	Ex-LGOC to B29.Body & parts to Lancia 3,1925
	1	AL 9410	AEC		016/16ROS		Extended and rebodied 030/28ROS, 1921
	4	AL 9411	Daimler Y		B38		Possibly extended,body trans. to Lancia 4, 1925
	18/20/19	NN 44/289/302	Daimler Y		018/16ROS		Ext.& rbd O34/30ROS.1921.[to BTL]1929.Bds to Gilfords Nos.113/33/112
1921	9	BH 0472	Daimler Y		018/18ROS	1920	Source unknown, conv.to B38,body & run.units to Lancia 9,1925
	21/22	NN676/1711	Daimler Y Barton		034/30ROS		[to BTL]1929.No.21 body to No.34 Gilford.
	14	NN 1269	Daimler Y	Thompson/Louth	B32C		Sold to NCT with Beeston route, 1.3.24
	7	LH 8139	AEC B		B31R	1914	Chassis from haulage fleet.Body to Lancia 7. 1924
	12	AL 2360	Daimler Y		B31R		Regn. and ?body from Thornycroft,body to Lancia 12
	10	AL 6306	AEC B		B20		Regn. from Ryknield lorry
			Straker Squire		0/ROS		Source unknown.Chassis & body poss. reused in extended form
	15	OE 1715	Daimler Y	Hora	B29C	1919	Source unknown.Sold to NCT with Beeston route, 1.3.24
1922	24	NN 2344	Daimler CB	Holmes	B36C		Sold to NCT with Beeston route, 1.3.24
	17	NN 2410	Daimler Y Barton		034/30ROS		[to BTL]1929. Body to No.32 Gilford
	25	NN 2503	Daimler Y	Eastbourne Aviation	B35C		Sold to NCT with Beeston route, 1.3.24
	28	NN 2508	Daimler Y		Ch20		Chassis ex-WD. [to BTL]
	29	NN 2509	Daimler CB		B39		Renum.26, body & regn. to Lancia 52,1925[to BTL]
	27	NN 2665	Daimler CB	Eastbourne Av.	B36C		Sold to NCT with Beeston route, 1.3.24 Chassis ex-WD
	26	NN 2666	Daimler Y	Hickman	B36C		Sold to NCT with Beeston route, 1.3.24 Chassis ex-WD
	30	NN 2714	Daimler CB	Hickman	B36C		Sold to NCT with Beeston route, 1.3.24 Chassis ex-WD
	31	NN 2789	Daimler CB		B40		Chassis ex-WD
	8	AU 115	Ford T				Source unknown
	8	NN 3489	Daimler Y Barton	Hickman	B60C		Chassis ex-WD. Sold to NCT with Beeston route,1.3.24 to B56C
	13	AL 4408	Daimler Y	Todd	B42C		Sold to NCT with Beeston route,1.3.24 Body & reg. from Thornycroft

Year	Fleet No.	Registration No.	Chassis	Bodywork	Type	Date New	Notes
1923	10	NN 3561	Daimler Y Barton		B66C		Chassis ex-Wd. to B56C 1924 [to BTL]
	34	NN 4514	Lancia-Barton		B32F		[to BTL]
	33/32	NN 4531/2	Lancia		B26F		
	36/41	NN 5081/5881	Lancia		B26		[to BTL] No.41 reg. no. to 114. 9.29
	35	NN 5011	Lancia		B26D		[to BTL]
	6	NN 5379	Daimler Y		B26		Body transferred to Lancia 6,1925
	38-40	NN 5823/4/5850	Daimler Y Barton		034/30ROS		[to BTL] 38 to Box van 11.29 in haulage fleet
1924	8	NN 7312	Lancia		B26		[to BTL]
	7	LH 8139	Lancia-Barton		B31R		Body trans. from earlier vehicle retain fl. & reg No.[to BTL]
	11/2/15	NN 8890-1/5	Lancia		B29F		[to BTL] 2 to B26F.Reg to 115. 15 to B32F 1928
	14	NN 8892	Lancia		B29F		Ext & conv. to 6W B32F by 1927.[to BTL]
	12	AL 2360	Lancia-Barton 6 wheel		B36R		Body trans. from Daimler 12 retain. fl.& regn.No.[to BTL]1928 Strachan & Brown body B32F. 1930 to 4 wheels
1925	30	NN 9420	Lancia		B32F		[to BTL] Conv. to 6 wheel 6.28. Reg. to 116
	24/42/43/ 46/47/49	NN 9815/RR 1136/ RR 1280/2123/ RR 2166/2623	Lancia-Barton 6 wheel		B39F		[to BTL] 42 reg.no. to 124 12.29. 47 to B36F 1929 24/43/49 to B32F by 1929, 43 reg to 59. 1.30
	25	NN 9936	Lancia		B31F		[to BTL]
	27	RR 443	Morris-Barton 6whl	Strachan & Brown	B24F		
	26	RR 469	Lancia		B31		[to BTL] to B32F, chassis ex-No.50. 1929
	45/48	RR 2074/2496	Lancia-Barton 6whl 6 wheel		B40F		[to BTL]
	44	RR 1753	Ford T		B24		
	50	NU 4622	Lancia		B20		ex-Hall & North, Horsley Woodhouse.w/d by 1.26 for spares & reb.
	3	LC 7379	Lancia-Barton		B29F		Body trans. from earlier vehicle retain fl. & reg. No.[to BTL] to B32F 1927-8
	6	NN 5379	Lancia		B26F		Body trans. from earlier vehicle retain fl. & reg. No.[to BTL] to B32F 1929
	9/4	BH 0427/AL 9411	Lancia-Barton 6 wheel		B38F		Body trans. from earlier vehicle retain fl. & reg. No.[to BTL] 4 to B32F and 4 wheels 1929. Commer engine 1931
	52	NN 2509	Lancia-Barton 6 wheel		B39F		Body trans. from earlier vehicle retain fl. & reg. No.[to BTL] Chassis to No. 69 body and body to Gilford No. 34 9.30
1926	31/55 59/61	RR 3074/4157 RR 4797/4968	Lancia Barton 6 wheel		B39F		][to BTL] 61 chassis to No. 95 body 9.31. 31/59 to B32F 1929]43Reg. no. & 80 body to 59. 1.30 B32
	29/53	RR 3423/4	Lancia-Barton 6whl		B40F		[to BTL] 1927 No.29 S & B B32F. Body to 128. 1930
	33/60	RR 4531/5087	Lancia-Barton 6whl		B26		[to BTL]
	32	RR 3492	Lancia		B26		[to BTL]
	51	NY 1917	Lancia		B14	1922	ex-Jones, Pontycymmer.w/d 12.26 for spares & reb.
	54/56/58	RR 4112/4597 RR 4636	Lancia-Barton 6 wheel		B39F		[to BTL]
	50	KK 7328	Lancia	Hickman	B20F	1923	ex-Autocar, Tunbridge Wells.[to BTL] Chassis to No. 26 1928
	51	KL 3279	Lancia		B20	1924	ex-Autocar, Tunbridge Wells. 1928 to B32F [to BTL]
1927	62	RR 5441	Lancia-Barton 6 wheel	Challand & Ross	B39F		Chassis ex-Irish Govt. [to BTL] to B36F.1929.Body to No.140. 11.30
	64/63/66/65 69/72/70/71 73-76	RR 5562-7/6406-7/ RR 6887/7087/ RR 7236-7	Lancia-Barton 6 wheel		B32F		[to BTL] 6.30 No. 63 body & reg.no. to No.66.1930 No.64 body to No.113.10.30. No.65 body to No.139. 9.30. No.69 chassis ex-52.1930 No.70/76 bodies to 138/136 & No.73 chassis & reg.no. to No.72.
	27	RR 5662	Lancia-Barton 6whl	Strachan & Brown	B24F		Body from old 27[RR 443][to BTL] to B32F. Body to 122
	44	MD 9403	Lancia		B24	1921	Ex-Motocar. poss. rec'd old 44[RR 1753] body[to BTL] 1929 body B32F. ex-67
	67-68	CC 4860/4958	Lancia Pentaiota		B26F	1924	ex-Pye, Heswall, Cheshire [to BTL].67 rebuilt with 68 chassis & 85 body. 'Crude oil' eng. 3.31.Commer eng. 6.32.Original body to 44.
	35	NN 5011	Lancia-Barton 6wl	Strachan & Brown	B32		Reblt as 4whl 1930. Commer eng. 6.31

Year	Fleet No.	Registration No.	Chassis	Bodywork	Type	Date New	Notes
1927	77/85-7	IJ 7049/7236/ XI 5768/01,6939	Lancia		B26		Sources unknown.Irish.77/86 reb/ext.1928. Strachan & Brown B32 1928 No.85 6 wheels and body ex-77. 1930 to 4 wheels
	78-9	XI 6375/01,6975	Lancia		B26F		Sources unknown,Irish. 78 fitted with Gardner 4L2 oil eng.3.30 to 7.30
	80-1	XI 4809/01,6985	Lancia		B24		Sources unknown,Irish. 80 reb/ext.11.28.S & B B32F.Commer eng. 1931
	82-4	RR 8023/01,6990/ RR 5663	Lancia		B26		Sources unknown
	88	GD 1004	Lancia		B26	1925	Reb/ext Strachan & Brown B32F 11.28.reg.no. exch 86
1928	89-91	RR 8436/8478/8628	Lancia-Barton 6 wheel	Strachan & Brown	B32F		89 to South Notts Bus Co Ltd[5] 1.30. 90 reb. as 4whl. 1930 91 to oil. eng. ex-No.78. Commer eng. 6.32
	50/92-3/95/ 9/99/103-4/ 8/36	RR 8510/8681/ RR 9112/9321/9671 /9816/9864/VO 65 /NN 7312/5081	Lancia-Barton 6 wheel	Challand & Ross	B32F		50 to Wards Bus Service Ltd 7.31-2.32. 4whl. 8.30 95/99 Commer engines 12.31 and 6.31.95 took 6whl. chassis ex-61, 4.31 8/36 bodies to Gilfords 32/112
	94	RR 9285	Lancia		B26		
	96-7	RR 9322-3	Lancia Pentaiota	Strachan & Brown	C26D		Ran as Cream Coaches during 1928/29
	98/105	RR 9501/VO 64	Commer 4PF	Challand & Ross	DP 32F		
	100	RR 9755	Lancia-Barton 6whl		B32		
	101	RR 9800	Gilford 1660T	Wycombe	DP32R		
	102	RR 9856	Lancia-Barton 6whl	Strachan & Brown	B26		Commer engine 6.31
	106/68	VO 167/CC 4958	Lancia-Barton	Strachan & Brown	B32F		68 to Wards 6.31-10.33.then renumbered 176
	107	VO 256	Lancia-Barton 6whl	Massey	B32F		Commer engine 1931
1929	108	RR 5763	Chevrolet		B14	1927	ex-H. Smith, Long Eaton, 3.29
	109		Thornycroft			?	ex-H. Smith, Long Eaton, 3.29
	110	VO 994	Barton-Meadows	Challand & Ross	B32F		
	108-9		Reo		B14F	?	ex-H.Boxall,Marlpool,4.29 [109 correction to text]
	111	RA 5758	Gilford		B30F	1928	ex-H. Boxall,Marlpool,4.29. To B32F by 10.29. To B26F
	112/32-4	VO 1376/1520/1675	Gilford 1660T		030/26ROS		Bodies ex-19/17/20/21/18.By 1931 all B32 bodies ex- 36/8/Witham/52/64
	113	VO 1949/2175					
	108-9	UE 7866/5	Gilford		C32F	1929	ex-Sales, Netherseal, Derbyshire 7.29. C26 by 9.29
	114	NN 5881	Lancia-Barton		B32		Registration ex 41, body ex 44. Commer engine 6.31
	115	VO 2398	Chevrolet LQ	Witham	B20		Body to Lancia-Barton 115 during 1931
	116	VO 2539	Chevrolet LQ	Ashwood	B20		Body to Lancia-Barton 116 during 1931
	117	RA 7857	Gilford		B26F	1929	ex-J. Turner, Findern, Derby, 11.29
	118	RA 9297	Gilford		B32F	1929	ex-J. Turner, Findern, Derby, 11.29
	119	RA 3721	Gilford		B26F	1927	ex-J. Turner, Findern, Derby, 11.29
	120	VO 2550	Barton-Meadows	Barton	B32		To South Notts Bus Co Ltd. 1.30-3.31
	121/123	VO 2634/2648	Morris	Ashwood	B20		
	122	VO 2635	Morris		B20		Body ex 27
	124	RR 1136	Lancia-Barton	Ashwood	B31		Registration ex 42
1930	125	VO 2930	Gilford 1660T	Barton	B32F		
	126-7	VO 3096/3136	Morris		B26		Bodies ex 83[126] and 81[127]
	128	VO 3151	Barton	Strachan & Brown	B32F		Body ex 29, Coventry Climax engine
	129/130	VO 3672/4094	Barton	Witham	DP32F		Coventry Climax engine
	131	VO 4253	Barton	Barton	B32		Coventry Climax engine
	132	VO 4296	Barton	Barton	DP32R		Gardner 5L2 engine, to Commer 6.32
	133	VO 4424	Barton	Witham	B32R		Coventry Climax engine
	134/137	VO 4425/4710	Barton	Barton	B24		Continental engine
	135	VO 4578	Barton	Barton	B32		Sunbeam engine, to Commer 1932
	136	VO 4582	Barton		B32F		Gardner 4L2 oil engine, to Commer 6.32. Body ex 76
1931	138	VO 5339	Barton		B32		Coventry Climax engine. Body ex 70
	139	VO 5439	Barton		B32F		Blackstone oil engine, to Gilford 5.31. Body ex 65
	140	VO 5990	Barton	Challand & Ross	B32		Leyland engine. Body ex 62
	141	BA 7656	Commer		B32	1929	Ex-Foster & Seddon, Pendleton, Lancs
	115	NN 8891	Lancia-Barton	Witham	B20		Body from Chevrolet 115, registration from 2
	116	NN 9420	Lancia-Barton	Ashwood	B20		Body from Chevrolet 116, registration from 30
	142-3	VO 6036-7	Leyland LT2	Leyland	B35F		
	144	VO 6615	Barton	Barton	B32		Commer engine, to B29

Year	Fleet No.	Registration No.	Chassis	Bodywork	Type	Date New	Notes
1932	145	VO 7318	Barton	Barton	B35		Commer engine
	147	VO 7574	Barton	Ashwood	32		Barton Bros crude oil engine, to Gilford 5.32
	146	RA 6950	ADC 426	Hall Lewis	B32	1928	[Acquired from J. Upton, Long Eaton 3.32
	148	RA 8601	Maudslay ML		B26F	1929	]as above.Then to Wards Bus Service Ltd 1.7.32.ret 10.33 as 175
	149	RA 3974	Star Flyer		B24	1927	]as above
	148	TE 9520	Leyland TD1	Leyland	L24/24R	1929	ex-Leyland demons.Reb.Duple L28/27F 1942.Chassis to 637,1951
	149	UT 9519	Commer F4		B32	1931	ex-Mrs N. R. Howe [Comfy] Beeston, Notts. 11.32
	150-9	VO 7401-10	Leyland LT5	Leyland	B35F		156/7 DP32F 1932, later B35F. 153/5/7/9 30 + 30 1942-45
	160-1	VO 8411-2	Leyland LT5	Leyland	B35F		
1933	162-9	VO 9462-9	Leyland LT5	Leyland	B35F		166/7/9 30 + 30 1942-45. 162 Rebuilt body 1947
	170-1	VO 9470-1	Leyland LT5	Duple	C32F		
	172	TO 7232	Maudslay ML4B	Vickers	B26F	1928	ex-Wards Bus Service Ltd, Calverton, Notts. 10.33
	173	VO 3329	Reo	EMCO	B26F	1930	ex-Wards Bus Service Ltd, Calverton, Notts, 10.33
	174	VO 297	Maudlsay ML4B	Vickers	B28F	1928	ex-Wards Bus Service Ltd, Calverton, Notts, 10.33
1934	176	RA 9593	Gilford 166SD	Strachan & Brown	B26F	1929	ex-S. Pounder, Ilkeston, 5.34. 176 to South Notts [18] 1934
	177	TO 8801	Minerva	Wilton	B26F	1928	ex-S. Pounder, Ilkeston, 5.34
	178-9	ARR 178-9	Leyland LT5A	Duple	C32F		
	192	ARR 992	AEC Regal I	Duple	C32F		
	180-91	ARR 180-91	Leyland LT5A	Brush	DP38F		Rebodied Duple DP39F 1940-1,182 chassis to 709 in 1953,186 oil eng. 1950
	193-4	AVO 193-4	Leyland LT5A	Willowbrook	DP 39F		Rebodied Duple DP39F 1940-2. [except 195-6/208/214] Nos.204/9 to DP39F by 1936.
1935	195-203/205-8	BAL 395-403/405-8	Leyland LT7	Duple	DP39F		196 rbd.Brush DP39F ex-350,1950. Chassis of 199/200/205 to 539/545/543
	212-5	BRR 295-8					respectively in 1953. 214 reblt 1949, Oil eng. 1950 in 196/212/214
	204-209	BAL 204/209	Leyland LT7	Duple	C32F		
	210	BAL 210	Leyland TS6	Duple	C32F		
	211	TV 7993	Bedford WLB	Rainforth	B24F	1933	ex-F. U. Charlton, Ilkeston, 1.35
	216	ANU 740	Dennis Lancet I	Willowbrook	C32F	1934	ex-Billingham Bros, Ilkeston, 7.35
	217	RA 9789	AEC Reliance	Willowbrook	B32F	1929	ex-Billingham Bros, Ilkeston, 7.35
	218	RB 280	Gilford		B26F	1929	ex-Billingham Bros, Ilkeston, 7.35
	219	RB 4619	Gilford 1680T	Willowbrook	B32F	1931	ex-Billingham Bros, Ilkeston, 7.35
	220	TV 6012	Bedford WLB	Duple	B20F	1932	ex-Billingham Bros, Ilkeston, 7.35
	221	RB 8482	Bedford WLB	Willowbrook	B20F	1933	ex-Billingham Bros, Ilkeston, 7.35
	222-3	JU 729-730	Commer Centaur		B20F	1932	ex-M. King, Long Clawson, 8.35
	224-5	UT 9027/RB 5093	Commer Invader		B20F	1931	ex-M. King, Long Clawson, 8.35
	226	UT 7721	Commer Invader		B20F	1930	ex-M. King, Long Clawson, 8.35
	227	JU 4506	Bedford WLB	Duple	B20F	1934	ex-M. King, Long Clawson, 8.35
	228	JU 5020	Bedford WLB		B20F	1934	ex-M. King, Long Clawson, 8.35
	229	JU 2983	Bedford WLB	Duple	B20F	1933	ex-M. King, Long Clawson, 8.35
	230	JU 731	Bedford WLB	Duple	B20F	1932	ex-M. King, Long Clawson, 8.35
	231	UT 6778	Morris		B18F	1930	ex-M. King, Long Clawson, 8.35 not operated
	232	UT 6776	Morris		B14F	1930	ex-M. King, Long Clawson, 8.35 not operated
	233	UT 4187	Morris	Willowbrook	B14F	1929	ex-M. King, Long Clawson, 8.35 not operated
	234	RR 9540	Thornycroft A6	Challand & Ross	B24F	1928	ex-M. King, Long Clawson, Chassis to carnival float 8.35
	235	UT 9016	Chevrolet		B14F	1931	ex-M. King, Long Clawson, 8.35.Not operated [corr. to text]
	236	ARA 322	Leyland LT5A	Brush	C32F	1934	ex-F. W. Chambers, Ilkeston, 11.35.DP38F 1936. Reb.Duple DP39F 1941
	237	VT 6530	TSM B10A2	Beadle	B31R	1931	ex-F. W. Chambers, Ilkeston, 11.35
	238	RY 9402	Dennis GL	Bracebridge	B20F	1930	ex-F. W. Chambers, Ilkeston, 11.35 [corr. to text]
	239	VL 3995	Bedford WLB	Bracebridge	B20F	1932	ex-Allen Bros, Hose, 11.35
	240	UT 6268	Guy OND	Guy	B20F	1930	ex-Allen Bros, Hose, 11.35
	241	DO 8821	Reo		B24F	1930	ex-Allen Bros, Hose, 11.35
	242	ARR 582	Leyland LT5A	Brush	DP 38F	1934	ex-Squires, Ruddington, 11.35
	243	VO 7051	Crossley Alpha	Willowbrook	B32F	1932	ex-Squires, Ruddington, 11.35
	244	VO 5568	Crossley Eagle	Willowbrook	B32F	1931	ex-Squires, Ruddington, 11.35
	245	VO 5268	GMC T30		B20F	1931	ex-Squires, Ruddington, 11.35
	246	VO 4408	GMC T30	Rainforth	B20F	1930	ex-Squires, Ruddington, 11.35
	247	AAU 621	AEC Regent I	Willowbrook	L25/27F	1934	ex-E. W. Campion & Sons, Nottingham, 11.35
	248	JF 223	AEC Regent I	Ransomes	H21/27R	1930	ex-E. W. Campion & Sons, Nottingham, 11.35
	249/250	TV 4021/3713	Commer Invader	Willowbrook	B20F	1931	ex-E. W. Campion & Sons, Nottingham, 11.35
	251	TV 5630	Commer Avenger	Willowbrook	B32F	1932	ex-E. W. Campion & Sons, Nottingham, 11.35

Year	Fleet No.	Registration No.	Chassis	Bodywork	Type	Date New	Notes
1936	252-67/	BVO 452-67	Leyland LT7	Duple	DP39F		253-6/9/61-7 Burlingham UB36F during 1944.258/64 exch.bodies 1946.
	272-5	CNN 864-7					253/4/6/8-9/61-2/7 Duple C39F,1949 & oil eng. 1950.264 body to 342, chassis to
	286-93	CRR 821-8					653,1950.255/60/3/6/93 chassis to 535-6/496/494/546 in 1953-4
	268-9	BVO 468-9	Leyland LT7	Duple	C32F		to DP39F during 1939. Oil engine 1950
	270-1	BVO 470-1	Leyland TS7	Duple	C32F		
	276-85	CRR 811-20	Leyland KPZ2	Brush	C20F		
1937	294-7	CVO 10-3	Leyland TS7	Duple	C32F		
	298-9	CVO 14-5	Leyland LT7	Duple	C32F		to DP39F during 1939. 299 chassis to 549,1954
	300	RB 2274	Minerva		C25D	1930	ex-E. Gregory, Ilkeston, 4.37. 300 not operated
	301	JL 701	Gilford 1680T	Willowbrook	B32F	1931	ex-E. Gregory, Ilkeston, 4.37
	302	RP 9593	Gilford 1680T	Duple	B32R	1930	ex-E. Gregory, Ilkeston, 4.37
	303	RB 5462	Gilford 1680T	Willowbrook	B32F	1933	ex-E. Gregory, Ilkeston, 4.37
	304	ANU 739	Dennis Lancet I	Willowbrook	C32F	1934	ex-E. Gregory, Ilkeston, 4.37
	305	CRA 992	Dennis Lancet II	Willowbrook	DP39F	1936	ex-E. Gregory, Ilkeston, 4.37
	306-11/	DNN 234-9	Leyland LT7	Duple	DP39F		]Chassis 306/8/11/19/20 to 547 /8/4/38/40 during 1952-3
	316-20	DRR 972-6					]316/9-20 oil engine 1950-1
	312-5	DRR 564-7	Leyland KPZ2	Duple	C20F		312/4 to 25-seat during war
1938	321-30	DRR 977-86	Leyland LT7	Duple	DP39F		327/9 chassis to 537/497,1953.321 oil engine 1950
	331-2	DVO 116-7	Leyland LT7	Duple	C32F		
	333-4	DVO 118-9	Leyland TS8	Duple	C32F		
1939	335-43	EVO 31-9	Leyland LT8	Duple	DP39F		341/2 rbd, bodies from 541/264,1951/1950.336/9/41-2 oil eng. 1950
	344-5	EVO 708-9	Leyland TS8	Duple	C32F		
	346-9	EVO 710-3	Leyland TD5	Duple	L26/27F		348 chassis to 652, 1951
	350-3	FNN 661-4	Leyland LT8	Brush	DP39F		350 body to 196, 1950. 351-3 oil engines 1950
	354-62	FNN 665-73	Leyland LZ5	Brush	DP39F		354/8/61-2 bodies to 492/485/499/498 during 1947
1940	363-7	FNN 674-8	Leyland LZ5	Brush	DP39F		
	368-76	FRR 142-50	Leyland TD7	Willowbrook	L27/27F		368 chassis to 707
	377	YG 7220	Gilford Hera 176	Wycombe	C32F	1934	ex-T. Winfield & Son, Awsworth, Notts 6.40
	378	CNN 393	Commer	Grose	C26F	1936	ex-T. Winfield & Son, Awsworth, Notts 6.40
	379	ARR 459	Leyland LT5A	Brush	C32F	1934	ex-R. Calcraft,London 7.40. reb.Duple DP39F 1941
	380-2/8-9	KR 6415/7/9/04/14	Leyland TD1	Short	H24/24R	1930	ex-Chatham & Dist.394/6/8/83/93 reb.Duple L28/27F 1941-2.389 bdy to 470,1947
	383/4/6-7	WE 4377/9/3-4	Leyland TD1	Leyland	L27/24ROS	1929	ex-Cleethorpes CT.16/13/14/15. Reb.Duple L28/27F 1941-2
	385	WW 8959	Leyland TD1	Leyland	L27/24R	1929	ex-Todmorden JOC 19, reb.Duple L28/27F 1941
1941	390/409-10	VX 5169/GC 1210/	Leyland TD1	Duple	L28/27F	1930	Chassis ex-LPTB, TD57/178/175/180
	413	07/12					
	391	DR 8816	Leyland TD1	Duple	L28/27F	1931	Chassis ex-Southern National O.Co. 3103,chassis to 638 during 1950
	392	KR 6407	Leyland TD1	Duple	L28/27F	1930	Chassis ex-Chatham & Dist. 386
	393-4/411	VK 3841/39/40	Leyland TD1	Duple	L28/27F	1931	Chassis ex-Tyneside T & T Co 11/9/10. 411 body to 455, 1947
	395	WW 8762	Leyland TS1	Duple	L28/27F	1929	Chassis ex-Hirst, Ripponden, Yorks
	396-9/412	KO 7358/60/	Leyland TD1	Duple	L28/27F	1928	Chassis ex-WSMT. 398 chassis to 639
		AG 2530/29/					
		KP 3062					
	400	CNB 215	Leyland TS7	Harrington	C32F	1936	ex-Hartley, Manchester
	401	JP 622	Leyland TS6T	Burlingham	C32F	1935	ex-Webster, Wigan. To DP39F
	402-3	JP 2189/91	Leyland LZ2	Santus	C32F	1937	ex-Smith, Wigan. Reseated to DP39F on entry into service
	404	CM 8723	Leyland TD1	Duple	L28/27F	1929	Chassis ex-Birkenhead CT 96
	405-6	TV 4943/7	AEC Regent I	Park Royal	H28/24R	1931	Loaned from Nottingham CT, 110/114, March to October 1941
	407	BU 9449	Leyland TS7	Mulliner	C32F	1936	ex-Happiways, Oldham
	408	WN 8073	Leyland TS6	Burlingham	C32C	1935	ex-Harris, Grays, Essex
	414/6	ARF 630/VT 9860	Dennis Lancet I	Willowbrook	C32F	1933	ex-Blue Services [Grainger Bros] Ltd, Ilkeston 10.41
	415	EW 7752	Dennis Lancet I	Willowbrook	DP32F	1933	ex-Blue Services [Grainger Bros] Ltd, Ilkeston 10.41
	417	JU 1852	Bedford WLB	Duple	C20F	1933	ex-Blue Services [Grainger Bros] Ltd, Ilkeston 10.41
	418-9	DRB 153-4	Bedford WTB 1	Duple	C26F	1937	ex-Blue Services [Grainger Bros] Ltd, Ilkeston 10.41
	420	GNU 815	AEC Regal II	Willowbrook	C32F	1939	ex-Blue Services [Grainger Bros] Ltd, Ilkeston 10.41

Year	Fleet No.	Registration No.	Chassis	Bodywork	Type	Date New	Notes
1942	421-2	FVO 322-3	AEC Regent I	NCB	UL27/28R		
	423	FVO 324	Dennis Lancet II	Strachan	UB36F		Not received. Diverted to Boyer, Rothley, Leics. Regn. to 426
	424	FVO 325	Leyland TS11	Willowbrook	UB36F		Reb. Duple C35F from 484 during 1948
	425-7	GAL 136/FVO 324/ GAL 224	Guy Arab I	Brush	UL27/28R		426 allocated regn. of 423. 427 platform doors 1955
1943	428	GAL 258	Guy Arab I	Roe	UL27/28R		
	429-30	GAL 241/389	Guy Arab I	NCME	UL27/28R		
	431-5	GAL 390-2/504-5	Guy Arab II	Duple	UL27/28R		432/3 platform doors 1954-5
1944	436-7	GNN 73-4	Guy Arab II	Roe	UL27/28R		
1945	438-49	GNN 506-7/544-5/ 703-10	Guy Arab II	Strachan	UL27/28R		439,443/5-8 platform doors 1954-5
1946	450-2	UG 1053-4/6	Leyland TD2	Roe	H30/26R	1932	ex-Leeds CT 15/16/18
	457-61	JF 2705-7/9-10	Leyland TD2	Brush	H26/24R	1932	ex-Leicester CT 258-60/62/3. 460 tree lopper 1951
	479	VO 7457	Bedford WLB	Bracebridge	DP20F	1932	ex-J. H. Starbuck, Cropwell Bishop, Notts 9.46
	480-3	HAL 654-7	Leyland PS1/1	Duple	C33F		
	475-7	JF 1531-3	Leyland TD1	Brush	H26/24R	1931	ex-Leicester CT 255-7
1947	455/470	HRR 942/JAL 987	Leyland PD1	Duple	L28/27F		Bodies ex-411/389. Chassis to 669/668 1953
	463/5/54/ 74/67/71	HVO 132-5/JNN 384/464	Leyland PD1	Duple	L29/26F		
	478	RB 5507	Leyland TD2	Leyland	L24/24R	1932	ex-Chesterfield CT 48
	484/6-9/ 491/3-7	HNN 712-3/HVO 123-131	Leyland PS1/1	Duple	C35F		Orig. body of 484 to 424,rbd Duple C39F,1948.Chassis of 494/6-7 to 713/715/718, orig. body and flt. no. to chassis and regn. no. of 266/263/329, 1953
	485/492/8-9	HNN 793/HVO 576 JAL 853/616	Leyland PS1/1	Brush	DP39F		Bodies ex-358/54/62/61. Chassis to 727/24/26/25, 1954
	490	HVO 729	Leyland PS1/1	Barton	DP39F		Chassis to 738, 1956
	500	EK 7260	Leyland TD1	Leyland	L24/24R	1929	ex-Wigan CT 2
	501-5	EK 8108-12	Leyland TD1	Leyland	L24/24R	1931	ex-Wigan CT 68-72.
	520-4/6-7	HRR 421/563/995/ HVO 387/596/JAL 592/JNN 174	Bedford OB	Duple	C29F		524/7 Perkins P6 oil engines 1951.525 Chevrolet eng. 1950, to C24F 6.54 524-6 reduced to 20 seats 1951, 527 to C27F 5.51
	525	JAL 30	Bedford OB	Duple	C27F		
1948	508/466/456/3/ 62/472/512/1/473/ 513/468/510/509/ 514/464/506-7/ 469/515-6/518/7/ 9/572-4/1/0/5-9	JNN 630/655/742/ 793/920/JRR 68/ 261/403-5/751-2/ 930-2/JVO 229-38/ 881/KAL 51/114/ 146/256/374/507-8	Leyland PD1	Duple	L29/26F		462/519 chassis to 878/902, 1960. 510 rebodied 1961 with 1949 Alexander L27/26R body ex-Ribble Motor Services 2078. 472 body to 753, 1962. 511 chassis to towing lorry 41, 1962 577 chassis to 901. 1960
	528-31	JNN 573/JRR 114/ JVO 148/749	Bedford OB	Duple	C29F		Seating reduced 1951. [529-31 Perkins P6 oil engine 1954-5]. 528 to 20. 529-31 to 24, 5.51 then 530-1 to 20 7.51
	535-45/7-8/6/9	JRR 915-29	Leyland PS1/1	Duple	C35F		535-49 chassis to 714/711-2/716-7/719/651/720/722/730/710/723/729/721/728. 542 body to 709.Bodies & flt nos. of 535-40/3-9 ftd to chassis & regn. nos of 255/260/327/319/199/320/205/311/200/293/306/308/299. 541 body to 341
1949	532	KAL 683	Bedford OB	Duple	C29F		Perkins P6 oil engine 11.52, to C24F 5.51
	533-4	KRR 297/KVO 148	Bedford OB	Duple	C24F		533 to South Notts [65] 3.57. 534 to C29F
	550-6/9/65/57/ 60-2/58/63-4/6-8	KAL 147-52/203-5/ 381-3/501-6	Leyland PS1/1	Duple	C39F		Chassis of 551/60/3-4 to 736/735/737/734, 1956. 552/6/62/8 to 790/789/788/ 787, 1957. 550/561 to 795/799, 1958. 565 reduced to 38 seats from 5.56
	580	KNN 254	Leyland PD1A	Duple	L29/26F		
	581-4	HL 9064-5/59/7	Leyland TD5	Roe	L27/28R	1939	Ex-West Riding Automobile Co Ltd, Wakefield, 535-6/530/528/515/513/430/ 505/516. 586 had been rebodied 1943 [430]. 585 converted to tree lopper 1961. Seating capacity of 581-5 increased from 24/24 before entry into service.
	585	HL 8613	Leyland TD5	Roe	L27/28R	1938	
	586	HL 8611	Leyland TD5	NCB	UL27/28R	1938	
	587	HL 7432	Leyland TD4	Roe	L27/28R	1936	
	588	HL 6072	Leyland TD4	Roe	L27/28R	1937	

WARDS BUS SERVICE LTD

Acquired 6.31 and operated as an associated company until 9.33. Finally wound up as a company 11.54.

Year	Regn. No.	Chassis	Bodywork	Type	Date New	Notes
1931	VO 297	Maudslay ML4	Vickers	B28F	1928	]Taken over with the business of Wards [Arnold] Bus Service 6.32, and
	VO 3329	Reo	EMCO	B26F	1930	] transferred to Barton 10.33 as 174/173
	CC 4958	Lancia-Barton	Strachan & Brown	B32	1928	Ex-Barton [68] 6.31, and returned as 176, 10.33
	RR 8510	Lancia-Barton	Challand & Ross	B32F	1928	Ex-Barton [50] 7.31 and returned 2.32
1932	RA 8601	Maudslay		B26F	1928	Ex-Barton [148] 3.32, and returned as 175, 10.33
	TO 7232	Maudslay ML4B	Vickers	B26F	1928	Acquired by Barton from Mrs N. R. Howe, Beeston, Notts 11.32, and trans. direct to Ward. Passed on to Barton as 172, 10.33

Notes and Abbreviations

The standard codes adopted by the national enthusiasts societies have been used to describe body types, which are detailed for general guidance.

B - Single-deck service bus.
DP - Dual-purpose single-decker.
Ch -Charabanc - separate entry to each row of seats, and no fixed top.
C - Coach.
O - Open-top double-deck bus.
H - Highbridge double-deck bus.
L - Lowbridge double-deck bus.
F - Full fronted cab.
U - Utility.

These letters, which are combined where relevant, are followed by seating numbers of the bus. The upper-deck capacity, where known, is given first, ie 28/27. A plus sign followed by a number denotes maximum capacity of standing passengers. Suffixes to the seating indicate doorway positions.

F - Front.
R - Rear.
C - Centre.
D - Dual entry/exit.
RD -Double-deck bus fitted with rear platform doors.
ROS- Rear open staircase.
Thus L28/27RD indicates a lowbridge double-decker, seating 28 upstairs and 27 on the lower deck, fitted with rear platform doors. DP44D is therefore a dual-purpose single-decker with 44 seats and dual-entry/exit.

Saloon - When referred to within the text of this book, describes a general service vehicle either to bus or dual-purpose standards. A coach will be described as such throughout.
Several companies abbreviated their titles for sales purposes, whilst others are commonly known in the abbreviated form. These are listed together with their full titles.

ADC - Associated Daimler Co Ltd.
AEC - Associated Equipment Co Ltd, Southall, Middlesex.
BMMO - Birmingham & Midland Motor Omnibus Co Ltd, Edgbaston, Birmingham.
COD - Central Ordnance Depot.
E & T - Excursion and Tours.
GMC - General Motors Corporation of America.
GWR - Great Western Railway.
LGOC - London General Omnibus Co Ltd.
Lincs.RCC - Lincolnshire Road Car Co Ltd, Lincoln.
LMS - London Midland & Scottish Railway.
LNER - London & North Eastern Railway.
LPTB - London Passenger Transport Board (1933-47)
MGOC -Midland General Omnibus Co Ltd, Langley Mill, Derbyshire.
Midland Red - See BMMO
NCB - Northern Coachbuilders Ltd, Newcastle-upon-Tyne.
NCME - Northern Counties Motor & Engineering Co Ltd, Wigan
NCT - Nottingham Corporation Tramways (1897-1927).
- Nottingham City Transport (1928-).
Pop. - Population.
ROF - Royal Ordnance Factory.
Trent (TMT) - Trent Motor Traction Co Ltd, Derby.
TSM - Tilling-Stevens Motors Ltd, Maidstone, renamed TSM Ltd, before reverting to original title in 1937.
Western SMT - Western Scottish Motor Traction Co Ltd, Kilmarnock.

Services Operated

AUGUST 1919

Nottingham [G] - Sandiacre - Long Eaton
Nottingham [G] - Beeston - Chilwell
Long Eaton - Draycott

JUNE 1929

No.	Route
1	Nottingham [G] - Gotham - Loughborough
1B	Long Eaton - Nottingham [G] - Barton in Fabis
2	Nottingham [G] - Melton Mowbray
3	Nottingham [P] - Long Eaton - Castle Donington
	Nottingham [P] - Swadlincote
4	Sandiacre - Arnold
4	Sandiacre - Beeston - Arnold
	Stanton by Dale - Arnold
5	Nottingham [P] - Derby
6	Nottingham [P] - Birmingham
7	Nottingham [T] - Epperstone
7A	Nottingham [T] - Lambley
7B	Nottingham [T] - Lambley - Newark - Balderton
8	Nottingham [P] - Oxton - Newark - Claypole
9	Birmingham - Nottingham [P] - Skegness
10	Nottingham [P] - Kegworth - Loughborough
11	Nottingham [G] - Coalville
12	Nottingham [P] - London
14	Nottingham [G] - Leicester
15	Long Eaton - Ilkeston

[G] Greyfriar Gate
[P] Upper Parliament Street
[T] Trinity Square

The Duple-bodied Bedford OB, No. 530, was operating a road-cruise when photographed on Princes Street, Edinburgh. The list of 1919 and 1929 services, [left], will be seen to be local to Nottingham. By the mid-'thirties they had spread to cover Britain.

Bibliography

Although very little has been written on Barton Transport Ltd, the following were useful references:-

Chapter 9 Extended tours by motor coach by E. L. Taylor from **The Omnibus** - David & Charles 1971.
Buses Illustrated 14 and 18 contain an article by Roy Marshall on Barton Transport Ltd.
Barton Transport Ltd produced three leaflets, **A brief history of Barton Transport Ltd**, **Barton Story** by David Edgar and **Prelude to Progress** by John F. Speed.
Valuable background information was obtained from:-
Various editions of **Commercial Motor** and **Motor Transport**.
The forgotten railways of the East Midlands by P. Howard - David & Charles 1973.
Victorian Nottingham Vol.1/19 and **Edwardian Nottingham** Vol. 1 by R. Illiffe and W. Baguley - Nottingham Historical Film Unit.
The History of British Bus Services by John Hibbs - David & Charles 1968.
The Leyland Bus by Doug Jack - Transport Publishing Company.
Various Guides and street maps produced by Local Authorities in the operating area.

Photo Credits

Unless otherwise stated photographs are from the Barton Transport Ltd collection of photographs.

G. H. F. Atkins	49,67,77(upper),81,83,90,101(top right),105(both),106(top & both lower),107(top right),109(all except top left),110(left),111,112(top left & bottom right),113(top),115 (upper right),116(top),120(top right),121(top right),125(lower left),126(lower left)
Mrs A. Barton and family collection	14(lower),106(top right)
E. P. Barton	15(both),18
Brush/TPC Library	71(upper),110(lower)114(upper left)
Richard J. Butler	91,124,125,127(top left & both bottom)
John Clarke	118(lower right)
John Clarke collection	36,58,71,103(top right),107(top (left),108(top left),109(top left), 118(lower left)
Commercial Motor	32(lower right),37,39
Duple Coachbuilders Ltd	86,107(lower),115(lower right), 117(lower),125(upper)
Peter Edgington	66,85
Eddie Harrison collection	64(both),74,89
W. J. Haynes	108(top right & lower),122(lower left)
Lens of Sutton	123(top right)
Leyland Vehicles Ltd	51,54,55(both),104(lower)
Roy Marshall	77(lower),78(lower),79,80,112,113 (lower left),117(top),119(all),120 (all except top right),121(both left), 122(top & bottom right)
Roy Marshall collection	16,22,47,103(lower),113(right),114 (lower right),115(upper left),116 (lower left),126(top & bottom right),127(top right)
A. W. Mills collection	116(lower left)
Motor Transport	96(top right),98(lower right)
Nottingham Historical Film Unit	33,98(top left)
Alan F. Oxley	11,57,61(lower),73(lower left), 103(top right)
Alan F. Oxley collection	14(upper),28(upper),40,50,53,93 (lower right),94(top & lower left), 98(centre),100(top right),102 (right),103(centre),110(top & centre right),114(lower left), 121(lower left)

Note: The above credits are also for drawings and plans.

Acknowledgements

Perhaps the most satisfying aspect of preparing a book of this nature, is meeting many interesting people from which friendships have developed and flourished. Firstly I must mention various members of the Barton family, who willingly gave information and have been listed individually in the photographic credits. John Clarke and David Fowler from Melton Mowbray have been most helpful, in particular John, who has recorded much of the early days in his area. Thanks to Alan Mills who read and corrected my original draft, an ideal person having knowledge of the East Midlands and in particular Barton, with first hand experience as a conductor during his student days. Contributions from employees of the Company, past and present, came from Harold Tuckwood (a driver from 1916 until 1950), Muriel Harpham, Ken Wilson, Eddie Harrison and Jo Parker. Jo provided detailed information on chassis, bodywork, oil replenisher and many other items. To Mal, the elite of photographers for first class prints, my thanks. I am grateful to the Directors of the Company for their assistance, in particular the Chairman for writing the Foreword.

I have spent many hours in the archives in the area, and in particular thanks go to the staff of all the local libraries, too numerous to mention, and Bernard Malkinson of the Long Eaton Advertiser Co Ltd. The records of the Omnibus Society and PSV Circle were invaluable. Luckily in this area we have three outstanding photographers who have recorded on film many vehicles which otherwise would have been forgotten, Geoff Atkins, Richard Butler and Roy Marshall, who also gave additional information as did Peter Edgington, Peter Badgery, Chris Taylor and E. Tuxford. To anyone who has been omitted, my abject apologies and thanks.

Finally a mention to all the ladies who gave their services in typing the manuscript — Margaret Chambers, Elizabeth Frost, Pat Clarke, my wife Barbara, and to the members of TPC, not least to Series Editor Alan Townsin who made many useful suggestions. Robin Hannay, Roy Marshall and Doug Jack kindly read the final proofs.

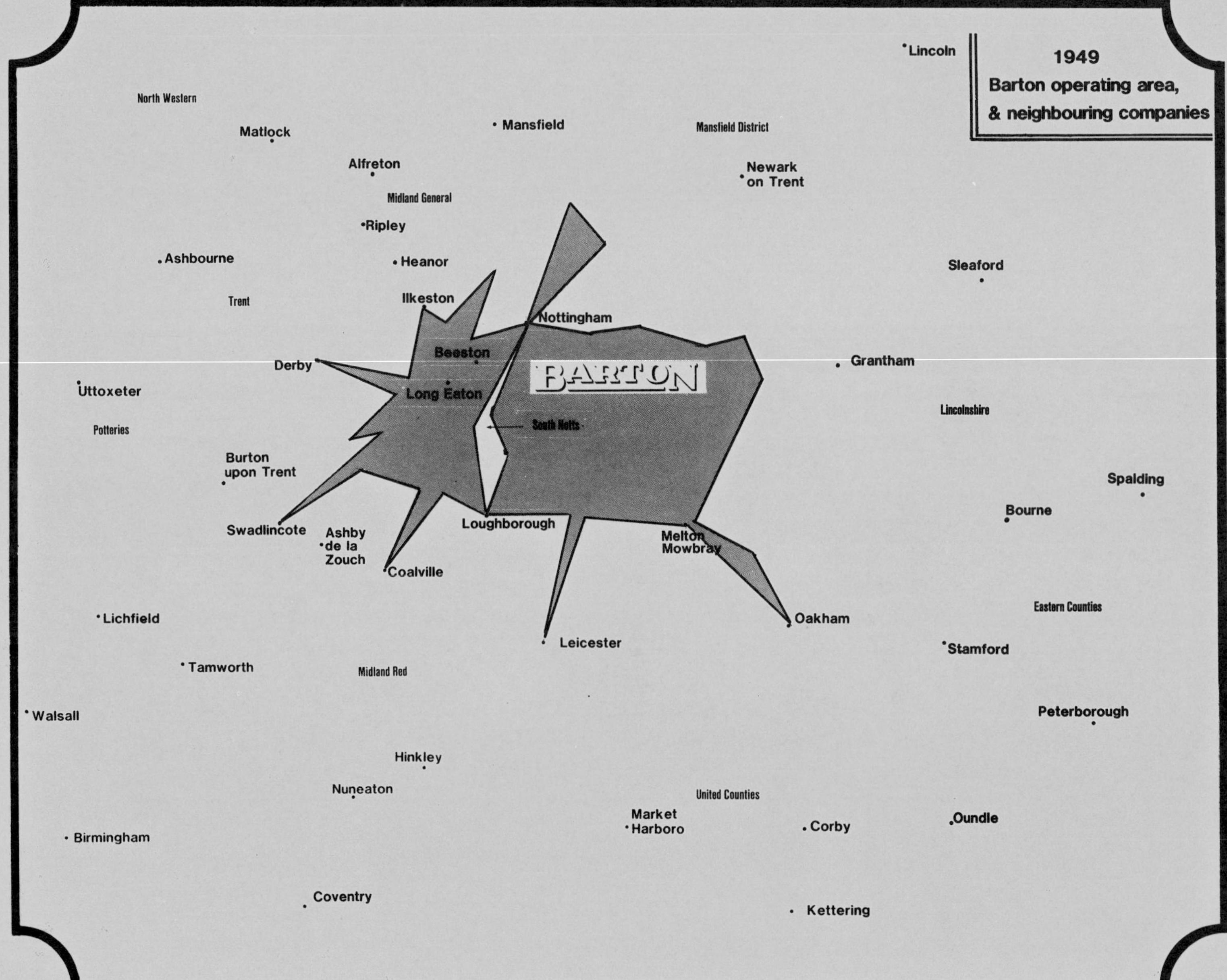
1949
Barton operating area,
& neighbouring companies
Lincoln
North Western
Matlock
Mansfield
Mansfield District
Alfreton
Newark on Trent
Midland General
Ripley
Ashbourne
Heanor
Sleaford
Trent
Ilkeston
Nottingham
Beeston
Derby
BARTON
Grantham
Uttoxeter
Long Eaton
South Notts
Lincolnshire
Potteries
Burton upon Trent
Spalding
Bourne
Swadlincote
Ashby de la Zouch
Loughborough
Melton Mowbray
Coalville
Eastern Counties
Lichfield
Oakham
Leicester
Stamford
Tamworth
Midland Red
Walsall
Peterborough
Hinkley
Nuneaton
United Counties
Market Harboro
Corby
Oundle
Birmingham
Coventry
Kettering